EXPORTING DEMOCRACY

ALSO BY BOB RAE

From Protest to Power:
Personal Reflections on a Life in Politics

The Three Questions:
Prosperity and the Public Good

Canada in the Balance

BOB RAE

EXPORTING DEMOCRACY

THE RISKS AND REWARDS
OF PURSUING A GOOD IDEA

McClelland & Stewart

LIBRARY AND ARCHIVES CANADA CATALOGUING IN PUBLICATION
Rae, Bob, 1948-
Exporting democracy : the risks and rewards of pursuing a good idea / Bob Rae.
ISBN 978-0-7710-7289-5
1. Democracy–History. 2. Democratization–History–21st century.
3. World politics–21st century. 4. New democracies. I. Title.

JC421.R33 2010   321.809   C2010-901553-3

We acknowledge the financial support of the Government of Canada through the Book Publishing Industry Development Program and that of the Government of Ontario through the Ontario Media Development Corporation's Ontario Book Initiative. We further acknowledge the support of the Canada Council for the Arts and the Ontario Arts Council for our publishing program.

Published simultaneously in the United States of America by
McClelland & Stewart Ltd., P.O. Box 1030, Plattsburgh, New York 12901

LIBRARY OF CONGRESS CONTROL NUMBER: 2010923469

Typeset in Janson by M&S, Toronto
Printed and bound in Canada

This book is printed on acid-free paper that is 100% recycled, ancient-forest friendly (100% post-consumer waste).

McClelland & Stewart Ltd.
75 Sherbourne Street
Toronto, Ontario
M5A 2P9
www.mcclelland.com

2   3   4   5   14   13   12   11   10

In memory of my father, Saul Forbes Rae

—

"It is not our affluence, or our plumbing, or our clogged
freeways that grip the imagination of others.
Rather, it is the values upon which our system is built."

JAMES WILLIAM FULBRIGHT,
remarks in the U.S. Senate, June 29, 1961

CONTENTS

CHAPTER I

THE WORLD IN OUR IMAGE:

The Challenge of Sharing Democracy and Human Rights

Today it's possible for people in almost half the countries of the world to say, "We're democrats now." This does not mean that democracy can be taken for granted, that history is over, or that different people mean the same things when they say these words. But it does mean that what was, for much of the last two hundred years, a Western idea has become widely adopted as the political gold standard. From Indonesia to Estonia, from Chile to Iraq, people have claimed the democratic idea as their own. As I write these words, people are in the streets of Thailand campaigning for democratic accountability. In Afghanistan, women are worrying that "reconciliation" will mean their rights are abandoned. In Russia, demonstrators hold simultaneous rallies across the country to reaffirm that they want their rights respected and their government held accountable. It would seem that Thomas Jefferson was right. Democracy is truly an infectious idea.

Many governments say they value democracy deeply, but their practices often fall far short of their ideals. What should the rest of the world do when countries flout human rights? Does the standard of what to do vary depending on whether that country is rich or poor, powerful or weak? Should cultural traditions trump equality rights?

These questions seem simple enough. But after listening to a wide range of opinions over the past several years, and working in a number of countries, I have learned that the answers are never easy.

If Karl Marx and John Stuart Mill were to meet today in a Highgate coffee shop in London, they would no doubt scratch their heads at the state of the world around them. Each in his own way – and using very different arguments – was convinced that a more rational world would lead to a decline in religious zealotry. In Marx's view, a well-led proletariat, conscious of its economic role, would overthrow the institutions and prejudices of feudal and bourgeois societies. The result inevitably would be a better world, one of scientific production, material abundance, and general enlightenment, where the division of labour, which alienates man from his true self, would be no more. Mill's view was less utopian, less grandiose, and more practical, but no less optimistic: progress would be steady, rational, and benign as the world became more prosperous, tolerant, open-minded, and liberal.

Their century, the nineteenth, was a time of radical and optimistic ideas, but it was also a time of expanding empires, of ideologies based on racial superiority and hatred. Nationalism arose from the need of communities to have their voice heard, but it came with a price – the harsh view that "my tribe is better than yours." Ultimately, these competing empires and ideologies clashed in the first and second world wars.

The twentieth century was both the most liberal and the most barbaric in human history. Fanaticism, religious hatred, ideological zealotry, and an infinite capacity for cruelty proved to be deadly when combined with technological prowess and an insatiable appetite for empire and control. Hence Gandhi's entirely apt response when asked what he thought of Western civilization: "It would be a good idea."

Yet during these dark times other ideas emerged: the importance of international law in dealing with disputes between nations, and the creation of institutions to enforce these laws. The recognition of a community of nations in 1648 at Westphalia, which ended thirty years of religious warfare in Europe; the condemnation of slavery in 1815 at the Congress of Vienna; the creation of the

Red Cross in 1863 and the signing of the first Geneva Convention a year later; the establishment of the World Court in 1908; the League of Nations in 1919, and in 1945 the founding of the United Nations; the judgement at Nuremberg; and the signing of the Universal Declaration of Human Rights, followed three years later by the Convention on Genocide; in 2002 the International Criminal Court; and in 2006 the Security Council Resolution on the Responsibility to Protect – these are all the result of the effort to create an international order whose purpose is to express our common yearning for security, peace, and the chance to fulfill our ambitions as human beings in a co-operative world. None of these accomplishments has come easily, and these aspirations are frequently dashed by politics.

When we talk about democracy, what do we actually mean? The word means "rule of the people," but it is only relatively recently that its meaning is complimentary. Few people today who aspire for public support would fail to describe themselves as democrats." It has become the common working assumption of politics. For many thousands of years this was not the case. The citizens of ancient Greece were the first to adopt democracy, and Pericles of Athens was among the first recorded to sing its praises: "We Athenians decide public questions for ourselves or at least endeavour to arrive at a sound understanding of them. . . They want to be free and to rule." (Dunn, 28-29)

But far from everyone in Athens was a citizen and entitled to these rights – women, slaves, and foreigners were excluded. And just a generation after Pericles, Plato insisted that the rule of virtue and of the virtuous was far preferable to the rule of the people. When Plato's student Aristotle wrote of the *demos*, he meant the mob, the unruly majority who could be mobilized and swayed one way or the other by the unscrupulous. Democracy was not, for the ancients, the most desirable of systems, because it could lead to a world out of balance. The best government was one that encouraged the arts, prosperity, and the pursuit of learning. It required leaders who understood this, and who themselves accepted limits to their power.

The democratic idea went into hibernation after its earliest emergence some twenty-five hundred years ago. It would take the Protestant Reformation and the Enlightenment to give it new life, and the American and French revolutions to give it the vibrancy that is still with us today.

In the 1950s, C.B. Macpherson, the Canadian scholar and teacher of politics, wrote about "the real world of democracy," in which different kinds of democracy competed with each other. Macpherson tried to make the case that the countries of both the Soviet bloc and the Third World had as much right to claim they were democracies as the liberal, capitalist democracies of the West. Liberal democrats should not, he argued, think their model is the only form of democracy.

Macpherson was way off the mark about the state of democracy in the Soviet Union and its satellites, to say nothing of China. Today, the idea that "non-liberal" systems like the Soviet Union had a "genuinely historical claim to the title democracy" seems perverse. Just because regimes use the word *democracy* doesn't mean they are democratic. Poland in the 1950s was a communist dictatorship that called itself a "workers' democracy." The abuse of democracy is widespread, and no regime's propaganda proves its own legitimacy.

Human rights, the rule of law, the independence of judges, and respect for constitutional order are all values that today seem intrinsic to liberty and democracy. Yet, in the eighteenth and nineteenth centuries, the workers' movements that ultimately gave rise to social democracy were fighting for freedom. Freedom, they argued, didn't just mean the right of employers to buy and sell labour. It had to mean the right of workers to form unions and to use the political process to force governments to ensure universal access to health care, pensions, a minimum standard of living for everyone.

There are other key elements to our sense of democracy. Freedom of speech and association mean little without a free press of diverse opinions and political parties able to mobilize oppositions as well as governments. It is not enough that there are courts. There also have to be judges at liberty to make rulings.

Democracy, freedom, and the rule of law may not be technically synonymous, but in the West they are intimately connected in our minds and political practice. Democracy means being able to choose our governments and our leaders. But it is about far more than elections. It's about being fairly treated by the police and courts, about being able to make a living and keep something for ourselves as well as contribute to common services through taxes. It's about being able to make our way without being told that the door of opportunity is barred because of the colour of our skin, or the language we speak, or the religion we practise, or our gender, or our sexual orientation. The equality we seek is not absolute equality of condition or outcome, but it is about being treated fairly and without discrimination.

The expansion of democracy to include everyone has meant several dramatic changes. Today, being a property owner is not a requirement for political participation. We take this for granted, but it is a relatively recent phenomenon. Fear of the *demos* was used to limit the franchise, to ensure that constitutional order and social privilege were protected by keeping most people down, out, and under control. Even as he was contemplating an expanded political and social order, John Stuart Mill was arguing that university graduates should have more than one vote, that the wise guidance of the more intelligent was needed to offset the risk of too much power in the hands of an unguided people.

Property qualifications limited the franchise throughout the industrialized world until well into the twentieth century. But property was not the only barrier. In the United States, for example, Thomas Jefferson, an architect of the Declaration of Independence and advocate of the revolutionary cause, was a slaveholder, as were

George Washington and many of the "founding fathers." Even those, like the great English reformer William Wilberforce, who argued against the injustice of slavery in the British Empire and around the world, would not have accepted non-whites as equal citizens and as voters. Lincoln came to sign the Proclamation that freed the slaves in the middle of the Civil War only when he saw that it was politically the wiser and necessary course. At its outset, the Civil War in the United States was not about freeing the slaves; it was about maintaining the union.

Slavery was widespread at the time of the Declaration of Independence, a fact that even today we gloss over when we talk of the "wisdom of the Founding Fathers." The exclusion of slaves from citizenship was set out in detail in U.S. Supreme Court Chief Justice Roger Taney's decision for the majority in the Dred Scott case of 1857.

Dred Scott, his wife, Harriet, and their two daughters were slaves brought back from a "free state" (Illinois) to Missouri by their owner, John Emerson. After Emerson died, Dred Scott sued his widow for his freedom, on the grounds that he had gained his freedom and was no longer a slave. After the suit was dismissed, he sued again in federal court, this time against John Sandford, the executor of Emerson's estate. The ultimate decision of the U.S. Supreme Court was that a "free negro of the African race," whose ancestors were brought to the United States and sold as slaves, was not a citizen within the meaning of the Constitution. The decision of the court was delivered by Chief Justice Roger B. Taney:

> In the opinion of the court, the legislation and histories of the times, and the language used in the Declaration of Independence, show that neither the class of persons who had been imported as slaves, nor their descendants, whether they had become free or not, were then acknowledged as a part of the people, nor intended to be included in the general words used in that memorable

instrument. . . . This opinion was at that time fixed and universal in the civilized portion of the white race. It was regarded as an axiom in morals as well as in politics which no one thought of disputing, or supposed to be open to dispute, and men in every grade and position in society daily and habitually acted upon it in their private pursuits, as well as in matters of public concern, without doubting for a moment the correctness of this opinion. . . . And, accordingly, a negro of the African race was regarded by them as an article of property, and held, and bought and sold as such, in every one of the thirteen colonies which united in the Declaration of Independence and afterwards formed the Constitution of the United States. (Supreme Court of the United States)

Taney exaggerates the unanimity of opinion about slavery in 1776. John Locke, one of the intellectual fathers of modern liberalism, was a critic of slavery, and the anti-slavery movement had its roots deep in British Protestant thought. Neither Thomas Paine nor Edmund Burke were supporters, and slavery was abolished in Upper Canada, for example, only twenty years after the Declaration of Independence. But the Taney judgment is important because it reminds us how deeply engrained slavery was in the first avowed democracy in the world.

Abraham Lincoln freed the slaves in 1863 but it took another hundred years of struggle before the passage of civil rights and voting legislation ensured the minimum legal protection for African Americans seeking to exercise their franchise.

Racial exclusion was the rule in many countries at the time. The expectation of the conquerors of the Americas was that native populations would be either wiped out or completely assimilated, in rapid order. Throughout the hemisphere, European settlement was a brutal business. Disease and military adventure took a terrible toll, with deaths in the millions across both continents. The

Beothuk of Newfoundland were annihilated by disease, and aboriginal populations everywhere were treated as savages to be converted, corralled into reservations, abused as workers, and disregarded as human beings until they assimilated. Grotesque efforts to "take the Indian out of the child" by governments and churches led to severe personal and cultural trauma, and have left a legacy of poverty and exclusion.

From Baffin Island in the north to Cape Horn in the south, every country in the Americas is wrestling with diversity and competing traditions and memories. Democracy in all of these countries has to deal with the terrible gap between peoples. New legal and constitutional structures are being created to come to terms with this world in a way that is respectful of human rights and different ways of life. But the pace of change is slow and uneven, and it is always those without power and resources who pay the price for delay.

This issue plays itself out in every part of the globe. The imperial experience has left huge scars. South Africa's apartheid system enshrined different rights, different places to live, work and play, in a grim pyramid of inequality and prejudice whose relatively peaceful dismantlement has to be seen as one of the triumphs of our time.

We cannot understand the politics of China and India and so many other countries of the Third World unless we make the effort to imagine what the "opening up" of these countries was like when Europe, and later the United States, took it upon themselves to make the world over in their own images. The spread of "Western values" was not just about the rule of law and better education. It was about the subjugation of vast swaths of the world to the economic benefit of the imperial power. It was also, unavoidably, about racial superiority, keeping natives out, labelling people by race and colour, creating hierarchies of worth and wealth. That was as true for the British in Africa and Asia as it was for the Dutch in Indonesia and the Americans in the Philippines.

Property and race were not the only ways of keeping the people at bay. Sex and gender have also been a battleground for centuries, and overcoming these barriers has been at the heart of the long movement toward democracy.

One of the most trenchant critiques of Edmund Burke's assault on the French Revolution (which we'll come to in the next chapter) came from a remarkable woman, Mary Wollstonecraft. She followed her *Vindication of the Rights of Men* (1790) with her powerful *Vindication of the Rights of Woman* (1792), which was at least as revolutionary a concept as the abolition of the monarchy.

The politics of most of history have been patriarchal, and in many places still are. Women were to be protected or abused, confined to the world of the home and family, denied the right to hold or inherit property, put on a pedestal of virtue or treated as sexual playthings – but never to be treated as equals. The battle for equality – which is still being waged – has taken many generations to make a difference. The Supreme Court of Canada in 1928 ruled that since women were not legally "persons" in 1867 – the time of Canadian Confederation – they were not eligible to be "summoned" to the Senate. The judges quoted at length from an 1868 English common law decision that "chiefly out of respect to women, and a sense of decorum, and not from their want of intellect, or their being for any other such reason unfit to take part in the government of the country, they have been excused from taking any share in this department of public affairs . . ."

The court's logic was simple enough: "For the public offices thereby created women were, by the common law, ineligible and it would be dangerous to assume that by the use of the ambiguous term 'persons' the imperial Parliament meant in 1867 to bring about so vast a constitutional change affecting Canadian women, as would be involved in making them eligible for selection as Privy Councillors" (Supreme Court of Canada).

In rejecting this argument– "not eligible then, not eligible now" – Lord Sankey of the Imperial Privy Council in London, which was then Canada's highest court of appeal, took a different view. "The exclusion of women from all public offices is a relic of days more barbarous than ours. . . . The British North America Act planted in Canada a living tree capable of growth and expansion within its natural limits," he wrote (Judicial Committee). And so women were indeed persons, and the BNA was not a shackle to the emancipation of women.

In Western nations, women did not begin to get the vote until the second decade of the twentieth century. The reform of family and property laws was achingly slow, and even today glass ceilings, wage discrimination, and inadequate child care, to say nothing of never-ending "culture wars," make women's equality a goal but not yet a reality. Most institutions in the West, from governments to corporations, were set up by men to suit themselves. Altering their structures and processes to accommodate women will not happen overnight.

Democracy is the working assumption of modern politics in the West. But it has to be understood as having a range of meanings and a long history. It did not come without a long struggle. It is, without a doubt, a European idea, but it speaks to universal values.

The difficulty is that the sharing or exporting of democracy comes with heavy baggage, the baggage of imperialism. To a great extent, the history of the world is the history of empires, their rise, dominance, and fall, and of how they inevitably clash with other, competing empires. Intrinsic to the imperial idea is the assumption that the values of the centre of the empire are inherently universal and superior to others, that the conquering nation has both a right and an obligation to proselytize and impose these superior values, even by force.

If pluralism, the rule of law, and equality are simply grafted or imposed onto all societies as a kind of universal good, to be adopted quickly, or worse, to be swallowed with a gun to the head, the democratic exercise is bound to fail. Our own experience in embracing these ideas and making them work in the West has had a long, difficult, and often violent history. But these ideas now lie at the heart of what we understand democracy to be, so it is not possible for us to simply abandon them in a fit of misplaced relativism. This tension takes us down some difficult paths.

Take, for example, the question of homosexual rights, something not found in the Declaration of the Rights of Man, the Universal Declaration of Human Rights, or most national constitutions. Over the last fifty years, most of the West has gone from criminalizing gay and lesbian sex between consenting adults to respecting sexual behaviour as a matter of privacy ("There's no place for the state in the bedrooms of the nation," in Trudeau's words) and now to the understanding that expressing one's sexuality is fundamental to being human, and that society should celebrate all consenting relationships and, indeed, according to many courts has a positive obligation to do so. While it is still vehemently opposed by a minority in the West, the right of homosexuals to marry is being extended by the courts in many jurisdictions.

This change has been dramatic, but in many parts of the world there is no progress.

When Iranian President Ahmadinejad spoke at Columbia University in 2007, his assertion that "there are no gays in Iran" was greeted with laughter. But behind this stupid comment lies a dark reality: gays and lesbians are executed in Iran. Hitler's regime was convinced that Jews were not human and therefore could be slaughtered without guilt. It treated homosexuals and the mentally disabled in the same way. Ahmadinejad's argument takes us down the same path.

Prejudice and even hatred against gays are still widely prevalent, and rooted in the popular culture and legal structures of many countries throughout the world. People are being harassed and killed not because of what they say, but because of who they are.

The struggle to change this will take enormous effort. It will go against the political grain. It will offend many people who will see homosexuality as a Western depravity. But we know that homosexual identity is natural, that repressing it causes misery, and that failing to provide legal protections denies people the right to be themselves – and so we have no choice but to use what leverage and influence we have to argue that gay rights are human rights, period.

Breaking down the walls of prejudice will not happen quickly. Most of the constitutions in the world today are silent on this question. But from the Canadian experience (our Charter of Rights and Freedoms does not explicitly include sexual orientation under its equality rights), we know how quickly opinion can and does shift. But it doesn't shift on its own. It requires that arguments be made, that issues be joined, that lies be exposed.

It is impossible to separate foreign policy from the issues of poverty, pollution, climate change, or of the migration of peoples in response to natural disasters, wars, ethnic conflict, and the personal desire for mobility and prosperity. Yet these issues have traditionally been treated as if they were separate from the world of diplomacy. That's simply wrong-headed. So is the notion that we can usefully talk about foreign and domestic policies in separate compartments. This is not just quaint, it is dangerous.

In many countries of the West, and especially in Canada, it must be said that we are in the world, and the world is in us. We cannot live our lives with different needs and desires in watertight compartments. Our own basic needs – clean air to breathe, water to drink, food, security, shelter – do not start and stop behind a firewall of our own making. What we want for ourselves is not that complicated, although there will always be room for choice and argument. I know no one who chooses squalour and starvation, abuse and suffering, no work, no home, no money, no dignity, no relationships. No political architecture can make us all happy all the time. But politics can change things, can make things better, for ourselves and for others.

The tendency to isolate ourselves leads some to say that not much can be done for the poor, the starving, and the persecuted because their problems are as much about their character as they are about politics. But most people are poor or badly governed through no fault of their own. The creed of self-satisfaction is ultimately bankrupt, but not just because it is morally unedifying. It is worse. It is unwise. Sticking our collective head in the sand doesn't make our problems go away.

This book is a discussion of the things we value: freedom, democracy, respect for human rights, pluralism, equality between men and women, to mention just a few – and the difficulty of defending and promoting them in the world. The central argument is that we need to think more strategically about how these values can take root in places where their absence is the source of much hardship and human suffering.

This conclusion may seem startlingly obvious, but the failure to apply it has caused much damage in the world. The military invasion of Iraq, led by the United States and the United Kingdom, and the subsequent civil war in that country, has proved a dangerous adventure. The failure to consider beyond the immediate justification for a policy to its practical consequences is always costly in human lives, dollars, and increasing insecurity. The refusal to put the question of whether a policy will work on an equal plane with the question of whether it is right will always lead to decisions that are surrounded by a self-righteous aura but have little prospect of eventual success.

As I write, Canadian and NATO troops in Afghanistan are fighting a difficult and dangerous insurgency. How do we better ensure success in that mission? What are the consequences of failure?

In subsequent chapters, I trace the history of both democratic ideas and institutions, and then look at some modern conflicts through the lens of a debate that dates back centuries. This book is not an academic or philosophical treatise, but a reflection by a practising politician who occasionally likes to think.

CHAPTER 2

CAN THE WORLD BE BORN ANEW?
An Age-Old Debate Still Resonates

O ne of the ironies of our time is that much political commentary in the West makes a point of drawing a sharp distinction between the stability and tolerance of the "democratic world" and the violence and repression of other regimes. It's ironic because it ignores or dramatically underplays the violent and revolutionary nature of the conflicts that gave rise to our democratic world. For a full one hundred years, Europe was torn asunder by the political fallout from the Protestant Reformation, which paved the way for democracy. Millions died in the name of both political and religious ideology. The English Civil War and the American and French revolutions were not about abstract categories in which competing ideas strutted across the stage of history. They were violent, bloody conflicts.

It took violence, and the lessons drawn from it, to overthrow the old feudal order and usher in the new: governance that allowed for differences of opinion without bloodshed. Thomas Paine and Edmund Burke were among the leading political writers and thinkers of their day. Their different visions of politics and democracy have had dramatically different consequences. Paine's world was a place of great ideals. There were people of virtue fighting empires of evil. Burke, by contrast, spoke to a very different spirit: for him institutions were more important than ideas, and were the embodiment of values strengthened by time and experience. To ignore them was to ignore what we know of history and human nature. It is an irony of our time that the forces of the conservative right speak more happily in the tongue of Paine and many on the left are borrowing the language of Burke, although neither are particularly steeped in either.

I doubt very much if Fox News commentator Glenn Beck realizes that Paine demolished the Christian religion in the *Age of Reason*, and pointed to the triumph of the welfare state in *The Rights of Man*. One wonders if social democratic trade unionists know they sound a little like Edmund Burke when they talk of "organized rights" and protecting past entitlements.

Writing in the winter of 1776, Thomas Paine, a passionate Englishman, took up the cause of the American Revolution as his own and found the language to make the case for democracy and independence simple, dramatic, and compelling. "These are the times that try men's souls," he wrote in one famous phrase, and went on:

> The summer soldier and the sunshine patriot will, in this crisis, shrink from the service of his country; but he that stands by it now, deserves the love and thanks of man and woman. Tyranny, like hell, is not easily conquered; yet we have this consolation with us, that the harder the conflict, the more glorious the triumph. What we obtain too cheap, we esteem too lightly: 'T is dearness only that gives every thing its value. (Paine, 117)

Thomas Jefferson, a few months earlier, also found compellingly simple words for his contribution to the American Declaration of Independence. That document speaks of "truths" that are "self-evident," and declares that "all men are created equal, that they are endowed by their Creator with certain unalienable Rights, that among these are Life, Liberty and the pursuit of Happiness."

Paine's and Jefferson's words are quoted often and almost always with great favour. In the United States especially, the values and virtues they describe as "self-evident" are considered to be worth fighting for, worth dying for, and by implication worth killing for. By extension, it is also believed that tyrants who fail to recognize the universality of these rights and the inherent goodness and inevitability of democracy must be scorned, reviled, and defeated. Life is more complicated than this. There are practical challenges to these premises and assumptions that seem on first glance to be so transparent.

All societies need a common acceptance of some form of authority to survive. The English Civil War a century and a half before the American and French revolutions had turned on apparently simple questions: where does this authority come from, and why should it be accepted? The issue of whose authority should prevail had its origins deep in medieval society, where the power and authority of church and state were hierarchical (and hereditary in the case of the Crown) and linked by the mystery of faith and ritual and the loyalties of family, tribe, and clan.

This world was shattered by the Protestant Reformation, which insisted there was no need for interlocutors between the believer and God. Thus individual conscience (based on individual literacy) alone was legitimate. The acceptance of this idea made the Reformation much more than just a religious revolution. It was also political, as it threatened the power and authority of the monarchy. In Britain, the theory of the divine right of kings, which dates to medieval times, was dear to the hearts of the Houses of Tudor and Stuart, and was a deeply held belief of both King James I and his son and successor Charles I. The notion that the monarchy was above the law and the people, that its power and authority stemmed from God and not from the nation, became increasingly incompatible with the idea that there was a profound, intrinsic equality in the human condition and that no one, not even the monarch was above it or beyond it.

The great British economic historian R.H. Tawney traces how the political and religious ideas of the Reformation had a parallel in the economic change that was also underway, in his brilliant book *Religion and the Rise of Capitalism*. A growing, successful merchant class would not accept the heavy hand of aristocratic and feudal authority. The guilds and monopolies at the base of the feudal economy had to be broken for the new economic order to succeed. The medieval "moral economy," which bound master and serf, king and nobleman, had to be shattered and replaced by a system that allowed capital freedom to move and where political authority reflected the power of a new, literate, ambitious merchant class that was insisting on its place and its rights, and would not rest until the old order disappeared.

As a Christian and a member of the Labour Party, Tawney does not celebrate this transformation. He rightly points out that social solidarity was shattered by the acquisitive spirit and that much hardship accompanied the destruction of "the commons." But it would be wrong to interpret the turmoil of that period as being just about the emergence of a thrusting capitalism. A small island kingdom of a few million people was being racked to its core by violence, poverty, and religious fanaticism, as well as by these changes in the economy. It took the conjunction of all these forces to set the stage for the emergence of the "democratic idea" as a truly revolutionary force. As in other times of political turmoil, the army itself became a focal point of the great debate.

The overthrow and execution of King Charles I in 1649 after seven years of civil war – unimaginable a short few years before – was the beginning not the end of the argument about what kind of political order should follow the end of the monarchy. Leading members of the army under the command of Oliver Cromwell gathered in Putney, then a London suburb, where they argued at length and without resolution about how far the principle of equality should be taken.

Marshall McLuhan has reminded us that the invention of the printing press around 1440 made the Protestant Reformation possible. Within a few years, Scotland, one of the poorest countries anywhere, became the most literate community in Europe, a literacy based on the widespread availability of the Bible in English and Gaelic. Literacy challenged the authority of "God's middlemen," the bishops and priests who for centuries had controlled the interpretation of the Bible, and the beliefs of the clergy and the laity, through their command of Latin. The ideas that every soul needed saving, and that salvation comes from within each individual, were incompatible with the hierarchy of feudal society. The middlemen had to go. The biggest middleman of all was the king.

This was the backdrop of the war of "all against all" that Thomas Hobbes would describe in *Leviathan* and *Behemoth* as the consequence of societies where authority, power, and legitimacy were contested and no fundamental consensus could be reached on how to organize sovereignty. The debates at Putney focused on a simple question: what's next after we've killed the King and want a new political order?

There are remarkable parallels among the debates that unfold in societies besieged by arguments about fundamentals. Twice in my life I have felt a small whiff of the excitement such moments can bring: in Baghdad in the years just after the capture of Saddam Hussein, and in Sri Lanka in the months after the 2001 ceasefire when goodwill had, however briefly, replaced the cynical antagonism of the past. We shall be looking at these examples later, but it is important to realize they have their historical antecedents.

Soon after I was first elected to Parliament in 1978, a violent dispute broke out in a Sikh temple in my constituency between those members of the temple who believed food should be eaten only while seated on the floor and those who said eating at tables while sitting on chairs was acceptable – this was neither the first nor the last of these disputes. Neighbours to the temple – not many Sikhs among them – lamented at a public meeting about how "silly" this argument seemed. "Hardly worth fighting about," some said.

I pointed out at this meeting that it took Christian Europe several hundred years to decide that arguments about ritual, the language of religious service, whether windows should be decorative or plain, whether priests should face the congregation or face the altar and the cross, were not worth dying for. Tens of millions died before the heat drained so far out of the argument that its contemporary version could seem silly.

In the seventeenth century, which was the height of the conflict in Britain, the debate took on a political as well as a religious tone. If the execution of the king simply meant that Cromwell would take over and not much else would change, the deeper potential of the revolution was being lost. An early pioneer of democracy, Colonel Thomas Rainsborough, argued at the Putney Debates that he was not fighting for property or order, but for democracy: "Really, I think that the poorest he that is in England hath a life to live, as the greatest he; and therefore truly, sir, I think it is clear that every man that is to live under a government ought first by his own consent to put himself under that government; and I do think that the poorest man in England is not at all bound in a strict sense to that government that he hath not had a voice to put himself under." To which Colonel Ireton for the establishment famously replied: "No man hath a right to an interest or share in the disposing in the affairs of the kingdom . . . that hath not a permanent, fixed interest in this kingdom" (Lindsay, 13).

So the issue was joined. To the earlier debate about religious belief and the consolidation of state power around a national church and a national king was added the potent fuel of democracy itself. For a brief, dramatic moment it seemed that the argument would be won by those who believed no one should submit to an authority he had no hand in creating.

It did not last.

Colonel Ireton won the battle of ideas for a considerable time. After Cromwell died, the monarchy was restored relatively peacefully in 1660, more with a whimper than a bang. Then a bloodless coup in 1689, known as the Glorious Revolution, confirmed that the British Crown would be forever Protestant, that the nation would be governed by consensus of Crown and Parliament, and that religious disputes would no longer be at the heart of political life. This cemented the notion in the British Constitution that religious tolerance (for Protestants initially, and much later for others), independent judges, and a Parliament increasingly responsible to a slowly expanding electorate were the hallmarks of a law-abiding society. Democracy would only come much, much later, and be built firmly on this liberal base.

The changes that occurred over this 150-year period were dramatic. At the outset, religious belief was everything. Protestants and Catholics killed each other because they could not imagine coexisting. Fighting about what was right and who should triumph was more important than civic order, social peace, or making money. Over time, collective exhaustion set in. In 1651, British philosopher Thomas Hobbes, much affected by the Civil War, published the book *Leviathan*. In it, he made a simple argument: order must triumph before anything else can get done. Sovereignty was not about the victory of a particular ideology; it was about ending civil war, order over chaos, and the monopoly of effective control. Religious beliefs had to recede as the exclusive basis of civil authority, because they were so divisive. Faith became a private matter. This is no trivial achievement – indeed it can be said that a key difference between political and religious extremists and the rest of us is that they believe their ideas or philosophy or theology are more important than anything else, and we believe in a world of freedom and security where religions and political differences are kept within bounds and limits.

These are in part the issues being played out in Iraq and Afghanistan, and in the Middle East, Pakistan, and Kashmir. We are in the middle of a long struggle whose conclusion will only come when a social consensus emerges that the costs of conflict are simply too high.

Not much of the British consensus that emerged during the Glorious Revolution was written down in a new constitution.

Indeed the Constitution of Great Britain and Northern Ireland is nowhere to be found, or rather it is everywhere to be found. It is found in the Magna Carta, in statutes, legal decisions, and precedents, all subject to change and interpretation. There was then, of course, as there is today, an enormous hubris and complacency in Britain about "the genius" of its common law and the allegedly unique character of the freedom and integrity of justice shared by British society. Like the arguments for American exceptionalism, they are tiresome to the rest of the world.

No one expressed this idealization of the historical and cultural character of "British liberty" better than Edmund Burke. An Irishman who went to London as a young man in the 1750s, Burke devoted his life to the House of Commons. Matthew Arnold said of Burke that he "saturated his politics with thought." This in itself would make him a little unusual for a member of Parliament. The fundamental premise of Burke's political thinking is that it is the shared experience of great institutions over time that create the social and cultural conditions of liberty. Emphasizing that "there is nothing more dangerous than governing in the name of a theory," Burke was adamant that freedom is not something to be thought of in the abstract.

Burke's position as an MP gave him an insider's perspective on politics. He became a key member of the parliamentary group led by the Marquess of Rockingham, known as the Rockingham Whigs. Burke served briefly in a ministry in the 1760s, and for the rest of his parliamentary career – which lasted until his death in 1794 – was not in government. But he was a man of both influence and inspiration.

His political beliefs rested on a few central themes: the need to understand and appreciate the balance between competing forces that underlay the evolving British constitution; the premise that man is weak but the species is strong, which meant that institutions both of government and religion deserved great respect because they reflected the collective wisdom of the ages rather than the temporary whims of the moment; and that the abuse of power happened most dramatically when people chose to govern in the name of abstract theory rather than with respect for institutional wisdom.

Burke applied these principles to the great issues of his time: the relationship between the Crown and Parliament; the exclusion of Roman Catholics from political and economic rights, which he thought unjust and futile; the rebellion in the American colonies; the corruption within the East Indian Company, which *was* the British Empire in the Indian subcontinent; and finally, the French Revolution and the risk that its ideas and influence posed to European civilization.

Writing about Ireland and Catholic emancipation in 1765, Burke said: "There are two, and only two, foundations of law . . . equity and utility. [Equity] grows out of the great rule of equality, which is grounded upon our common nature . . . The other foundation of law, which is utility, must be understood, not of partial or limited, but of general and public utility" (Burke, 214-15).

This gives some flavour to Burke's s thinking. The "mother of justice" is the equality of human beings. This is "grounded upon our common nature," our shared humanity. But the second principle is "utility," by which he means the exercise of rationality or judgment to ensure that the law reflects the broadest public interest.

When Burke's party was attacked for briefly reversing the unpopular taxes on the American colonies that had produced such a strong reaction that there was serious talk of independence, he answered with characteristic vehemence: the Tory insistence on an across-the-board tax based on an exaggerated sense of unlimited parliamentary sovereignty was bound to fail because of its simple lack of "utility." Parliament technically could implement any tax it wanted, but doing so was simply misguided, because "politics ought to be adjusted, not to human reasonings, but to human nature, of which the reason is but a part, and by no means the greatest part" (Burke , 102).

Burke held the post of agent for the State of New York between 1771 and 1775, and he took a deeply practical interest in the steady deterioration in the relationship between Britain and the American colonies. He objected vociferously to what he saw as abusive behaviour by the Crown, which he thought paralleled the abuse of Parliament by the courtier "cabal" around King George III. In his Speech on American Taxation (1774), Burke insisted that if Britain continued to view every objection to its taxing measures as tantamount to insurrection, the conflict would only escalate. But if another route could be found, reconciliation was entirely possible:

> The spirit of practicality, of moderation, and mutual convenience will never call in geometrical exactness as the arbitrator of an amicable settlement. Consult and follow your experience . . . Revert to your old principles . . . Leave America, if she has taxable matter in her, to tax herself. I am not here going into the distinctions of rights, nor attempting to mark their boundaries. I do not enter into these metaphysical distinctions; I hate the very sound of them. (Burke, 149)

Burke went on to remind his audience that America was not a small place, but a whole continent, with a rapidly growing population and a burgeoning economy. This meant that any effort to subdue the colonies by force would be hugely difficult, if not impossible.

> . . . the use of force alone is but temporary. It may subdue for a moment; but it does not remove the necessity of subduing again; and a nation is not governed which is perpetually to be conquered . . . Terror is not always the effect of force, and an armament is not a victory. If you do not succeed, you are without resource; for, conciliation failing, force remains; but force failing, no further hope of

reconciliation is left. Power and authority are sometimes
bought by kindness; but they will never be begged as alms
by an impoverished and defeated violence. (Burke, 157)

It was not just population and commerce that made Britain's
policy folly, it was the fact that force and intimidation were
running up against the "fierce spirit of liberty," which Burke saw
as the essential public character of the American people. As for
the exasperated notion of locking them up and throwing away the
key, Burke was blunt. It was simply not possible to "draw up an
indictment on an whole people."

Conciliation and concession had to be tried, he argued, and
Burke's resolutions were sweeping: the colonies should be recognized as self-governing, free from the burden of imperial taxation,
able to pursue their destinies within an empire that recognized
both rights and limits. This practical spirit had seen its advantages
at home. The right approach to the colonies called for a new spirit
in the empire, a kind of federal co-operation, where authority
would arise from common values, not from force:

> Let the colonies always keep the idea of their civil rights
> associated with your government – they will cling and
> grapple to you, and no force under heaven will be of
> power to tear them from their allegiance. But let it be
> once understood that your government may be one thing
> and their privileges another, that these two things may
> exist without any mutual relation – the cement is gone,
> the cohesion is loosened and everything hastens to decay
> and dissolution. (Burke, 184)

Burke's essential point about America is that it did not will its
way to a revolution based on abstract principles. It was pushed
into rebellion by the fatuous insistence of George III and his ministers that the Crown and Parliament had the absolute right to do

as they wished, to impose their taxes and authority wherever and however they wanted.

Burke argued that the expression of absolute power contained in the phrase "sovereignty of Parliament" always had to be exercised with discretion and good judgment. The real constitution is always evolving. Practical realities and good governance, public opinion itself, are always barriers to absolute authority. Parliament can only do whatever it wants in theory, not in practice.

As we well know, George III won the argument, and Britain lost America. But Burke's arguments provide critical insight into the nature of authority that remain relevant to the modern state. Legitimacy is based on consent, on opinion. The Hobbesian state of enforced order alone would not survive without consent, a moral consensus. Short-term power might come from the barrel of a gun, but long-term authority and legitimacy require something else: a deeper and shared acceptance of the rule of law based firmly on the principles of equality and utility, on a shared humanity and on what will work in practice.

If the American Revolution gave Burke inspiration to warn Parliament of the consequences of imperial overreach, his epic confrontation with Warren Hastings, the governor of the East India Company, took the argument even further.

Hastings had been appointed governor of Bengal in 1772, and during his lengthy tenure was accused of corruption and abuse of power. Burke became a serious student of Indian history and politics, and after joining the Parliamentary Select Committee in 1781 he became, in effect, Hastings's chief prosecutor. The cause became something of an obsession for Burke, and many of his critics concluded that he had lost perspective and was blaming Hastings for every act of injustice committed in India.

Burke was, in effect, using Hastings as a proxy for putting imperialism on trial, but it never occurred to him that the empire itself was illegitimate, just as he had ruled out the possibility of British withdrawal from America in his speeches on reconciliation.

He admitted that "all these circumstances are not, I confess, very favourable to the idea of our attempting to govern India at all. But there we are; there we are placed by the Sovereign Disposer; and we must do the best we can in our situation. The situation of man is the preceptor of his duty" (Burke 378-79).

It shows the limits of political debate that such a comment would go unchallenged in the House of Commons of the time. It would be several generations before anti-imperial movements in the colonies would be matched by liberal, radical, and socialist opinion at home that rejected the idea that the "Sovereign Disposer" had simply placed British financial and economic interests smack in the middle of India. Despite this limitation, Burke's conclusions about the East India Company's rule in India were dramatic, as was his remedy: "An oppressive, irregular, capricious, unsteady, rapacious, and peculating despotism, with a direct disavowal of obedience to any authority at home, and without any fixed maxim, principle, or rule of proceeding to guide them in India, is at present the state of your charter-government over great kingdoms" (Burke, 379).

In his speech opening the impeachment trial in 1788, Burke was scathing in his attack on Hastings's main defence, that politics and administration in India could not be judged by the standards of the West:

> These gentlemen have formed a plan of geographical morality, by which the duties of men, in public and in private situations, are not to be governed by their relation to the great Governor of the universe, or by their relation to mankind, but by climates, degrees of longitude, parallels not of life but of latitudes; as if, when you have crossed the equinoctial, all the virtues die. . . .
>
> This geographical morality we do protest against. Mr. Hastings shall not screen himself under it . . . the laws of morality are the same everywhere, and . . . there

is no action which would pass for an act of extortion, of peculation, of bribery, and of oppression in England, that is not an act of extortion, of peculation, or bribery, and oppression in Europe, Asia, Africa and all the world over. (Burke, 395-96)

This is the core of Burke's argument and a critical precursor of international law. The fundamental premises of law he described earlier in his statements on natural law are richly applied as he refutes the defences of "just following orders" and "East is East and West is West." They would echo almost 160 years later at the prosecutions in Nuremberg in 1945, and, decades after that, in international courts convened in The Hague and Arusha.

Burke was emphatic. India was a great civilization, not a land of savages and despotism. He defended both Muslim and Hindu systems of justice and administration as sophisticated and carefully crafted, which contrasted dramatically with the actions of the young men brought over by Hastings to steal the wealth of the region.

Hastings was eventually acquitted by the House of Lords, but Burke's main points were conceded. The administration of India would henceforth be public, not private. What had been a purely commercial enterprise would become a massive imperial regime. And for the next two hundred years, Western societies would be debating the legitimacy of imperialism itself.

Burke had told his electors in Bristol in 1774 that a member of Parliament had the duty to "sacrifice his repose, his pleasure, his satisfactions, to theirs . . . but his unbiased opinion, his mature judgment, his enlightened conscience, he ought not to sacrifice to you, to any man, or to any set of men living." And the events of the last few years severely tested Burke's conscience and character. An architect of the Whig party and the loyalties due to the "little platoons" that are critical to the establishment of responsible government, Burke ultimately broke with his party, although he insisted that his fellow Whigs broke with him. A lifelong opponent of the king and his courtiers in Parliament, he nevertheless accepted a pension from the Crown. This disillusioned many of his supporters and forced him into a defence of his life just as it was ending.

What pushed Burke to this extreme was the French Revolution, but the conflict had been present all along in Burke's writing. Even as a young man who abandoned formal legal studies to become a "philosopher in action," Burke's earliest work had brought him into direct conflict with the thinking of Rousseau, Diderot, and the philosophers of the Enlightenment.

"Man is born free, but is everywhere in chains" wrote Rousseau in the *Social Contract*. This was to Burke a nonsensical and even dangerous notion. It assumed a society of free people whose true nature was perverted by institutions that were intrinsically limiting and corrupting. The Enlightenment reasoning was that churches, political regimes, culture, customs and traditional beliefs were all systems of power and authority whose legitimacy had to be called into question by men whose capacity for reason would provide the key to freedom.

UN diplomat and political writer extraordinaire Conor Cruise O'Brien, who has published a biography of Edmund Burke, wrote that Rousseau's aphorism could just as well be "Sheep are born to eat meat and everywhere are herbivores." Burke thought it was simply wrong to argue that man was inherently good but corrupted by the artifices of society. He held that this was the reverse of what was true: that man's imperfections and failings were made less so by the institutions built over centuries. As he once put it, "Liberty, too, must be limited in order to be possessed."

In his reviews of Rousseau's books in the Annual Register in the 1750s and 1760s, Burke made it clear what he didn't like about Rousseau – by pushing every argument too far, taking it to its extremes, the man living in exile in Geneva was "unsettling our notions of right and wrong" (Burke, 89). "He never knows where to stop . . . He is therefore frequently tiresome and disgusting by pushing his notions to excess; and by repeating the same thing in a thousand different ways. Poverty can hardly be more vicious than such abundance " (Burke, 95).

Burke followed events in France closely, worried about the atheism and "excessive rationalism" he found in salon society, and wrote as well about the excessive debt of the country, which placed such a burden on the citizenry that it was hard to predict the consequences. Many around him, notably his Whig colleague Charles James Fox, were enthused by what they saw and heard in the early days after the French Revolution started in 1789. Outside Parliament, societies of all kinds sprang up in support of "the rights of man." Radical and dissenting groups that could trace their inspiration to the Levellers of the time of Cromwell came alive, emboldened by the spirit not just of liberty, but of democracy itself.

On November 4, 1789, a sermon was delivered by Dr. Richard Price, a leading Nonconformist minister, praising the revolution in France as the legitimate inheritor of Britain's own Glorious Revolution a hundred years earlier. Writing a year later, Burke said, "I looked on that sermon as the public declaration of a man much connected with literary caballers and intriguing philosophers, with political theologians and theological politicians, both at home and abroad" (Burke, 429).

Burke saw the revolution as the triumph of ideology over experience. Everything about it offended him: its deep anti-clericalism and assaults on established religion; its personal and vituperative attack on the king and queen; its radical undermining of property rights and relations; its extraordinary populism, which offended his deep sense of order and civility.

But what took Burke's critique further was his sense that, as he wrote in 1790, this was no mere radical upset. The world was entering a new and dangerous phase, where politics knew no bounds and where the revolution would consume all. In that regard he predicted and understood the Reign of Terror better than those around him. He was called every name in the book, an Old Tory, a sell-out who, in the words of Thomas Paine, "pitied the plumage more than the dying bird" in his descriptions of the treatment of Marie Antoinette.

Like George Orwell a couple of centuries later, Burke had a powerful sense of just how ominous destructive revolutions can be. Alexis de Tocqueville would write in 1835 about the tyranny of the revolutionary idea, "[T]he oppression which threatens people in a democracy will be unlike anything we have seen before. None of us can find its likening in our memory. Our words like 'dogmatism' and 'tyranny' do not do it justice. It is a new thing. We shall have to define it before we name it." Burke shared this sentiment when he wrote of the new, all encompassing world of revolutionary politics:

> The pretended rights of these theorists are all extremes; and in proportion as they are metaphysically true, they are morally and politically false. The rights of men are in a sort of middle, incapable of definition, but not impossible to be discerned. The rights of men in governments are their advantages; and these are often in balances between differences of good, in compromises sometimes between good and evil, and sometimes between evil and evil. Political reason is a computing principle: adding, subtracting, multiplying, and dividing, morally and not metaphysically or mathematically, true moral denominations. By these theorists the right of the people is almost always sophistically confounded with their power. The body of the community, whenever it can come to act, can meet with no effectual resistance. (Burke, 454-55)

Burke believed that an all-consuming politics would sweep away everything in its path; all advantages, all privacy, all dignity, all real rights. Thus a "barbarous philosophy, which is the off-spring of cold hearts and muddy understandings" meant a politics that knew no limits. In 1790, long before the execution of the French royal family and the debauchery of the Terror, he wrote prophetically, "In the groves of *their* academy, at the end of every vista, you see nothing but the gallows" (Burke, 459). The fury of the mob would produce more havoc than could ever come "from the dominion of a single sceptre . . . those who are subjected to wrong under multitudes are deprived of all external consolation; they seem deserted by mankind, overpowered by a conspiracy of their whole species. " (Burke, 485)

Burke's conclusion was clear: there could be no compromise with these revolutionary doctrines. They had nothing to do with freedom or good governance, nothing to do with an ordered politics that knew its limits or with a rule of law based on tradition and a reverence for institutions whose efficacy had stood the test of time. The "will of the people" and the "rights of men" on the French model would honour no religion and respect no differences. It would assert that every arrangement in life had to fall to the justice of the revolution and "men would become little better than the flies of a summer" (Burke, 469).

In what is perhaps his most famous passage, Burke wrote:

> Society is, indeed, a contract. Subordinate contracts for objects of mere occasional interest may be dissolved at pleasure; but the state ought not to be considered as nothing better than a partnership agreement in a trade of pepper and coffee, calico or tobacco, or some other such low concern, to be taken up for a little temporary interest, and to be dissolved by the fancy of the parties. It is to be looked on with other reverence. (Burke, 471)

Burke would have none of the argument that things in France had gotten so bad that the only cure was a deep revolution. The monarchy could be reformed, the clergy could mend their ways, and the approach of improving what was already in place always made better sense. The notion that "everything old should be new again" was fatuous nonsense. Instead,

> A man full of warm, speculative benevolence may wish his society otherwise constituted than he finds it; but a good patriot, and a true politician, always considers how he shall make the most of the existing materials of his country. A disposition to preserve, and an ability to improve, taken together, would be my standard of a statesman. (Burke, 501)

The last years of Burke's life were marked by sadness and controversy. His son died before him. Many of his friends abandoned him when he led the Old Whigs to support a Conservative coalition, led by William Pitt the Younger that took the revolutionary threat seriously, at home and in Europe. He was knighted as Lord Beaconsfield and received a handsome pension from the king, whom he had once vilified, for his years of public service. But he did not go quietly into the night. When two of his former friends, the Duke of Bedford and the Earl of Lauderdale, took it upon themselves to hammer away at him for having abandoned his principles and becoming a pensioned courtier, Burke wrote his last pamphlet, "A Letter to a Noble Lord." No one today remembers much about Bedford or Lauderdale, but Burke's spirited response is a gem of vindication. He had some fun with the contrast between his pension, which he felt was fair compensation for a lifetime of public service, and the inherited (and vast) wealth of his critics, but Burke saved the best for his main point. These naïve and fatuous aristocrats did not understand that the revolutionaries across the English Channel would soon be eating *their* dinner as well. What was happening in France was not some well-meaning reform. It was a "dreadful innovation" that would sweep all in its path, including the duke and the earl.

What the "Noble Lord" did not understand was that all the while he was expressing fond hope for reason and change to prevail in France, "like the print of the poor ox that we see in the shop-windows at Charing Cross, alive as he is, and thinking no harm in the world, he is divided into rumps, and sirloins, and briskets, and into all sorts of pieces for roasting, boiling, and stewing. " (Burke, 578-79) It is hard to imagine a more compelling illustration of the phrase "done like dinner."

Burke died in 1797 at the age of sixty-eight, convinced that the battle for liberal values meant that Britain had no choice but to take on the threat of a spreading Jacobinism with force of arms. Two years later Britain was at war with France and her allies, and remained so until 1815. During those years, the forces of democracy within the country faced serious repression, with trade unions and political activists arrested and deported. The full power of the state was brought to bear against those who felt that "English liberty" had to mean rights for the people and not just the privileged few.

Burke fully understood the dangers of revolution that shook his time, and shakes ours still today, but he failed to comprehend the flaws in the "dying bird," to return to the analogy penned by Thomas Paine. Burke's defence of the established world more than once led him to the dangerous stance of "whatever is, is right," a reverence for tradition that meant he was oblivious to what needed to change and a complacency for the unearned blessings of the lives of the privileged. His politics were unmoved by even an ounce of populism, although in his writings on Ireland and America he did know and understand what a deep sense of grievance could mean and the futility of repression. But the plight of "the people" in those countries never led him down the path of revolution. In seeking to get the king to reconcile with the colonies, Burke was still the parliamentary insider. His was always an argument for change from within.

On America, for example, Burke wrote about the conflict almost as if the Declaration of Independence didn't contain Jefferson's powerful words about the "self-evident" nature of man's equality and the right to life, liberty and the pursuit of happiness. While it is true the spirit of the American Revolution drew many of its principles from the theories of a balanced constitution that Burke embraced, there was also an underlying sense of deeper change, a sense that institutions like the monarchy and the established church had to give way to the force of reason and first principles.

We shall never know whether the American Revolution could have been averted by a more conciliatory Britain, any more than whether the full force of the Terror in France could have been prevented, as Burke certainly believed, by the French adopting the virtues of the balanced constitution celebrated by Montesquieu but reviled by Rousseau.

The radical spirit of democracy and of the rights of man was better expressed by Thomas Paine than by anyone else of his time and generation. Born in Norfolk County in 1739, the son of Quaker parents, Tom Paine failed as a stay maker and excise man and was penniless in 1774 when he decided to venture to the American colonies at the age of thirty-five.

Paine wrote a few years later, "When the country, into which I had just set my foot, was set on fire about my ears, it was time to stir. It was time for every man to stir." (Paine, 7) And stir he certainly did. Paine's powerful pamphlet "Common Sense," written in 1776, had an extraordinary impact as soon as it appeared. It sold over a hundred thousand copies, which made it the bestselling book of its time next to the Bible. Its argument and its language were passionate and blunt.

Few pieces of political writing have done more to capture and express the spirit of the moment. According to George Washington, none was so successful at persuading Americans that the path to independence was the only right road. Jefferson, no slouch himself in the writing department, said, "No writer has exceeded Paine in ease and familiarity of style, in perspicuity of expression, happiness of elucidation, and in simple and unassuming language" (Paine, 32).

"Common Sense" appeared before the Declaration of Independence, in the winter of 1776. It was a critical and difficult year. The colonies were divided, there was much debate about the wisdom of the conflict with the king, and many of the colonists were searching for a way out, for what Burke called "conciliation."

Paine's was a powerful call for independence: "The cause of America is in a great measure the cause of all mankind . . . The laying a Country desolate with Fire and Sword, declaring War against the natural rights of all Mankind, and extirpating the Defenders thereof from the Face of the Earth, is the concern of every Man to whom Nature hath given the Power of feeling" (Paine, 65-66).

For Paine, conciliation was neither possible nor wise. Too much blood had been spilled; too much division had come to America. A peace in 1776 would have split the colonies, and forced brother against brother. The die was cast. There was no turning back.

Burke thought that reforming the constitution was all about achieving a better balance. While the power of the king to name his placemen had to be limited, and accountability to Parliament had to mean something, balance between the Crown, the Lords and the Commons had to be maintained, with each respected.

Paine would have none of this. Men were born equal, the ranks and differences that ate away at the egalitarian soul of society were merely the products of wars and thefts of an earlier time. Neither the monarchy nor the aristocracy (what he called "the no-ability") had any reason for existence apart from histori-cal accident and brute force. Invoking the old, radical argument of the "Norman Yoke" – that ancient English institutions had been usurped by the invasion of William the Conqueror in 1066 – Paine wrote, "A French bastard landing with an armed banditti, and establishing himself king of England against the consent of the natives, is in plain terms a very paltry rascally original – It certainly hath no divinity in it . . . that William the Conqueror was an usurper is a fact not to be contradicted. The plain truth is that the antiquity of English monarchy will not bear looking into" (Paine, 76, 77).

"Common Sense" crackles with democratic fervour. Its argument is simple, its language plain. It laid the foundation for the idea of American "exceptionalism" that is espoused by many in the United States today: "We have it in our power to begin the world over again. A situation, similar to the present, hath not happened since the days of Noah until now. The birth-day of a new world is at hand" (Paine, 109).

The myth that the "noblest, purest constitution on the face of the earth" could be created in a single stroke was thus born. Paine's was a remarkable performance. Fresh off the boat from England, he filled a void and his passionate rhetoric helped turn a tax revolt into a revolution. He quickly made friends, and also enemies, and as time progressed his prescription for what needed to be done and could be done was challenged both by his adversaries and the times.

Paine had a simple, if not simplistic, view about constitutions. They should express the will of the people, and should change as that will changes. The job of the courts was to apply the law, not to make it, and that is why a constitution needed to be in writing. He never ceased to make fun of what he saw as the fiction that Britain had a constitution. How could it? It wasn't written down.

The American political leadership was hardly of one mind when it came to what should happen next, and Paine was not an easy colleague. He drank a lot and had no family. He was quick to take offence and never felt recognized for his contribution to the revolutionary cause. His correspondence is filled with vituperation and constant requests for money and recognition. He thought his opponents were rascals. They responded in kind, the prickly John Adams writing:

I know not whether any man in the world has had more influence on its inhabitants or affairs for the last thirty years than Tom Paine. There can be no severer satyr on the age. For such a mongrel between pig and puppy, begotten by a wild boar on a bitch wolf, never before in any age of the world was suffered by the poltroonery of mankind, to run through such a career of mischief. Call it then the Age of Paine. (Paine, 28-29)

Paine gave as good as he got. In an extraordinary diatribe written in 1795 after his release from a French prison, he let loose against all those "reactionaries" – George Washington, John Adams, Alexander Hamilton, John Jay – who he felt had betrayed the revolution, by limiting democracy in the Constitution of 1787, by toying with the idea of a hereditary presidency, by ceding power to the Senate, by an obsequious treaty with Britain. Washington was "treacherous in private friendship . . . and a hypocrite in public life" who took credit for winning a war that really belonged to France (and presumably to Paine, who arranged a critical loan and the presence of French ships during the colonies' revolt). John Adams, whom Paine particularly loathed, "is one of those men who never contemplated the origin of government, or comprehended anything of first principles" (Paine, 495). The diatribes continued right up until Paine died – alone, angry, and penniless – in 1806.

At the time of the American Revolution, he served as an aide-de-camp to a revolutionary general, and as secretary to the Committee of Foreign Affairs of the Congress, and he travelled to France to get much-needed financial and military support for the rebellion. On his return, frustrated and penniless, he asked Congress for money. He was refused, although two states helped him out, Pennsylvania with $500 in cash and New York with a farm in New Rochelle. He aspired to be an inventor, and in the 1780s was as interested in his scheme for an iron bridge as he was in constitutional arguments. But it was a new revolution, not an engineering method, that gave Paine a renewed purpose, and the world his second great contribution to thinking about democracy.

He had returned to England in the spring of 1787 (ironically the year in which America would adopt its new Constitution). He quickly fell in with the crowd of radicals and dissenters who saw in the democratic ideas of the American Revolution renewed inspiration for change at home and elsewhere in Europe. Before leaving for Britain, Paine had expressed these thoughts remarkably clearly in his "Letter to the Abbé Raynal," a review of a French account of the American Revolution. Paine felt that the abbé had missed the key point about what had happened in America. It was more than just a tax revolt: "Our style and manner of thinking have undergone a revolution more extraordinary than the political revolution of the country. We see with other eyes; we hear with other ears; and think with other thoughts, than those we formerly used. We can look back on our own prejudices, as if they had been the prejudices of other people" (Paine, 163).

It was the American Revolution, and the alliance with France, that created this transformation, which could not now be stopped or contained. What had worked in America could and should work everywhere. The language echoes St. Paul and the expectation of religious conversions was no less profound: "A total reformation is wanted in England. She wants an expanded mind – a heart which embraces the universe . . . It is not now a time for little contrivances or artful politics" (Paine, 165).

In the winter of 1789, Paine was in France, where he was widely fêted as a Citizen of the World. He liked what he saw, the principles of reason and equality being applied to destroy moth-eaten institutions that belonged in the dustbin of history.

Enter Edmund Burke. His *Reflections on the Revolution in France*, itself a reply to a sermon by Dr. Richard Price (whom Paine described as "one of the best-hearted men that lives"), as we have seen, took dead aim at the central notion of democratic thinking: that the people or the nation had a right to choose their own governors, "to cashier them for misconduct, and to frame a government for ourselves" (Paine, 202).

Point counterpoint: Paine wrote *The Rights of Man* as a response to Burke's *Reflections*. Paine easily won the publishing stakes, Part II of the *Rights of Man* is said to have sold nearly 1.5 million copies during Paine's lifetime, versus about 30,000 for *Reflections*. To say that Paine struck a nerve is an obvious understatement. Just as *Common Sense* captured the spirit of 1776, *The Rights of Man* spoke for the democratic urges unleashed by the fall of the Bastille.

A simple view would be that the democratic pamphleteer had the better argument, and that the hoary elitism of Burke at twilight was no match for Paine's rhetoric. And yet. We saw that Burke, writing long before the execution of King Louis XVI and the full force of the Terror, had exceptional insight into the full force of what the French Revolution meant in reality. Paine's first argument is that Burke's portrayal of Dr. Price and the French National Assembly was quite exaggerated:

> Notwithstanding Mr Burke's horrid paintings, when the French Revolution is compared with the revolutions of other countries, the astonishment will be that is marked with so few sacrifices . . . Among the few who fell, there do not appear to be any that were intentionally singled out. They all of them had their fate in the circumstances of the moment, and were not pursued with that long, cold-blooded, unabated revenge which pursued the unfortunate Scotch in the affair of 1745 [the defeat of Bonnie Prince Charlie at Culloden]. (Paine, 211-12)

Paine's take on the essence of the French Revolution presages the comment by the American journalist Lincoln Steffens on the Russian Revolution: "I have seen the future and it works !" Score one for Burke in the insight department. But, to be fair, Paine did have a point when he noted how insensitive Burke was to the injustices that fuelled revolutionary fervour, in his comment about Burke caring more for the plumage than the dying bird. Score one for Paine.

Paine's argument in *The Rights of Man* is weakened throughout by constant personal attacks on Burke as a pensioner who had been bought off by the Tories. This is all the more ironic because Paine felt he deserved to be recognized for his service to America. But personal invective aside, there are two central arguments in Part I of the *Rights of Man*. The first is that, just as in the case of the American Revolution, the events in France forced the world to return to first principles, to remind itself about the essential questions of what politics and society are all about: "What we now see in the world, from the revolutions of America and France, are a renovation of the natural world order of things, a system of principles as universal as truth and the existence of man, and combining moral with political happiness and national prosperity" (Paine, 260).

The second is Paine's dismissal of the notion that some past agreements or understandings should prevent a people from exercising their full sovereignty and power as a dangerous nonsense that was nothing more than the tyranny of the past over the present and the future. Burke's idea of a "long contract," Paine said, was a cover for tyranny.

> I. Men are born and always continue, free and equal in respect of their rights. Civil distinctions, therefore, can be founded only on public utility.
> II. The end of all political associations is the preservation of the natural and imprescriptible rights of man; and these rights are liberty, property, security, and resistance of oppression.
> III. The Nation is essentially the source of all Sovereignty; nor can any INDIVIDUAL, or ANY BODY OF MEN,

be entitled to any authority which is not expressly derived
from it. (Paine, 260)

An advocate of limited but effective and efficient government,
Paine argued that societies based on these principles would no
longer have oppressive governments over them. The natural
harmony of things would be restored, corruption would cease, as
would excessive taxes, patronage, and the burden of unnecessary
"place" aristocrats, and assorted hangers-on.

Listen to Paine:

The vanity and presumption of governing beyond the
grave, is the most ridiculous and insolent of all tyrannies.
(Paine, 204)

A greater absurdity cannot present itself to the understanding of man, than what Mr Burke offers to his readers.
He tells them, and he tells the world to come, that a
certain body of men, who existed a hundred years ago,
made a law; and that there does not now exist in the
nation, nor ever will, nor ever can, a power to alter it.
Under how many subtleties or absurdities has the divine
right to govern been imposed on the credulity of mankind?
Mr Burke has discovered a new one, and he has shortened
his journey to Rome by appealing to the power of this
infallible parliament of former days; and he produces
what it has done as of divine authority, for that power
must certainly be more than human, which no human
power to the end of time can alter. (Paine, 205)

When Burke criticized the harsh discrimination against Irish
Catholics, he fully accepted that the equal treatment of all people
before the law was a hallmark of a moral society. He accepted the
notion that people had rights. The core issue separating him and
Paine was that Burke did not believe rights could be asserted in

the abstract as absolutes. "Rights with what consequences?" And if the exercise of universal rights gave rise to the oppression of the majority, despite legal contracts and acquired rights, then the doctrine of rights would give rise to a new era, not of liberty, but of oppression.

In Paine's second argument, there is a fascinating tension between the principle of popular sovereignty and the idea of constitutional government. Like Jefferson, Paine was deeply troubled by the way in which arguments about constitutionalism quickly became limits on the pure democracy that had been such a source of inspiration for him during revolutionary times. The complex balance we see today between judges and legislators, with courts reviewing parliamentary decisions, would have filled him with horror, as would any notion that the Supreme Court of the United States had the right and obligation to test the will of legislators against the "intentions of the Founders" as expressed in the Constitution and the Bill of Rights.

But in reality this is what written constitutions are all about. Arguments of interpretation and application are unavoidable, which is why the independence of the judiciary, and the protection of minority opinion and rights, are at the heart of constitutional thinking. John Adams understood that. So did the Federalists. Paine did not.

Paine's root-and-branch attack on the evils of the monarchy, aristocracy and the purveyors of oppression in Britain gave *The Rights of Man* a dangerous flavour in a country increasingly obsessed with national security. The second part of the book went even further, setting out an ambitious plan for pensions for the people, full employment, and an end to imperial wars. Paine set the agenda for progressive politics for the next two centuries. He also set the authorities against him for asserting that the revolutions in America and France would be but a prelude to a revolution in the system of government in Britain.

Paine was charged with seditious libel and fled to France in September of 1792. In a pamphlet published just after he left England, Paine wrote these stirring words:

> If to expose the fraud and imposition of monarchy, and every species of hereditary government – to lessen the oppression of taxes – to propose plans for the education of helpless infancy, and the comfortable support of the aged and distressed – to endeavour to conciliate nations to each other – to extirpate the horrid practice of war – to promote universal peace, civilization and commerce – and to break the chains of political superstition, and raise degraded man to his proper rank; – if these things be libellous, let me live the life of a libeller, and let the name of Libeller be engraven on my tomb . . .
>
> A man derives no more excellence from the change of a name, or calling him king, or calling him lord, than I should do by changing my name from Thomas to George, or from Paine to Guelph. I should not be a whit the more able to write a book because my name was altered; neither would any man, now called a king or a lord, have a whit the more sense that he now has, were he to call himself Thomas Paine. (Paine, 370-71)

In August 1792 this same Tom Paine was awarded the title of "Citizen of France," and in September was elected to the new National Convention in Paris. A remarkable turn of events, by any definition. For Paine it was a chance to be lionized once again as the first Citizen of the World and the foremost champion of democracy. A year later he was in jail, and came within a hair's breadth of going to the guillotine.

Appointed to the Committee of Nine to write the French Constitution, Paine found himself caught in the crossfire of the

battle between Jacobins and Girondins, the bewildering mael-
strom of competing ideologies and personalities that quickly put
the lie to his earlier fond notion that the "few who fell were not
intentionally singled out." He argued for an end to the monarchy,
but against the execution of the king. For all he was now a citizen
of France, the war between France and England after 1793 made
him suspect in the eyes of his detractors, including Robespierre,
who arrested and imprisoned him. His optimistic vision of democracy did not include the irrationalities of the Terror.

Paine spent his time in prison writing *The Age of Reason*, his
assault on organized religion. He was released from prison after a
series of entreaties from American ambassador James Monroe,
and proceeded to stay at the American embassy for several months,
confirming his reputation as one of the world's great schnorrers.
He wrote relatively little about France after the revolution, com-
pleting *Agrarian Justice* before returning to the United States in
1802. His religious views earned him the lasting opposition of the
followers of established religion, and he remained a bitterly controversial and increasingly lonely figure until his death in 1809 at
the age of seventy-two.

Two lives devoted to politics in an era of revolution and of swirl-
ing controversies about rights, freedoms, empire, and democracy.
What does it all mean today? What do these old debates and diatribes have to tell us?

The short answer is "a great deal." Current arguments about
human rights, constitution making, good governance, humanitarian intervention – you name it – trace their roots back to what was
let loose in the two great revolutions of the eighteenth century and
to the lessons and conclusions subsequent generations have drawn
from them, have misunderstood, or have misapplied. It is not a
simple matter of choosing between Burke and Paine, right or
wrong, but of understanding the wisdom and limits of each man's
approach to democracy. Paine's life was about the democratic urge,

a passionate appeal to social justice and human rights that still leaps off the page today. It is no surprise that President Barack Obama quoted Paine in his inaugural address, just as President Reagan did twenty-five years earlier. The premises that the world can begin anew and that the values of America are universal have become fundamental to Americans' understanding of themselves and the world.

To which Burke would say, "Hold on. Think of consequences as well as rights. Beware of governing in the name of a theory. And understand the limits of your understanding." To repair the world is different from making it anew. The millenarian passion that lies behind so much religious and political thinking, that souls, nations, planets can be redeemed, has driven much of human activity and history. But unless tempered with a healthy dose of Burkean realism, this passion has and will continue to lead us dangerously astray. A wise friend once described himself as a member of the "Up to a Point Party." It's a party whose membership needs to grow. We stub our toes on difficult facts, and this forces us to slow down and watch what we're doing. It does not mean we lose our values, but it does mean we have to figure out how better to put them into effect.

The arguments that swirled through eighteenth-century Britain, France and North America produced different versions of the idea of democracy. One of the realities of our time is that when we talk about exporting and sharing our values, we are often talking of very different things. The debate in Britain centred on Parliament, the monarchy, the rise of the middle and working classes, and how a new constitution could emerge that would reflect an ever-changing social consensus. It could be argued that Britain lost its appetite for violence at home after its Civil War, and opted instead to fight on other people's lands as the British Empire entered its next phase after the loss of the American colonies. We will explore in subsequent chapters some of the consequences of the imperial and colonial experience for those who had to live through it.

The emergence of modern political parties can be traced to the gatherings of those more loyal to either the monarch or Parliament, and then to those advocating for deeper social change. But through it all, the British notion of Parliament being at the heart of democracy, with representatives winning separate constituencies, and (eventually) governments becoming accountable to Parliament, remains the core institutional framework of democracy.

The creation of the United States added several critical differences to this concept. First, that the Congress and the presidency, in form a likeness of Parliament and monarch, would be elected bodies. True, there was some flirtation with the notion of a hereditary presidency, and it might be said that with the dynasties of the Roosevelts, the Kennedys and the Bushes there is still some residual element of monarchism even in the American system. Second, that the Supreme Court would quickly emerge as the institution with the critical responsibility to interpret the written constitution, and that it would have the power to limit the ability of the executive or Congress to have its way. It was this that Paine and Jefferson objected to so strongly, but their objections faded in significance as more and more disputes found their way to the Supreme Court, and powerful justices like John Marshall and Roger B. Taney in the early 1800s made the court a separate pillar of power.

An elected Congress and president quickly gave rise to organized, and well-financed political parties in the United States. George Washington was the last president whose right to office was uncontested. He warned against the power of "faction" as he left office, as he saw the Federalists and Anti-Federalists lining up to succeed him. The bitter contests for the presidency between Thomas Jefferson and John Adams were marked by expensive campaigns, vicious personal attacks, and deep partisan divides – all of which continue in the American political system. So of course does federalism, a major innovation that gave individual states sovereign powers while ensuring the national government had sufficient independent power to knit the country together. The continued existence of slavery, which both Burke and Paine deplored, meant that it would take a civil war to reset the balance between the power of the states versus the centre, and to establish what modern human rights really meant.

What then of France? The revolutionary ideas of Jefferson and Paine about the "sovereignty of the people" reached their full expression, not in the United States (where "the people" had many different institutional nooks and crannies in which to express themselves), but in the revolutionary France that lasted for only a few years and then met its Thermidor (and its Napoleon). But the notion of a sovereign people expressing itself through street demonstrations, of popularly elected institutions capable of doing whatever was required and justified by an appeal to the majority of the people, resonated long after 1789, and indeed does to this day. Burke reminds us of the sheer cost of the revolution, but that has not tarnished its romance, nor its rhetorical (and practical) power. In Venezuela, President Hugo Chavez dissolves a federation because the states get in the way of the people's will. He nationalizes companies because of popular sovereignty, and insists on his direct relationship to the people, which is affirmed by referenda and his "unique understanding" of what the people want. Property rights and other freedoms must bend to the will of the people. *Vox populi, vox dei*. And, of course, *vox Hugo*.

In short, the democratic idea is not a simple one. There are many who claim to be democrats; indeed their number is growing. But not all who claim to be really are, and even then we have to ask, "What kind of democrat are you?" The answers are always interesting.

CHAPTER 3

BATTLE OF THE "ISMS":
The Nineteenth-Century Roots of Current Conflicts

The French Revolution ended, not with the establishment of millennial rule by beneficent tribunes of people in red caps, but with the rise of a deeply ambitious military officer determined to bring the chaos to an end. Every revolution has its Thermidor, the phase when fervour starts to fade and the political pendulum swings back toward the status quo ante. (Thermidor was the month, in the revolutionary calendar, when Robespierre was executed.) Napoleon Bonaparte's ambitions went well beyond ruling France. The wars that shook Europe from the 1790s to 1815 were about competing national claims, and fed on the internal turmoil in many countries, which was exploited by the extraordinary ambitions of both France and its emperor.

Most revolutions have difficulty staying home. This was certainly the case with the American and the French: the ideas of greater equality, national legal codes, and stronger and more efficient administrative states were part of the Napoleonic plan that had its champions all over Europe. The industrializing countries of Europe needed more effective governance than the old feudal system provided, and France was able to attach its vaulting imperial ambition to this need and desire for change. The result was a continent at war.

France defended its invasions and ambitions as a response to the attempts by the old order to encircle this radical presence in the heart of Europe, and to the urgent demands and requests from people everywhere to be freed from feudal oppression and the monarchy. It was not the first nor would it be the last time that foreign troops were portrayed as liberators responding to the needs of a beleaguered population. But the liberators reached too far. Napoleon's long trek into the bleak cold of Russia was a disaster, and he lost what proved to be the final battle, at Waterloo, in what is now Belgium.

Napoleon's defeat led to the largest peace negotiation in history over the course of seven months in 1814-15. The Congress of Vienna brought together representatives from all the warring countries of Europe. It was not (as was Versailles one hundred years later), an assembly of victors. France played its role, with chief negotiator Talleyrand determined to salvage her historic boundaries and avoid a brutally imposed peace. The Congress of Vienna and its architects had their detractors. The Ottoman, Holy Roman, and Russian empires were pillars of reaction that had held down their peoples for one hundred years, and they rightly feared any change on the continent. But the Congress was not seeking justice or a new world order. It merely wanted a working pact that would keep Europe whole and at peace.

Count Metternich dominated the proceedings and fashioned the principles of balance and restoration. He was in charge of the Austro-Hungarian Empire for the better part of a century, and was the leading conservative politician of his time. (Onetime U.S. Secretary of State Henry Kissinger found much to admire in Metternich.) His vision was simple enough: a balance of power between competing heads of state and principalities, and the restoration of monarchy and established order in a Europe that would repress the forces of revolution and democracy. It is hard to gainsay the remarkable achievements of the diplomacy of that time. Napoleon was first exiled to Elba, and then, after his escape and march to Waterloo, to a more distant and lonely fate on the South Atlantic island of St. Helena. But he was not executed. France's gains in war after 1792 were taken away, but there were no permanent armies of occupation.

There was even a modest advance in international humanitarian law. The movement for the abolition of slavery, which had come to life in the British Parliament under the leadership of William Wilberforce, was recognized as an important objective. The Congress of Vienna drew the borders and boundaries of Europe and established a rough balance of power that would last until imperial ambition once again unleashed a drive to war in 1914.

The American and French revolutions were not just about the idea of democracy. They were also about the idea of nation, about the meaning of both the United States and France for their own citizens and the rest of the world. In both cases, it is impossible to separate the sense of national mission from the broader ideas of citizens' rights and accountable government. The American Revolution both inherited and affirmed the underlying idea that the settlers of the American colonies and their descendants were in some sense a chosen people, whose persecution in Europe had led them to escape to a great land over which a beneficent God presided.

Nationalism's emergence in the modern world is deeply connected to the idea of citizenship. People have rights in a state, as members of a community defined by bonds of culture, language, religion, and shared memories and beliefs. These rights may well have universal significance, but not (or so the nineteenth-century argument would go) in the abstract. These rights have force in real countries in the real world.

This connection of the national idea to the democratic idea is what gave rise to the powerful movement for independence in Latin America in the nineteenth century, an extraordinary transformation that not only destroyed the Spanish Empire but created separate and distinct states across the continent in remarkably short order.

In Europe, both Italians and Germans discovered their common identities and national dreams, which sent centuries-old walls and barriers between various principalities, duchies, and city-states tumbling down.

The national idea had a galvanizing effect around the world. But it had its problems and its limits. The French sociologist Ernest Renan summed them up in a trenchant lecture he delivered at the Sorbonne in 1882 entitled "What Is a Nation?" Renan pointed out that it was far too simplistic to assert that the basis of nationalism in France was race, or religion, or language, as the modern world made such rigid homogeneity impossible. France had an important Protestant tradition and various regional languages, and it was impossible to trace a unique French tribe or ethnic group. Renan's answer to his own question is a quotation familiar to many Canadians. A nation is people "having done great things together and wishing to do more." In other words, a country is a continuing exercise in political will and choice, the declaration that "we are a country because we can remember common achievements and we want to continue into the future." It is not a compelling call for nationhood, but it ensures a greater sense of civility than the drumbeats of either tribe or religion.

The problem with nationalism is what George Orwell, writing years later, would call its "dirty little secret": that it doesn't get past tribalism but rather declares that my tribe is better than yours. The shift from the argument that "I need self-government because of the uniqueness of my culture" to the view that "my culture is actually better than yours" has infected political discourse since the French and American revolutions, and remains a powerful problem today. When ideas of mission and empire are added to nationalism, we have something else again.

In the Christian tradition (as in the Muslim), salvation is not simply a personal or private act. Going forth and multiplying the numbers of true believers, convincing others, showing them the way – these are part and parcel of the Gospel. A world of sinners needs conversion and those without faith must be saved. Both the Glorious Revolution of 1689 and the American Revolution were seen at the time as the redemption of a people. The great evangelizing drives of the Protestant Wesleyan movement in England, which held that faith was a matter of personal salvation and piety, were too powerful to be kept at home. There were millions of souls to be saved locally but there were billions in Asia and Africa. God's word and Christ's redemptive powers knew no national boundaries.

In an earlier time, the two great proselytizing religions had fought head to head. After the collapse of the Roman Empire and, later, the birth of Islam, tens of millions of people in Europe, North Africa, the Middle East, and Asia found themselves at the mercy of crusading armies determined to spread the faith and "civilization," each convinced of the rightness of their cause and the extraordinary benefits of either the Kingdom of Christ or the Caliphate. Both Islam and Christianity had this profound sense of mission, the core belief that revealed truth has to be shared, because there is only one true path to salvation. Islam's truly remarkable march through Central Asia, the Middle East, and across North Africa to southern Spain put the Christian kingdoms on notice. For two hundred years, Christian armies fought Muslim armies, especially for control of the Holy Lands, each side convinced they were engaged in a battle for civilization itself. By the 1440s, the Christians were exhausted by two hundred years of war, and the Holy Lands soon became part of the rapidly expanding Ottoman Empire. After recovering from the Crusades, Christian Europe looked to take its mission elsewhere, and hitched its wagon to the great voyages of discovery to the New World.

Canadians (like all inhabitants of the Americas) know only too well the deep and close connection between religious belief and imperial conquest. The church of the time believed it was spreading civilization, sharing values, bringing a "savage" population to God and a better way of life. That first contact was also marked by the spread of disease, pestilence, and cultural destruction is only now being fully understood. Whether by sword or by disease, the effect was the same: the conquest of indigenous inhabitants and the start of settlement by Christian Europeans.

Europeans' "discovery" of the rest of the world came in dramatic phases, first with the voyages to America, then the circling of the globe. During these conquests, the flag and the cross were almost interchangeable, and with the establishment of the great trading companies, money was not far behind. A mercantile empire was founded in Canada by the Hudson's Bay Company in 1670. Like the East India Company founded seventy years earlier, it was the de facto government in vast areas of these newfound lands.

The exchange with Africa was different. It was the slave trade that dominated the relationship between the Arab world, Europe, and Africa for several hundred years, with horrendous consequences and scars that are still deeply felt. The battle against slavery began in earnest only in the late eighteenth century, and its abolition in the British Empire took full effect only when slavery no longer made economic sense. In the United States only a civil war would finally bring it to an end.

Thomas Paine left the United States in a state of great disappointment when he realized that the American Constitution in 1787 was more about federalism and limited government than about the spirit of a democratic revolution. It allowed states that permitted slavery to continue to do so. As the authors of the *Federalist Papers* made clear, a strong central arrangement was necessary to bring the states together, but the sovereignty of each state was also deeply entrenched. James Madison, one of its authors, wrote that power needed to be divided and dispersed lest it be abused, and other key architects of the American Constitution, in particular John Jay and John Adams, believed that democracy was more to be forced than expressed. In his remarkable survey of the United States written in the 1830s, Alexis de Tocqueville gave a trenchant account of a nation where local government and participation were as important as any central institution. While he fully admired the egalitarian spirit of work in the country, de Tocqueville also noted some central contradictions: America sought conformity as much as it encouraged dissent, and the fate of both the aboriginal and the black populations was in direct contradiction to the lofty goals of American society.

The issues of states' rights and slavery were deeply intertwined, and the expansion of America westward brought further conflict with the native peoples. As each new state was formed west of the Alleghenies, the proponents of slavery argued vociferously against any ban in the newly constituted territories. But the movement for abolition, powerfully linked to the American Protestant tradition of New England, would not allow slavery to spread.

This fight, which took hold in the 1840s and 1850s, led to the Civil War or, as southerners call it to this day, the War between the States. Abraham Lincoln, elected to the presidency in 1860, was not in the hard abolitionist camp. Rather, his central tenet was that the union could not be allowed to break up. He only signed the Emancipation Proclamation in 1863 when he concluded that freeing the slaves was a political necessity to realign the integrity of the union. There would be no more talk of secession.

The war was won by the forces of the Union, but it would take another century before the rights of black people were advanced in comprehensive legislation. Segregation and racial discrimination remained ugly scars on American democracy for a hundred years after the Civil War. What the Civil War did accomplish was to shift power from the individual states to the central government.

It was the race for spoils in Asia and Africa by the European powers in the nineteenth century that gave rise to even greater contradictions. Burke's campaign against Warren Hastings and the East India Company began a great tradition in that it married an assumption of British primacy and superiority to an intense preoccupation with doing empire right. Taking empire seriously meant an extraordinary devotion to systems of government, administration, military dominance, and education. The liberal approach to imperialism meant that the justification of empire was no longer the extension of power and domination for their own sake or for the sake of profit and exploitation, although these interests remained substantially political, but was rather the exportation of superior values, religion, morals, and culture.

This shift naturally gave rise to the sharpest accusations of hypocrisy. When Lord Macartney, appointed by Britain as its envoy to China, first visited the Middle Kingdom in 1793, he wrote in his journal:

> The Empire of China is an old, crazy, first-rate Man of War, which a fortunate succession of vigilant officers have contrived to keep afloat . . . The breaking up of the power of China (no very improbable event) would occasion a complete subversion of commerce, not only of Asia, but a very sensible change in the other quarters of the world . . . Her ports would no longer be barricaded; they would be attempted by all the adventures of all trading nations, who would search every channel, creek and cranny of China for a market, and for some time be the cause of much rivalry and disorder. (As quoted in Wikipedia)

The emperor dismissed Macartney and his delegation; China did not want or need contact. This exchange tells us much about what would become of the not so splendid isolation of China. A self-contained system incapable of change and adaptation faced a brutal assault from the West that resulted in 150 years of ruthless exploitation and in the Chinese Empire's collapse.

In the 1840s, Britain (the same country that had produced Rainsborough, Paine, Burke, and Wilberforce) forced China at gunpoint to open itself to the opium trade, all in the name of profit. That the opium traders were followed by missionaries may have left Britain with a self-righteous glow, but this was lost on generations of Chinese addicted to opium and caught in battles between emperors and foreign invaders not of their making.

The race to colonize Africa starting in the mid nineteenth century also led to abuses, ones whose effects are still being felt today. As described in Adam Hochschild's powerful 1998 book, *King Leopold's Ghost*, the Belgians annexed the Congo as a private domain of the royal family, destroying millions of lives in the process, and ruling the country with a grim brutality rivalled by countless other examples whose memory now haunts us.

The grimmest face of empire is its sense of racial superiority. That Africans and Asians were seen as inferior – even sub-human – was the underlying premise of the European imperial exercise. This is its terrible legacy, which resonates in public opinion, jokes, stereotypes, and public policy.

Slavery was truly the ugliest side of the imperial idea, only possible because whites believed that blacks were not truly human, but other forms of race hatred emerged as the dark side of nationalism. The most deadly of these was anti-Semitism, which was deeply ingrained in the Christian teaching that the Jews were responsible for the death of Jesus Christ. Jews were dispersed from their ancestral lands in the Middle East after the collapse of the Roman Empire, establishing themselves in North Africa, Central Asia, and Europe. They lived as a people apart, more or less tolerated depending on the time, place, and circumstance. The unintended beneficiaries of a ban by the Roman Catholic Church on the payment of interest on loans between Christians, Jews in Europe were also resented for their prosperity. In 1656 Oliver Cromwell allowed Jews back after their expulsion from England in 1290 only because he needed their financial assistance. The Spanish Inquisition, starting in 1478, required them to convert or be expelled. The Holy Roman, Russian, and Ottoman empires allowed Jewish communities to exist, but the folk culture of the time all too often erupted in violence as the myth of Jews drinking the blood of Christian children was passed on from generation to generation. It took the French Revolution and Napoleon to establish the notion that in a secular state Jews had the right to be citizens like anyone else.

The rise of nationalism collided with this spirit of emancipation, particularly when combined with racial theories that used bogus science to back them up. Charles Darwin had no views on racial evolution or superiority, but social darwinists did, and reactionaries like Joseph de Maistre in France and Herbert Spencer in England began developing social and political theories that trumpeted the survival of the fittest.

We can trace modern anti-Semitism to these roots. Theories emerged claiming that different "races" were like species with different traits and characteristics, some superior, some intractably inferior. The eugenics movement took hold, with the notion that inferior beings should not be allowed to reproduce, and certainly should not be allowed to mix their inferior genes with other, better genes. Theories of racial superiority also helped justify imperial rule in Africa and Asia. Ideas of empire, nation, race, and rights swirled around the nineteenth century in a heated competition for dominance. The other most potent ingredient in the mix, besides racial superiority, was the idea of an economic and social order that truly reflected man's equality and destiny to live in peace and solidarity: socialism.

There were many pre-industrial expressions of the socialist idea, closely tied to the religious fervour of the Protestant Reformation and the ferment of social and economic change in Europe, which came with the collapse of the old medieval and feudal order. Both the English Civil War and the French Revolution brought forward groups and thinkers who were convinced that the only true expression of social justice in this world would be found in societies that enforced the strict equality of both rights and outcomes. The Levellers and the Sans Culottes had this basic notion in common. They believed that the distinction between rich and poor had to be razed to the ground, and that the dominance of the wealthy was no more valid than the rule of monarch or priest.

These ideas ultimately proved to be far too revolutionary for their time, and were put in their place by Cromwell and Napoleon. But they never died. They were the sparks that burst into flame when two powerful ingredients were added – the Industrial

Revolution and the philosophies of Georg Hegel and Karl Marx.

A world economy is obviously vastly different from a life of small production, subsistence agriculture, and exchange by barter. It did not happen overnight: the spread of the Spanish and Dutch trading empires was based on the search for gold and other goods and treasure, and not on the integration of a manufacturing economy, but this would come with the great revolution of production precipitated by the invention of steam power and the mechanized manufacture of goods.

This Industrial Revolution quickly led to two critical things. First, a truly global economy in which goods and services were exchanged on a world scale, with cotton grown in India supplying the mills of Manchester, to name but one example. Second, it meant the creation of a working class brought together in great cities in unprecedented numbers The forging of common ideas and values among industrial workers would take decades and even generations, but it did happen, just as surely as those caught up in the global economy in every part of the world eventually voiced the injustice inflicted on them by these changes and by foreign domination.

There were revolutions in the world of philosophy to match what was happening in the economy and in society. As Thomas Paine was writing of the brotherhood of man in the political world, the German intellectual world was discovering the mutual obligations of universality in the writings of Kant and Hegel. Nothing less than universal prescriptions would do: Immanuel Kant's simple proposition that moral behaviour requires one to ask, "What would happen if everyone did what I do?" became the basis of theories or war and peace, international harmony, and justice.

Hegel's notion of universality was different and even more powerful than Kant's. The underlying assumption of his philosophy is that everything in the world, spiritual and historical, natural and political, fits together. History is not just one damn thing after another, a jumble of events, but the steady march of truth revealing itself to the world, the systematic spread of enlightenment to match the economic and social integration of the world itself. Everything makes sense, everything fits, if only we have the philosophical determination to categorize and understand the evolution and progress of the world, in both the realm of ideas and in real life. The ultimate expression of this painful march was a world of rational, free men living in a system where goods were exchanged freely, where governments enforced the rule of law thoughtfully and without discrimination, and where wise rulers took their instruction and enlightenment from philosophers.

Marx shared certain key assumptions with Hegel. Both believed it was possible to explain the world in a comprehensive way whose objectivity lent validity to the idea that it was "scientific." Both thought that the history of the world was a complex, but fundamentally understandable, march toward human freedom and liberation, in which the oppressive aspects of human society would be overcome and transcended. For Hegel it was the "cunning of reason," which revealed itself in dialectical fashion. For Marx it was man himself who would triumph, by refashioning the world around him. Dialectical materialism was a science, but the agent of change was more than the individual; it was man acting as a member of his class.

Marx's shift from the imperative to explain the world to the need to change it came in the 1840s – his early writings made him seem like a romantic democrat, seeing man's "alienation" from his true nature in the confining industrial world that was growing up all around him in Europe. A wave of revolutionary upheavals in 1848 throughout Europe – the "turning point which failed to turn"– threw the ruling classes of the continent into a panic, with arguments for accountable, open, democratic government shaking almost every country. Even Canada had its moment, with Baldwin and Lafontaine calling for responsible government. In the end, less happened than first met the eye. But it was the year *The Communist Manifesto* first appeared, which would have an impact on the world comparable that of *The Rights of Man* more than half a century earlier.

"A spectre is haunting Europe . . ." the pamphlet begins, "the spectre of communism." According to Marx and co-author Friedrich Engels, the Industrial Revolution was transforming feudal Europe, creating a working class whose common interests and culture would inevitably lead to a political and economic revolution. Just as the bourgeoisie had triumphed because of the truly revolutionary nature of capitalism, the proletariat would soon find its place in the sun. But, as they say, there's a catch. This proletariat would realize its potential only if it were properly led by a party that understood its "true consciousness" and true interest. This party, the Communist Party, understood better than any other (indeed than others combined) what needed to be done:

> The communists . . . are . . . the most enhanced and resolute section of the working-class parties of every country . . . they have . . . the advantage of clearly understanding the line of march, the conditions, and ultimate general results of the proletarian movement . . . the theoretical conclusions of the communists are in no way based on the ideas of principle that have been invented, or discovered by this or that worker or would be universal reformer. They merely express, in general terms, general relations springing from an existing class struggle, from the historical movement going on under our very eyes. (Marx, 79-80)

Economists and sociologists from a variety of ideological and intellectual backgrounds all note Marx's keen insight into the nature of the new industrial economy, the impact of technology on development, and the emergence of a global economy. But Marx's politics were and are cancerous. They are based on the premise that an elite had unique scientific insight that entitled them to leadership. At the core it is a view incompatible with democracy.

By the end of the nineteenth century, Europe was getting ready to blow. There were battles within states and between states, within Europe and far beyond. The internal battles were partly about the growing demand for greater democracy and a state better able to respond to the needs of the people. They were also about ethnic nationalism that the empires of the day were not able to contain. Britain was facing rebellion in Ireland. The Austro-Hungarian Empire had to cope with the deep instability of the Balkans; and the Ottoman Empire was tormented by growing conflict in Greece, Bulgaria, and beyond.

These demands and rebellions were initially met with force and repression, but the rebels refused to submit to the imperial yoke. Violent repression can be an effective way of showing power, but it cannot convey legitimate authority. Burke was right – empires fail when they try to make criminals of an entire people.

The conflicts were not just internal. The race for colonial supremacy in Africa and Asia produced even greater instability, and the conflicts in Europe proved impossible to contain. War between Russia and an alliance of Britain, France, and the Ottoman Empire erupted in Crimea in the 1850s. France and Germany went to war in 1870: Germany's victory and seizure of Alsace-Lorraine created a hostage to fortune that would bedevil relations between the two countries for the next century.

As empires expanded in their ambitions, they refused to accept the old rules of the game. British naval supremacy was an assumption of Pax Britannica. German naval rearmament was all about a long-term quest to end this British monopoly of sea power once and for all.

All these powerful tensions lay behind the long and slow descent into war in 1914. The socialist parties of Europe had been meeting as members of the Socialist International for thirty years. All that time they debated the evils of imperial conflict, the futility of the growing arms race, the failure of their countries to respect workers' rights. But this solidarity too would founder on the rocky shoals of national ambition. The drumbeat of each platoon became too strong, and a deep and terrible conflict became inevitable.

The First World War was a war like no other before it. While the principal theatre of the conflict was in Europe, it spread to Africa and the Middle East, as these outposts of empire were dragged in. Armies on both sides numbered in the millions, and so did the casualties. The battles whose names are etched forever in our memories – Ypres, Passchendaele, Verdun, Vimy – were conflicts in which hundreds of thousands of young men were slaughtered as a couple of metres of mud were exchanged back and forth between the warring sides.

Despite having campaigned in 1916 to keep the United States out of the war, President Woodrow Wilson found himself in a deep quandary. Germany took the naval conflict to the Atlantic and sank American ships bound with supplies for Britain. The most infamous attack was on the joint British and American liner RMS *Lusitania*, which went down with 1,198 drowned, in 1915. The United States was being dragged into the conflict. The sheer bloodiness of the war, to say nothing of its massive expense, made it impossible to sustain. The first to buckle under the strain was Russia, whose tsarist regime was completely incapable of dealing with the deep revolt within its army and its people and paid the price by being toppled from the Russian throne. Its initial replacement was a weak parliamentary coalition led by Kerensky, who failed to appreciate the deep antipathy to the war that animated the Russian people. He felt duty bound to continue the conflict and was the next to pay the price.

Lenin felt no such scruples. He took the Marxist principle that the socialist movement required strong communist leadership a further step: communism could only succeed if an even smaller cadre, the Bolsheviks, seized the moment and took the party in the direction necessary to take and hold power. Leninism was not about building coalitions, it was about destroying them. Social democrats, Mensheviks, trade unionists, activists of all kinds – they were as much the enemies, and victims, of Lenin's ruthlessness as the aristocracy and the tsarist generals.

Having seized power, Lenin quickly sued for peace with Germany, not because he intended to stick with what he was negotiating at Brest-Litovsk, but because he needed to satisfy the public's thirst for peace.

Just as quickly as public opinion in Europe had been whipped to a nationalist frenzy when the war broke out, it turned hard and fast in the opposite direction as casualties mounted into the millions, and the illusion that the war would be over in a few months was replaced by the sickening realization that it – and the mounting death toll – could last forever.

In taking his country into the war in 1917, Woodrow Wilson had to express America's objectives in terms that went beyond the usual nationalist rhetoric. Harold Nicolson, a witty and wise observer of international politics who was present as a young British diplomat at the Conference of Versailles in 1919, describes his own faith as a young man in the principles of "Wilsonism":

> I was conscious . . . that there was in his pronouncements a slight tinge of revivalism, a touch of Methodist arrogance, more than a touch of Presbyterian vanity. Yet I was not deterred by these disadvantages. 'The United States', I read, 'have not the distinction of being masters of the world – (Mr. Wilson was speaking in 1914) – but the distinction of carrying certain lights for the world that the world has never so distinctly seen before, certain guiding lights of liberty, and principle and justice.' I was disconcerted neither by the biblical, nor yet by the Princeton savour of these words. I like to think also that, with nerves frayed by the duration of the war, I still retained my faith in Wilson as a prophet of human reasonableness. (Nicolson, 37-38)

The world would be made new again. The old diplomacy of secret deals and cynical self-interest would be replaced by a public-spirited idealism that would lead the world to abandon force for all time. Nicolson goes on to describe his mood and thinking at the time:

> Not only did I believe profoundly in these principles, I took it for granted that on them alone would the Treaties of Peace be based. Apart from their inherent moral compulsion, apart from the fact that they formed the sole agreed basis of our negotiation, I knew that the President possessed unlimited physical power to enforce his views. We were all, at that date, dependent upon America, not only for the sinews of war, but for the sinews of peace. Our food supplies, our finances, were entirely subservient to the dictates of Washington. The force of compulsion possessed by Woodrow Wilson in those early months of 1919 was overwhelming. It never occurred to us that, if need arose, he would hesitate to use it. 'Never,' writes Mr. Keynes, 'had a philosopher held such weapons wherewith to bind the Princes of the world.' He did not use these weapons. He was not (and the slow realization of this was painful to us) a philosopher. He was only a prophet. (Nicolson, 41-42)

John Maynard Keynes's views were the subject of his brilliant polemic "The Economic Consequences of the Peace," which he wrote in 1920 after resigning from the British delegation. The greatest economist of his generation, he was also a mordant observer of politics. Keynes describes in one paragraph the world that was before 1914:

> The greater part of the population, it is true, worked hard and lived at a low standard of comfort, yet were, to all appearances, reasonably contented with this lot. But escape was possible, for any man of capacity or character at all

exceeding the average, into the middle and upper classes, for whom life offered, at a low cost and with the least trouble, conveniences, comforts, and amenities beyond the compass of the richest and most powerful monarchs of other ages . . . He could secure forthwith, if he wished it, cheap and comfortable means of transit to any country or climate without passport or other formality, could despatch his servant to the neighbouring office of a bank for such supply of the precious metals as might seem convenient, and could then proceed abroad to foreign quarters, without knowledge of the religion, language, or customs, bearing coined wealth upon his person, and would consider himself greatly aggrieved and much surprised at the least interference. But, must important of all, he regarded this state of affairs as normal, certain and permanent except in the direction of further improvement, and any deviation from it as aberrant, scandalous and avoidable. The projects and politics of militarism and imperialism, of racial and cultural rivalries, of monopolies, restrictions, and exclusion, which were to play the serpent to this paradise, were little more than the amusements of his daily newspaper, and appeared to exercise almost no influence at all on the ordinary course of social and economic life, the internationalization of which was nearly complete in practice. (Keynes, 11-12)

In his ironic way Keynes was describing how this world was shattered by the war, and how its assumptions could not continue. He despaired at Versailles because he believed that, contrary to the lofty Wilsonian principles set out in the Fourteen Points, what ultimately happened would be a peace of the victors, a pact whose cost would be the permanent impoverishment of Germany and Austria and continuing instability in Europe. He was brutal in his assessment. Woodrow Wilson was no saviour. His mindset was

more theological than political; he was outsmarted and out-
manoeuvred by French Prime Minister Georges Clemenceau and
British Prime Minister David Lloyd George, who had committed
to their publics that Germany would be held fully accountable for
the war and would be made to pay – hence the clauses in the
Treaty of Versailles on war guilt and reparations.

The result was that only by "Jesuitical exegesis" could the
treaty be made compatible with the Fourteen Points, and so an
elaborate process of insincerity began.

> Now it was that what I have called his theological or
> Presbyterian temperament became dangerous . . . He
> would do nothing that was not honourable; he would do
> nothing that was not just and right; he would do nothing
> that was contrary to his great profession of faith. Thus . . .
> the Fourteen Points . . . became a document for gloss and
> interpretation and for all the intellectual apparatus of
> self-deception, by which, I daresay, the President's fore-
> fathers had persuaded themselves that the course they
> thought it necessary to take was consistent with every
> syllable of the Pentateuch . . . Then began the weaving of
> that web of sophistry and Jesuitical exegesis that was
> finally to clothe with insincerity the language and sub-
> stance of the whole Treaty. (Keynes, 50-51)

In her book *Paris 1919*, Margaret Macmillan recreates the
passion of the crowds that greeted Woodrow Wilson in London
and Paris as the discussions began, and the tortuous route that the
discussions took on a vast array of subjects. The end result was not
a stable peace, but an uneasy truce that was bound to end in a
resumption of the conflict. It was not the "war to end all wars,"
but rather a prelude to an even more bloody and brutal confrontation that would ensure that the twentieth century would become
the most violent in history.

If we take just the first of Wilson's Fourteen Points and look at what happened, we realize how great can be the gap between lofty pronouncements and a complete failure to deliver. The first point reads: "Open covenants of peace openly arrived at, after which there shall be no private understandings of any kind, but diplomacy shall proceed always frankly and in the public view." Even as these words were being written, secret agreements were being reached in Europe that would have a dramatic effect not only on Versailles but on future events. The Italians had been made promises to get them into the war that were not disclosed, and that affected debates at Versailles about the future of Trieste and the Tyrol. Two diplomats, Sir Christopher Sykes from England and François Georges-Picot from France, had met secretly in Paris in 1916 to discuss the future of the Middle East with the collapse of the Ottoman Empire. Kurdish and Arab leaders were not consulted, and borders and boundaries, together with "spheres of influence and quasi-imperial responsibilities, were drawn up in an agreement that both governments signed. Lebanon and Syria would go to the French; Palestine, Transjordan and Iraq to the British, whose role in Egypt and Sudan was confirmed. The result was that the Kurds of eastern Turkey, Syria, and Iraq, to say nothing of Iran, would be divided. Even today one can drive along the border between Turkey and Syria and realize that the villages on either side of a heavily armed fence were once part of the same world.

Anyone who has read T.E. Lawrence's *Seven Pillars of Wisdom* or seen David Lean's film *Lawrence of Arabia* knows that the British promised Sayyid Hussein bin Ali, the self-proclaimed King of Hejaz, sovereignty and independence for Arabs in exchange for their participation in the overthrow of the Ottomans. The Sykes-Picot Agreement made a mockery of that promise, just as the continuation of secret diplomacy at the expense of much heralded public principles made postwar politics a continuing exercise in trying to square circles.

It certainly made things more difficult for Woodrow Wilson, whose life and career reached their dénouement at Versailles. Wilson's failure to consult the grandees of the Senate throughout the negotiations, and his inability to overcome Americans' profound reservations about being trapped in Old World politics, meant that the one victory he was seeking – America joining the League of Nations that would be able to ensure that the First World War really was the war to end all wars – eluded him. The stroke he suffered shortly after his return to Washington meant he spent the last year of his presidency in pain and disability, with his wife Edith assuming more and more responsibility, while the country was kept ignorant of the extent of his frailty.

So the postwar era began with the United States retreating to its home base and its own concerns and interests in the Americas and the Philippines, increasingly acting as Europe's banker but playing no role in building the League of Nations that Wilson had promoted at Versailles. Europe, in turn, faced an impoverished Germany, a devastated and dictatorial Russia, and a France and Britain whose imperial ambitions were intact but whose economies and societies were divided and poorer than they pretended to be.

Rather than creating the conditions for recovery, the Treaty of Versailles guaranteed that there would be constant battles about reparations. Germany was not a lemon to be squeezed; it was a rock, and there was nothing to be had there. The Weimar Republic staggered into an inflationary crisis of unheard-of proportions, which was soon followed by the devastating impact of the Great Depression, which swept around the world.

From the start, the League of Nations had a profoundly ambivalent relationship with imperialism. It granted the colonial powers in Africa and the Middle East mandates to govern where German and Ottoman powers had governed before. The difference between a colony and a mandate became impossible to determine, and this meant that the League simply justified earlier power grabs.

These were, in many ways, the darkest times for the democratic idea. The hope that the First World War, in ending the old empires of Europe, would give rise to democracy in the many new countries left in their wake, that the nations of the League would live in harmony, and that the world order would be overseen by this new international institution that would ensure the peaceful spread of the rule of law all proved wildly implausible. It was not so much the age of democracy as the age of empire, dictatorship, and ruthless ideology. And as the world economy failed to right itself in the months and years after the Wall Street Crash of 1929, the next decade could rightly be called the valley of despair.

The depression changed the face of European politics forever. Italy had already fallen in the face of Benito Mussolini's march on Rome in 1922. His appeal to national honour and imperial ambition took him to power and was followed by a putsch that quickly destroyed all vestiges of constitutional liberal democracy in the country. In Germany, Adolf Hitler's rise to power five years later was equally dramatic. Hitler, who had been thrown in jail in 1924 after attempting a coup in Munich, set out his ideas for the world to see in his book *Mein Kampf*. It claimed that Germany's strength came from its Aryan stock and its racial purity. This nation had been betrayed, by liberals, cosmopolitans, trade unionists, weak-minded democrats and, above all, by Jews, a people who he claimed owed no loyalty to anyone and who sucked the lifeblood of the nation. Surrender in 1918 and the subsequent negotiations at Versailles were betrayals of the greatness of the German nation. Only a national revolution would allow for the return of the country to the supremacy that it deserved. Germany's empire was not so much to be found abroad as to the east, where inferior Slavic nations would provide Germany with the "living space" (*lebensraum*) that it needed. Germany needed to get back what it had lost at Versailles, but the march forward would take the country further, to undeniable leadership in Europe and the world. What could be accomplished by negotiation would be done by negotiation, but military action was the next step. Hitler was convinced the so-called democratic nations were weaklings that would cave in the face of determined, concerted steps by Germany. If they fought back they would be crushed.

Hitler's rise to power was swift and brutal. His party never actually won an election. A powerful presence in a minority Reichstag (parliament) led some German conservatives to conclude that it was better to let Hitler into power so he could be better controlled. Hitler was made chancellor, and immediately consolidated his hold on power by throwing his opponents in jail, seizing control of every institution of the state, including the army, and putting his Nazi program and policies into effect immediately. The Nuremberg Laws of 1935 established Germany as a racist state, with laws defining who was "pure German" and who was not, beginning with the exclusion and persecution of the Jews. Laws were passed forbidding intermarriage and preventing Jews from participating in professions from which they had played a role in the national life of Germany for a century and a half.

Externally, Italy and Germany ploughed ahead with a policy of rearmament and expansion, which was matched on the other side of the world by a similar expression of ambition by Imperial Japan. Japan's response to the economic invasion of the West had been very different from China's. Lord Macartney's description of the chaos that would hit China as a result of Europe's imperial ambitions had proved to be correct. The Chinese emperors had been overthrown, but no democratic government was able to control territory and exercise sovereignty. From 1900 to 1949, China was what would now be called a failed state, with widespread crime and pillaging, and local warlords attempting to establish control where they could.

Japan had reeled from the impact of first contact with the West in the 1850s, but quickly recovered under an authoritarian regime that kept barriers up while adopting and adapting Western technology. Japan's industrialization was a marvel of change and growth, and took place behind massive tariff barriers that allowed for the growth of Japanese manufacturing for both domestic and export use. At the same time, its military insisted on the need for Japan to retain its samurai warrior tradition while adopting the latest technologies. Japan went to war with Russia in 1905, surprising everyone with the strength and quality of its navy, and invaded and occupied Korea in 1910. It entered the First World War as a British ally, and emerged from the Conference at Versailles as one of the "Big Five" of the new order. It joined the League of Nations even as it targeted China for its further expansion. The Japanese army invaded Manchuria from Korea in 1931, for which it was criticized by the League, and Japan withdrew from membership. In 1937, the army pushed south, where it was met by resistance from Chinese Nationalists, Communists, and even warlords who saw their empires collapsing.

But no expansion – Germany when it entered the Saar and the Rhineland, Italy when it invaded Abyssinia, Japan in invading China – met with any organized resistance from the rest of the world, or any effective response from the League of Nations. Attempts to impose sanctions proved fruitless. Canada's representative at the League was forced to change his vote on his own proposal in 1935 when Prime Minister Mackenzie King heard that the League was contemplating stopping all exports of oil, coal, and steel to Italy.

It was in Spain that the forces of resistance to fascism did their best to stand their ground. Again, neither Britain nor France did much when Franco decided to match Mussolini and Hitler and ordered his troops to take Madrid in 1936. Much of the country fell to the Nationalists, but Madrid held out for two years and the eastern part of the country, including Barcelona, remained under Republican control. The Thomas Paines of their time responded to the Republicans' call for help, and volunteered to join the fight. So did the Soviet Union. And therein lies a tale that speaks volumes about the risks and tensions in the fight for democracy.

No writer of the twentieth century better expressed the central dilemmas of his time than George Orwell. Born in India as the son of a civil servant, Eric Blair spent his childhood in boarding schools and then joined the Burmese Police Force in the early 1920s. Disillusioned by the experience of enforcing the ways of empire, Blair resigned his commission as a police officer and returned to England. He took up the pen name George Orwell, and began the life of a writer, finishing his novel *Burmese Days*, writing reviews and short commentaries, and becoming politically engaged. He found his voice as a democrat, a socialist, an acute observer of poverty and politics, and a novelist and satirist with "a facility with words and a power of facing unpleasant facts." (Orwell, *Facing Unpleasant Facts*, xv). His life was cut short by tuberculosis in 1950 at the age of forty-six. Orwell is best remembered for his last two novels, *Animal Farm* and *1984*, political fables that brought home to the postwar generation that the communist illusion was over, that exposing the lies and propaganda of totalitarianism was the political responsibility of every thinking person.

Orwell came to these conclusions through his engagement in the Spanish Civil War. An independent socialist, committed to the fight against fascism, he and his wife went to Spain in late 1936 to join the struggle, and after he was wounded, returned to England six months later to write a book about his experiences, *Homage to Catalonia*.

Like Thomas Paine before him, Orwell was quickly caught up in the warmth and romance of the revolution. In 1936 and early 1937, Barcelona, the capital of the region of Catalonia, was the exemplar of the rule of equality, of brotherhood, of solidarity. As Orwell put it in a book review:

There was occurring a revolution of ideas that was perhaps more important than the short lived economic changes. For several months large blocks of people believed that all men are equal and were able to act on their belief. The result was a feeling of liberation and hope that is difficult to conceive in our money-tainted atmosphere . . . No one who was in Spain during the months when people still believed in the revolution will ever forget that strange and moving experience. It has left something behind that no dictatorship, not even Franco's, will be able to efface. (Orwell, *Facing*, 87)

Peter Davison, the editor of *The Complete Works of George Orwell*, has summarized Orwell's experience of Spain:

The vision of a socialist society that he experienced on first arriving in Barcelona was not destroyed by Franco; it was betrayed by his Communist allies. As described by him in *Homage to Catalonia*, this has all the inevitability of tragedy. That 'peculiar evil feeling in the air – an atmosphere of suspicion, fear, uncertainty and veiled hatred' that he found on his final visit to Barcelona was precisely that of the miasma of evil and terror dramatised in his favourite Shakespeare play *Macbeth*. The effect of that experience marked all else he wrote and did until the day he died." (Orwell, *Facing*, 33)

The heady days of egalitarian Catalonia that Orwell experienced in January of 1937 were replaced a few short months later by intense street fighting in Barcelona as the Stalinist-backed Communist Party and the POUM, the party whose ranks Orwell had joined and one of two local workers' parties, struggled for control of the region. Orwell described the fight as "a reign of terror – forcible suppression of political parties, a stifling censorship of the Press, ceaseless espionage and mass-imprisonment without trial." (Orwell, *Facing*, 41) He lost many friends to disease and execution in prison. It was a life-changing experience.

It was not just that Orwell suddenly found himself persecuted by the very people on whose behalf he thought he was fighting. It was that communism in its political form in Spain took on all the characteristics of the enemy it was supposed to be fighting. It vilified its opponents, lied about them, arrested them, called them "fascists in disguise," tortured them, extracted false confessions from them. In short, it said white was black and black was white. As Orwell put it:

> And so the game continues. The logical end is a regime in which every opposition party and newspaper is suppressed and every dissentient of any importance is in jail. Of course, such a regime will be Fascism. It will not be the same as the Fascism Franco would impose, it will even be better than Franco's Fascism to the extent of being worth fighting for, but it will be Fascism. Only, being operated by Communists and Liberals, it will be called something different. (Orwell, *Facing*, 45)

In a letter written to a friend on his return from Spain in the summer of 1937 Orwell wrote:

> The most terrible things were happening even when I left, wholesale arrests, wounded men dragged out of hospitals and thrown into jail, people crammed together in filthy dens where they have hardly room to lie down, prisoners beaten and half starved etc etc. Meanwhile it is impossible to get a word about this mentioned in the English press. (Orwell, *Facing*, 53)

For Orwell, the last point rankled as much as the first. Truth was a casualty of this ideological world, with "progressive thinkers" refusing to allow even the possibility that the communists could be in the wrong, because that would "objectively" help the fascist cause. Orwell had particular contempt for Kingsley Martin, editor of the *New Statesman*, who refused to publish Orwell's reviews because "they are against the political policy of this paper."

Most of those who fought in Spain on behalf of the Republicans were in the International Brigade, which was controlled politically by the Communist Party and whose membership included recruits from all over the world, including Canadians who fought in the Mackenzie-Papineau Battalion. They were not caught up in the internal struggle between "revolutionaries" and "counter-revolutionaries." Most of those who survived went on to fight in the Second World War, and were described ironically as "premature anti-fascists." "Orwellian" is now an adjective used to describe a nightmarish world where lying is a matter of course, where propaganda is everywhere, where there is no logic to arrests and no explanation for imprisonment. Neighbours rat on friends; there is no trust, no truth, no warmth, no secure ground on which to tread. There is the knock on the door, the truncheon on the head, the shrieks of those being tortured, the betrayals of those beaten to confess.

Thomas Paine did not write much about his own experience of the Reign of Terror in France, and he seemed to lack insight into the nature of the beast around him. The same cannot be said of Orwell. His experience in Spain marked him, and has marked all of us. *Animal Farm*, a political satire that at first had difficulty finding a publisher because it took on the Soviet Union, Britain's ally in the war against fascism, has given us an unforgettable picture of a revolution betrayed, of revolutionary pigs becoming oppressors, of history and truth suddenly being changed, of inequalities previously taboo now becoming respectable. There is the unforgettable scene at the end where the pigs are entertaining the farmers in the neighbourhood. As the other animals look forlornly through the window at the scene of celebration they realize that it is impossible to tell the difference between pigs and men, their former oppressors.

Animal Farm's brilliant satire can still make readers laugh out loud, but the same can not be said of *1984*. It tells the story of

Winston Smith, the everyman who works as a cog in the totalitarian machine, and who tries to find a sliver of freedom in a world
where Big Brother is all-seeing, all-controlling, and inescapable.
The rigidly hierarchical world is terrifying, with no room for discussion, debate, romance, or family. Winston's small break for
freedom is destroyed by a jealous neighbour who denounces him
to the Thought Police. He is sent to jail, where he faces his deepest
fear, a cell full of rats. He confesses to crimes he never committed
and swears undying devotion to Big Brother.

Orwell thus unveils the totalitarian world, a world of no real
choices and ultimately no real life. Never having embraced communism, he could not preach about the god that failed, as many who
lamented Josef Stalin's ruthless implementation of communism did.
But he did set out for the world a crystal-clear understanding of
what this grim future required: determined and principled witnesses, never afraid to face unpleasant facts and to describe the
world as they saw it.

Better than anyone, Orwell understood the link between politics and language, the necessary connection between the abuse of
power and the abuse of communication. The pigs in *Animal Farm*
are experts at propaganda, and know that their hold on power
depends on their ability to hoodwink everyone else. Ever present
on the television screen, Big Brother knows this as well, and is not
afraid to exercise command over all methods and techniques of
lying to keep the proles happy and in the dark.

Orwell often talked about how words could be used to conceal
the truth, or what was really happening. His experience in Spain
taught him that all political movements, left and right, were
capable of lying to destroy the enemy. He also knew that there are
always those willing to be deceived, willing to believe despite the
overwhelming evidence in front of them.

Orwell's experience of communism would be shared even
more brutally by countless others who were experiencing first-
hand what disagreeing with Stalin really meant. But the ultimate

betrayal came with the signing of the Molotov-Ribbentrop Pact in August of 1939. The two powers and ideologies that had been at each other's throats in Spain and across Europe concluded a secret negotiation with a breath-taking deal in which they agreed not to invade each other and to divide up the spoils in Eastern Europe, with Poland and the Baltic countries in particular to be sacrificed in an act of cynicism without parallel in European history (which is saying a lot). It sent many idealists scurrying from the embrace of the Communist Party, as they came to realize the accuracy of Orwell's insight.

What Orwell and his contemporaries like Arthur Koestler understood was that fascism and communism shared some powerful features, which could be summed in the simple word "totalitarian." Politics and the power of the state would become such that the notion of a private sphere was destroyed, with single parties insisting on a rigid conformity enforced through brutality, intimidation, propaganda, and fear. Whether the ideology of such a regime was fascist, racist, nationalist, communist, or a combination of all of the above is ultimately less important than the fact of domination, the enforced adulation of an individual or collective leader, and the power of propaganda to sway people in one direction of another.

In 1939, the prospects for democracy seemed bleak. True, President Roosevelt had "saved democracy" by his ability to give a sense of hope and trust to the American people, but the United States was still a country where the black minority could not vote and faced widespread discrimination. To the north, Canada prevented aboriginal people and Chinese immigrants from voting, and to the south much of Latin America was home to military dictatorships that effectively disenfranchised the majority of their people. The Caribbean countries were colonies to Britain, and their people could not vote. Africa's only fully sovereign country, South Africa, was ruled by whites and completely excluded the black and coloured majority from participating in political life.

The rest of the continent was subject to colonial rule from London, Brussels, Paris, Madrid, and Lisbon, and while national movements for self-rule were being formed they were steadily repressed by imperial powers.

In the Middle East, the British and French mandates meant that no countries were effectively independent, and bitter fighting between Jewish settlers and Palestinians erupted on a steady basis. The Indian subcontinent was still the British Raj and the British Empire stretched further to Burma, Singapore, and Malaya. People fighting for self-rule faced jail and worse, with clear lines of conflict between Muslims and the Hindu majority in India beginning to emerge. China was in good part under Japanese occupation, as was Korea, and Japan's imperial reach extended deep into those parts of South Asia not under direct rule. France had colonized Cambodia and Vietnam and was in the middle of a violent fight with the Viet Minh, the Vietnamese independence movement, under the leadership of Ho Chi Minh. Indonesia was a Dutch colony, and again the incipient independence movement there was met by a firm hand of imperial resistance.

The writings of Hitler and Stalin were full of the notions that history was on their side, that there was a corruption and fatal weakness in democracy, that its idea of equality was unrealistic, that it was not able to deliver the goods of prosperity, and that economic and social success depended on strong leadership dominating the necessary collective effort. It took a second world war to turn the tide.

CHAPTER 4

THE FATE OF DEMOCRACY AND HUMAN RIGHTS:

from the Second World War to the Cold War

Europe, Britain, and their allies confronted Hitler's invasion of Poland in September of 1939 with the realization that the previous strategy of appeasement was a failure. Giving the Nazis what they wanted only showed that their appetite knew no bounds. It was not about Germany righting the wrongs of Versailles, or an understandable response to the depression and the humiliation of defeat in 1918. Nazism, with its attendant expansionism, was a different beast, to which there could be no other response than military engagement. The United States was still stuck in its isolationist mould, but President Franklin Roosevelt realized that the threat from both Germany and Japan might eventually require an American response.

Neville Chamberlain, the British prime minister who was the architect of appeasement in the 1930s, was the most popular political leader in the West when he acquiesced in the dismemberment of Czechoslovakia in March 1938. Winston Churchill, who had been a central figure in British parliamentary politics since the turn of the century, was at the nadir of his political career, a rogue bull excluded from government for his extreme views on empire and the need to confront the dictators of Europe. Widely scorned as a throwback and reactionary, he had further isolated himself by becoming a romantic and loyal supporter of King Edward VIII, whose determination to marry an American divorcée had shocked the British public to its Puritan core. When Churchill rose to speak against the Munich Pact that allowed Germany's annexation of Czechoslovakia in the House of Commons, he was booed. When he warned that nothing was gained by the pact, and stated that the British and French governments had betrayed democracy not only in Czechoslovakia but in all of Europe, he was ignored.

The one thing we know for sure about public opinion is that it changes. It responds to events, to arguments, to contexts that never stay the same. As it so happened, my father was writing his PhD thesis at the London School of Economics at this time. His subject was public opinion and its measurement, and his laboratory was England in those dark days before the war. A by-election in Oxford pitted the master of Balliol College, A.D. Lindsay, as the "anti-Munich" candidate against Quintin Hogg, the Tory stalwart who would later become Lord Hailsham. During the campaign, my father recruited Oxford undergraduates to conduct a poll, which ended up predicting that Hogg would win. He did. It was this work that came to the attention of George Gallup and led to my father's first job, with the Gallup organization in Princeton.

Because opinion changes, Chamberlain went from triumph at Munich in March 1938 to moral defeat after Germany declared war on Poland in September 1939, to complete political humiliation in May of 1940 when MP Leo Amery told him, "In the name of God, sir, go!"

The man whose growling views had kept him on the margins of public life for a decade was chosen as the next prime minister because he had been proven right, and was seen as the best man to lead the country in wartime. Churchill became the voice of democratic resistance to tyranny, which was an extreme irony to the leader of the Indian independence movement, Mohandas Gandhi, whose quest Churchill regarded as a dangerous delusion. Nor were all Britons pleased at Churchill's leadership role; many on the left saw him as a reactionary and a warmonger.

But to the vast majority of the British public, and indeed to much of the world, Churchill was the one man who understood the moment. Even as he was being chosen to lead the country in a process that was far from transparent, there remained political forces in Britain ready to make a deal with Mussolini and Hitler. France was on the edge of collapse, an invasion of Britain by Germany was a distinct probability, and British troops were being driven from the coast of France by a rapidly advancing German army. Surrender was not in Churchill's blood, and in May 1940 he stared down those dissenters in his own cabinet who were prepared to do a deal that would allow Britain to avoid a German invasion.

He did so because he understood the nature of the fascist dictatorship he was fighting. Peaceful coexistence with these forces was something he was unable to contemplate. He had established a line of communication with Franklin Roosevelt, who was not prepared to declare war but understood what side he was on. Roosevelt's challenge, like Wilson's a generation earlier, was to campaign for the presidency at a time when isolationist feeling in America was running high, without abandoning his freedom to manoeuvre to where he knew he had to go. Under his leadership, the United States saw itself as the "arsenal of democracy," providing Britain with a lifeline that would allow it to continue the fight. Even before the bombing of Pearl Harbor on December 7, 1941, Roosevelt made the grand gesture of meeting with Churchill on the high seas off Newfoundland to sign the Atlantic Charter, whose eight points are worth quoting in full because they represent a groundbreaking step, and set the framework for the postwar world:

> First, their countries seek no aggrandizement, territorial or other.
>
> Second, they desire to see no territorial changes that do not accord with the freely expressed wishes of the peoples concerned.

Third, they respect the right of all people to choose the form of government under which they will live, and they wish to see sovereign rights and self-government restored to those who have been forcibly deprived of them.

Fourth, they will endeavour with due respect for their existing obligations, to further the enjoyment of all States, great or small, victor or vanquished, of access, on equal terms to the trade and to the raw materials of the world which are needed for their economic prosperity.

Fifth, they desire to bring about the fullest collaboration between all nations in the economic field with the object of securing for all improved labour standards, economic advancement, and social security.

Sixth, after the final destruction of Nazi tyranny, they hope to see established a peace which will afford to all nations the means of dwelling in safety within their own boundaries, and which will afford assurance that all the men in all the lands may live out their lives in freedom from fear and want.

Seventh, such a peace should enable all men to traverse the high seas and oceans without hindrance.

Eighth, they believe all of the nations of the world, for realistic as well as spiritual reasons, must come to the abandonment of the use of force. Since no future peace can be maintained if land, sea or air armaments continue to be employed by nations which threaten, or may threaten, aggression outside of their frontiers, they believe, pending the establishment of a wider and permanent system of general security, that the disarmament of such nations is essential. They will likewise aid and encourage all other practicable measures which will lighten for peace-loving peoples the crushing burden of armament.

The Atlantic Charter followed an earlier speech to Congress in which Roosevelt had outlined his vision for the future. He had talked about freedoms of speech and religion, but went further, to emphasize freedom from want, "which translated into universal terms, means economic understandings which will secure to every nation a healthy peacetime life for its inhabitants – everywhere in the world." He also talked about freedom from fear,

> which, translated into world terms, means a world-wide reduction of armaments to such a point and in such a thorough fashion that no nation will be in a position to commit an act of physical aggression against any neighbor – anywhere in the world. That is no vision of a distant millennium. It is a definite basis for a kind of world attainable in our own time and generation. That kind of world is the very antithesis of the so-called new order of tyranny which the dictators seek to create with the crash of a bomb.

These texts of the Atlantic Charter and the Four Freedoms became the basis of the United Nations. The UN, to which the United States would remain profoundly committed from the outset, was to become the keystone institution in an effort to build a world order that went beyond force of arms.

After six long years of fighting the Allies eventually prevailed. Stalin's Russia had suffered the heaviest losses of any country, but with the liberation of the concentration camps the world came to grips with the realization that Hitler's most murderous objective was the elimination of an entire people, the Jews. It was not until the end of the war that the world saw what the Nazis really represented. Theirs had not been a war only of territorial conquest. Behind the frontlines, the Nazis had attempted to annihilate a people. The first Russian and American soldiers who liberated Auschwitz, Belsen, Buchenwald, and the other Nazi death camps could not believe what they saw. Intelligence officers in Washington and London certainly knew of the Nazis' plans, and so did Roosevelt and Churchill, but ordinary soldiers would have seen for the first time the full extent of the depravity that was the Holocaust. The news that six million Jews had been slaughtered, many of them in these camps, profoundly shocked the world. The views that Hitler set out with terrifying clarity in *Mein Kampf* had been carried out.

The Allies quickly decided that the conduct of the Nazis had been so horrific that only an international tribunal could express the opprobrium of the world. Nuremberg, which had been the place where the laws vilifying Jews were proclaimed, became the seat of judgment on those who had committed this crime against humanity. There began the painstaking documentation of tyranny and responsibility. While it will always have its critics as "victors' justice," Nuremberg meant something more and different. It was an effort to deal with the cruelty of the recent past by insisting that those who knew and were responsible should pay the price. It was the first implementation of this principle, and the work it started is carried on today by the International Criminal Court, successor to the International Criminal Tribunal.

The early postwar years were marked by a strange dichotomy between the excitement of creating a new world order, with strengthened international institutions working within a framework of law, and the harsh reality that victory in Germany and Japan was immediately followed by conflict between the Soviet Union and the West. Once again, the issue was democracy and power politics. The Soviet Union was not leaving the countries it had "liberated," and communist parties all over Soviet-occupied Europe were fighting for supremacy. Once again Churchill summarized the situation in a powerful speech, this time in Fulton, Missouri, in 1946, which he entitled "The Sinews of Peace":

> From Stettin in the Baltic to Trieste in the Adriatic, an iron curtain has descended across the Continent. Behind that line lie all the capitals of the ancient states of Central and Eastern Europe. Warsaw, Berlin, Prague, Vienna, Budapest,

Belgrade, Bucharest and Sofia, all these famous cities and the populations around them lie in what I must call the Soviet sphere, and all are subject in one form or another, not only to Soviet influence but to a very high, and in many cases increasing measure of control from Moscow.

The Cold War had begun in earnest, and with it the battle for democracy, human rights and the rule of law would take on a distinctly anti-communist tone and texture. Elsewhere in the speech, Churchill pointed out that the two "giant marauders," war and tyranny, still threatened the security and well-being of ordinary people around the world. In a comment that would anticipate by several decades our recent preoccupation with national and personal security, Churchill said: "What then is the over-all strategic concept which we should inscribe today? It is nothing less than the safety and welfare, the freedom and progress, of all the homes and families of all the men and women in all the lands." This ambitious, global project would require a UN with teeth, because "courts and magistrates may be set up but they cannot function without sheriffs and constables. The United Nations Organization must immediately begin to be equipped with an international armed force."

Churchill also called for regional alliances that would reinforce the security interests of the West, and allow it to meet the Soviet threat with force and determination, and at the same time to be unequivocal about the common objectives for which the "English-speaking peoples" would continue to strive:

But we must never cease to proclaim in fearless tones the great principles of freedom and the rights of man which are the joint inheritance of the English-speaking world and which through Magna Carta, the Bill of Rights, the Habeas Corpus, trial by jury and the English common law find their most famous expression in the American Declaration of Independence. All this means that the people of any country have the right, and should have the power by constitutional action, by free unfettered elections, with secret ballot, to choose or change the character or form of government under which they dwell; that freedom of speech and thought should reign; that courts of justice, independent of the executive, unbiased by any party, should administer laws which have received the broad assent of large majorities or are consecrated by time and custom. Here are the title deeds of freedom which should lie in every cottage home. Here is the message of the British and American peoples to mankind. Let us preach what we practise – let us practise what we preach.

It was precisely on this point of "walking the talk" that Churchill's own contradictions turned on him. The inconsistency, of course, was the British Empire. "Every cottage home" did not, for him, include the homes of the hundreds of millions who lived under imperial rule in Africa and Asia. The same man who stood up to the dictators of Europe now declared that he had not become prime minister to preside over the dissolution of the British Empire. The man whose first books were romantic accounts of his experiences on the Northwest Frontier of India and battling Afrikaners in South Africa was the quintessential imperialist of his time, and the notion that democratic self-rule should be given quickly to the vast array of peoples who had been subjugated under the empire was anathema to him. When he was excluded from Cabinet, in the 1930's, Churchill was as likely to attack the idea of appeasing Gandhi as he was the failure to face up to Hitler.

In this regard Churchill was hardly alone. The United States made a point of distinguishing itself from Britain, which it characterized as "the colonial power," just as Woodrow Wilson had earlier drawn the line between the corruption of the old world and the pristine values of the new. But this doesn't stand up to scrutiny. As we have seen, the United States was based on the revolutionary values of freedom and the rule of law, but it was also based on slavery, the notion of its manifest destiny on the American continent, a Monroe Doctrine for the Americas (which declared that further colonization by Europe in the western hemisphere would be viewed as an act of aggression), and with the invasion of the Philippines and the Spanish-American War an even greater drive to expansion. These drives had their critics – Lincoln himself had been an eloquent critic of the war with Mexico in the 1840s – but those who advocated them carried the day, the presidency, and Congress. So the United States' credentials as an "anti-imperialist" power were themselves questionable.

Nevertheless, one of the key tensions between these two allies would be the nature of the postwar world. Britain could not really afford her empire, and America was not completely certain of how its new supremacy in the West would be exercised. But one central point was clear enough: building an anti-fascist alliance to end the war had drawn on both ideas and institutions. The ideas were, on their face, democratic, and the institutions were of global reach. And the world after 1945 would inexorably turn around these twin realities. We live with their consequences today.

The United Nations Charter, proclaimed in June 1945, reflected in good part the values expressed in the Atlantic Charter cited earlier, but also took into account the power realities that emerged as the Second World War drew to a close. The purpose of the organization was described ambitiously as "to save succeeding generations from the scourge of war, which twice in our lifetime has brought untold sorrow to mankind." While the word "democracy" does not appear anywhere in the charter, "tolerance," "peace," "social advancement," "justice" and "larger freedom" all do, as do the principles of "self-determination" and respect for "human rights and fundamental freedoms."

There were important differences between the United Nations and the League of Nations. First, the United States was present at the creation of the UN, and used its participation to insist that the values and principles of the new organization reflect the underlying values that had taken America into the war. Second, on the issue of colonialism, the charter went as far as it could to reflect the desire for self-government and the steady dismantling of the old power structures. As we shall see, the collapse of empire would not be easy; it would cause deep divides and conflicts, and almost unimaginable chaos and loss of life in some instances. But the language of the charter pointed the way to the world that was struggling to emerge. The weakness of the UN was not so much in the charter as in the politics that began to unfold as the Second World War was ending. The UN was a creature of the war, and it gave permanent status on the Security Council to the major Allies: the United States, the Soviet Union, France, the United Kingdom, and China. But the principal difficulty was the provision of a veto for these five countries. The immediate rivalry between the Soviet Union and the West that followed the end of the war meant that the Security Council was deadlocked from its earliest days.

The UN Charter envisaged a robust capacity in the new organization to keep the peace. Two chapters of the charter – VI and VII – were explicitly designed to put the organization at the centre of resolving disputes between "parties," and further to take steps to deal with "any threat to the peace, any breaches of the peace, and act of aggression." A central tension was whether threats internal to a country could become the focus of international actions. The passage of the Genocide Convention in 1948 (whose implications are brilliantly outlined in Samantha Power's *A Problem from Hell: America and the Age of Genocide*) and the definition of "crimes against humanity" further contributed to a growing sense that the existence of national borders could not trump the scope of justice. Article 47 envisages the creation of a "Military Staff Committee to advise and assist the Security Council on all questions relating to . . . the maintenance of international peace and security, the employment and command of forces placed at its disposal, the regulation of armaments, and possible disarmament."

The use of atom bombs at Hiroshima and Nagasaki brought home to the entire world the reality that the scale of devastation wrought by future conflicts could well exceed anything contemplated or imagined before. For a brief time, the administration of Harry Truman, who succeeded Franklin Roosevelt after his death in April of 1945, gave serious thought to handing over control of America's atomic arsenal to the UN. This idea evaporated in the cold air of political reality, but the fact that it was even contemplated shows how seriously the administration took the technology that was in its possession.

The Iron Curtain that Churchill described with such clarity at Fulton was not just a figure of speech. The overthrow of democracy in Eastern Europe was chilling, brutal, and complete by 1948. Thousands were killed, imprisoned, and tortured as dictatorship returned to Budapest, Prague, Warsaw, and the other capitals of Central and Eastern Europe. What were originally "popular front" coalitions were quickly taken over by communist parties controlled by Moscow and sustained by the overwhelming presence of the Soviet army. Stalin claimed that this "sphere of influence" was tacitly agreed to in the wartime conferences in Tehran and Yalta – something the West never conceded. But Soviet control would not be challenged, except in Greece, where a bloody civil war followed liberation in 1945, and where British and American efforts succeeded in pushing back the communist offensive.

In Budapest today one can visit the headquarters of the secret police – the communists used the same building as the Nazis before them. It is eerie to see the parallels between the two regimes, the similarity of tactics; even the uniforms were virtually the same. Totalitarianism took on a new meaning as gulags and prisons were filled with political dissidents and those who dared to stand up to the fierceness of dictatorship.

George Marshall, Truman's secretary of state, had the foresight to understand that only a massive infusion of American assistance would allow Western Europe to rebuild itself quickly enough to withstand further communist penetration. In both Italy and France, large communist parties had won substantial control over the trade union movement. They remained a powerful political and social force in those countries for four decades, before finally collapsing after the Berlin Wall's destruction signalled a complete transformation of European politics. But those parties could go only so far, and no further, and while a powerful opposition presence in both countries, they were never able to form or join governments or affect their countries' loyalty to the Western alliance.

The Cold War would, in part, be fought by force of arms. The UN did respond to the invasion of South Korea in June 1950 with military force in a war that was long and violent but in the end only reached a stalemate. NATO was a military alliance founded to face down the military might of the Soviet Union, as Germany and Japan, after a lengthy occupation, each returned to the world stage with new, democratic constitutions and political structures that placed them firmly within the Western orbit.

But the struggle for freedom, the quest for security that Churchill described so eloquently in Fulton, also took on another dimension. The first was the determined subsidy and support of anti-communist groups in Europe and around the world. The 1950s was a time when American embassies and cultural institutes were flush with dollars for those intellectuals and trade unions who could be counted on to go toe to toe with the communists, fellow travellers, and even advocates of neutrality in a war of ideas. American foreign policy also supported relatively unsavoury regimes, like Salazar's in Portugal and Franco's in Spain, and equally or more repressive governments in Latin America and Asia, that could be counted on to oppose communism wherever it flourished.

Aid programs were designed to fight Soviet influence. Recipient countries quickly learned how to play each side against the other, the most notorious example being Egypt's construction of the Aswan Dam, which was started by the Americans but completed by the Russians. The so-called non-aligned countries, led by newly independent India, tried to create a third force to counter the notion that the world had to choose between these competing ideologies. Their ranks were joined by the countries of Africa and Asia as they emerged from a century-long experience of colonialism. Their economies were weak, their states were fragile, and their people were poor.

Just as the reaction to the French and Russian revolutions was marked by repression in much of Europe, and later in North America, the Cold War set in motion a heavy wave of intimidation that coloured the "fight for democracy." In the United States, the shutting down of freedom in Eastern Europe, and the triumph of another brand of communism in China, spawned a powerful force within American politics that looked for villains and scapegoats within. The House Un-American Activities Committee and Senator Joseph McCarthy's sustained campaigns to flush out and persecute American communists and subversives knew no bounds in its indiscriminate smearing of liberals and progressives, trade unionists, and Hollywood stars. McCarthyism had a profound effect on American and indeed Western society. Lives were ruined as even a casual affinity for radical activity back in the 1930s led to ritual "outing" and denunciation. For many of those targeted the choice was between recanting or being blacklisted. Journalist Alistair Cooke called it "a generation on trial." Police and intelligence services were widely used to track and follow all forms of radical activity, liberals and social democrats were routinely confused with communists (even though they were always the first to be targeted by Stalinists), and in virtually every country in the world an ideological "culture war" financed by the West ensued.

This focus on fighting communism to the exclusion of everything else took a heavy toll on democracy and liberalism, because profoundly illiberal means were used to ensure security. Authoritarian regimes of every stripe were supported because they were seen as fortresses of anti-communism: Verwoerd's apartheid South Africa, Franco's Spain, Pinochet's Chile, Mobutu's Congo . . . the list is endless. The need to distinguish between revolutionary communists, nationalists, social democrats, and others was lost, and Western interests became more often than not synonymous with the forces of reaction.

To cite just one example: Herbert Norman was the son of Protestant missionaries who had grown up in Japan. After he moved to Canada as a student in the 1930s, he won a scholarship to Cambridge University, where he wrote a brilliant study of the Meiji restoration in Japan. He joined the Canadian foreign service in 1940, and returned to Japan as General Douglas MacArthur's right-hand man during the U.S. occupation, becoming instrumental in the reforms of the Japanese educational system and the establishment of democratic rule. The culling of names and records that became a specialty of the American anti-communist movement produced Norman's name. The charges varied: he had been a communist at Cambridge, he was a Soviet mole, he was a KGB operative. No evidence to support these claims was ever produced. The pressure proved too much; in the fall of 1956, Norman, by then Canada's ambassador to Egypt, took his own life by jumping from the top of the office building that housed the embassy.

The Cold War led to a serious confusion about democracy: "our" autocrats were okay; "theirs" were a problem. The filter of anti-communism was applied to virtually every aspect of foreign policy. The result was a Western world blind to its own colonial abuses, reluctant to face the injustice of apartheid, quick to isolate and destroy democratically elected leaders who threatened American economic interests, such as Iranian Prime Minister Mohammad Mossadegh, Guatemalan President Jacobo Árbenz, and Chilean President Salvador Allende, and to countenance the subsequent abuses of Chilean generals, Argentinean majors, and Greek colonels.

The effort to promote democracy and good governance will always be marked by some necessary tensions. The language of the Atlantic Charter and the UN's Universal Declaration of Human Rights is powerful, speaking to "universal" aspirations of democracy and human rights. The realities of national and international politics rarely take us to such heights.

The powerful sense that is now widely shared, that democracy and human rights are central to the human project should not lead us to the conclusion that "governance is easy," that the replacement of brutal dictatorship and chaotic conflict in which poverty is rife and ethnic hatred is widespread, by regimes supported by an enlightened and high-minded population, is a straightforward proposition.

There is no avoiding the Hobbesian insight that the first task of politics is to overcome the brutal chaos of the "war of all against all." That means a government with the ability to extend its writ throughout a country, to establish peace and order before good government can become possible. But the technique a government uses to establish control can't just be brute force. Consent is the basis of legitimate authority. Governments – imperial or national – can't make criminals of an entire nation, to borrow Burke's phrase.

The conditions that lead to better governance are closely tied to education and economic growth. People have to decide that getting on with life is more important than fighting; that religion, identity and ethnicity have to assume a place that is not exclusive and all encompassing. This does not happen overnight, and it does not happen automatically. There are many forces at work that actively don't want it to happen. Bad leaders want power for its own sake, and to enrich themselves. They will kill and terrorize to achieve their objective, and thus far in history we haven't found a better way to deal with them than to fight back when conditions simply become too risky or too oppressive.

The imperial idea has always contained in it the notion that part of the purpose of annexation or colonization was to "improve" the subject countries with better governance. This attitude was 99 percent hypocrisy and wishful thinking even in the colonial era. As the postwar world turned into a post-colonial world, the West used "foreign assistance" as a practical and necessary way to fight communism. Peaceful coexistence also meant peaceful competition.

The competition was often less than peaceful. The Central Intelligence Agency became a key instrument of U.S. foreign policy, sometimes deciding which foreign governments would live and which would die. For example, in Iran, the decision in the early 1950s by democratically elected Iranian Prime Minister Mohammad Mossadegh to nationalize the Anglo-Iranian Oil Company (from which Iran received just 16 percent of oil profits) led the British and Americans to organize a violent coup d'état and overthrow Mossadegh, ensuring that a British–American consortium would control the oil business. They replaced the civilian administration with a government run by a general but controlled by the shah. The British had persuaded the Americans that Mossadegh was a Soviet puppet. There was no apparent justification for this claim, and the deliberate undermining of the will of the people of Iran had a profound effect on the politics of the region.

The 1954 Guatemalan coup was also directly organized by the CIA. A democratically elected President Jacobo Árbenz Guzmán undertook land reforms that offended both the United Fruit Company and local elites. The CIA-organized operation was extensive, involving training guerrillas, carrying on widespread propaganda (which had worked so well in Iran), and supporting the armed invasion and overthrow of Árbenz by the army in a military coup.

Just as in Iran, the excuse given was that Árbenz was a "communist" (he was a social democrat) and was a threat to American security. Guatemala remained mired in military dictatorship and deep conflict for generations. It is estimated that over the four decades since the coup the number of "disappeareds" could be as high as a quarter of a million people.

The coup that overthrew Salvador Allende in Chile in 1973 bears a similar pattern, although Allende's management of the economy and other measures had aroused much opposition within Chile. Both the Supreme Court and the Chilean Congress were profoundly opposed, and the country was in deep political deadlock. However, he also had substantial public support, and documents clearly show direct CIA support for strikes, economic boycotts, and other measures that destabilized the government. A CIA directive issued on October 16, 1970, was categorical when it said quite simply, "It is firm and continuing policy that Allende be overthrown by a coup . . ." President Nixon had written CIA director Richard Helms a month earlier directing him to "make the economy scream to prevent Allende from coming to power or to unseat him." The military coup by General Pinochet led to the arrest of tens of thousands of people, and the torture and murder of hundreds of others. Thousands fled Chile as refugees, and the Pinochet regime kept its hold on power for almost two decades. Happily, today Chile is a thriving democracy.

The "democracy fight" was not confined to the Third World. A generation of exiles from behind the Iron Curtain kept the cause of freedom and democracy in Eastern Europe alive, but their courage was nothing compared with that of those who worked within the seemingly impregnable Soviet system. These struggles were at once national, religious, and democratic. At a geopolitical level President Josip Tito's Yugoslavia was the first to break free from the Soviet orbit, although the hold of the Communist Party on the country was uncompromising. Yugoslavia joined India and others as a leader of the Non-Aligned Movement, but Tito did not hesitate to throw his own dissenters, like Milovan Djilas, in jail. He allowed some private participation in the economy, and for a time it was fashionable to argue that the country was a leader in creating a "third way" between communism and capitalism. But there should be no illusion about Tito's hold on power – the internal structure of the country was anything but open and democratic, and its economic successes would prove short-lived.

Popular revolts in East Germany and Poland in 1953, and Hungary in 1956, were crushed by the Soviet and local armies, and the Warsaw Pact, the Soviet Union's answer to NATO, ensured that Soviet troops were everywhere. Local communist parties got their orders from Moscow. The Soviet Bloc was a world frozen in time, undermined perhaps most effectively by jokes widely shared by word of mouth, such as this one: A Polish shopper in 1962 asks when it might be possible to buy a radio. The woman at the counter says there is a long lineup and it could take years. The woman is insistent. "Give me date."

"Okay, let's say January 2, 1966," the shopkeeper volunteers.

"Morning or afternoon?"

"What's it to you?"

"My phone's coming in the morning on that day."

The economies of the communist regimes can be summed up in the saying, "You pretend to work and we'll pretend to pay you." Every political effort was made to enforce orthodoxy, and dissenters were severely punished. Everyone was encouraged to report economic and political crimes, and reports of "hoarding" and dissent were duly noted, recorded, and kept for posterity. It would take an entire generation before these documents were released, in all their sordidness, for their appalled victims and the world to see.

Communism was based on several contradictions, the most telling of which is that it claimed to draw its inspiration from the deepest wells of humanitarianism and solidarity, yet it survived only because of the harshness of its repression. Soviet leader Nikita Khrushchev's denunciation of Stalin's excesses walked a fine line, because his premise was that Stalin had created a "cult of personality" that took him away from the true path that had been set out by Marx and Lenin. One could equally well argue that many of these "excesses" were started by his predecessors, and that the idea of the dictatorship of the party was the origin of the disease. Certainly Lenin's efforts after 1923 to suppress the intelligentsia and to eliminate political opposition, and the cynical brutality with which he changed course in order to maintain power, put him firmly in the pantheon of tyrants.

Khrushchev could not admit any of this without abandoning his faith altogether. But the contradictions within communism became clearer within the Soviet Bloc as Western Europe and North America's postwar economic recovery raised living standards to their highest point ever. Hundreds died trying to cross the Berlin Wall to the West. Radio, television, movies, music all crossed through the curtain. Dissent was everywhere, and often had nothing directly to do with politics: a new generation simply wanted to be able to live better and could find no way to do that under communist rule.

Nineteen sixty-eight was a year of rebellion in the West, from Washington to Paris, where street demonstrations led to the end of the de Gaulle government. But nowhere was feeling deeper than in Prague in the spring of 1968. An unlikely communist leader, Alexander Dubček, suggested that Czechoslovakia might best follow Yugoslavia in seeking an economic and political "opening." The West watched in frustration as Soviet troops moved in, as they had done in Poland in 1953 and Hungary in 1956, arrested Dubček and the Communist Party leadership and restored the status quo with a vengeance.

But seeds had been sown and their fruit could not be completely eradicated. Khrushchev's successor, Leonid Brezhnev, in what he thought was a stroke of genius, began engaging the West in a "thaw" of relations. He promoted the idea of peaceful coexistence that would recognize the integrity of the borders of postwar Europe. The West's price was to insist that any agreement had to contain commitments to human rights and freedom. The Soviets, having already signed the Charter of the United Nations and the Universal Declaration of Human Rights and not having implemented their provisions, agreed. In 1975, most countries of Eastern and Western Europe, along with the USSR, the United States, and Canada, signed the Helsinki Accords.

While some critics feared that signing the accords "gave respectability" to the Soviets, the opposite occurred: it gave credibility and respectability to human rights, and granted dissenters in Eastern Europe access to wider European and world opinion in an organized way. The Jews of the Soviet Union were among the first to insist on their rights under the accords, and established ties with supporters in the West, as well as in Israel. The determination of "refuseniks," such as Jewish spokesman Natan Sharansky, began to chip away at the supposedly impregnable Soviet state. At the same time, the Soviet Union's military occupation of Afghanistan, which began in 1979, was taking a heavy toll in lost lives and diminished prestige, and in economic cost. An economy that had been capable of sending a man to the moon was now having trouble supplying the basics of life to its people.

Mikhail Gorbachev, who came to power in 1985, was not at the outset a democrat and certainly not a reformer. But he was a younger man, born after the revolution, who realized that the status quo could not continue. The ideas of *glasnost* (openness) and *perestroika* (restructuring) were supposed to lead to internal reform of the Soviet Union and the Soviet Communist Party. What he did not fully realize was that once reforms began it would prove impossible to stop them. Thomas Jefferson's insight that there is something "infectious" in the democratic idea proved true in this case as Lithuania, Latvia, and Estonia all withdrew from the Soviet Union, as did Ukraine and the eastern "Stans" (Turkmenistan, Uzbekistan, Kyrgyzstan, and Kazakhstan): the system simply collapsed. Nationalism was an even more powerful force than the appeal of liberal democracy.

Vicious ethnic conflict was only one consequence of what the

West claimed was the "end of communism." Decades of central rule and a centralized economy had destroyed civil society, eroded trust, and despoiled the environment. Well-meaning outsiders recommended "shock treatment" for their economies, but the effects of this sudden change on the standard of living and quality of life of most people were devastating. Unscrupulous kleptocrats took advantage of massive privatization of public assets to enrich themselves and seize control of the national economies. The professors and dissidents who were among the first generation of new leaders in the post-communist world faced an impossible choice between working with old communist bureaucrats or a wholesale purging of the old order, which would place the inexperienced and incompetent in control.

The reunification of Germany after the collapse of the Berlin Wall in 1989 continues to cost far more than anyone imagined, but it is impossible to imagine the alternative. The slow but steady integration of the countries of Eastern Europe into the European Union has made for dramatic transformations in their societies and economies that few could have imagined even twenty years ago.

The tearing down of the Berlin Wall was the key symbol of an end to the debate about whether capitalism or communism was the better way of creating wealth and governing societies. But it did not bring an end to history, or mean that the American way of life would triumph for all time. Several issues have emerged as the central challenges of our era.

Ethnic conflict has devastated the former Yugoslavia and parts of the former Soviet Union, and been the fuel of disputes in parts of Eastern Europe. It has also deeply affected much of Africa, the Middle East, and Asia. In each case, it is not simply about people not getting along. It is about how the appeal to tribe, race, and religious prejudice by cynical leaders is used to secure control. Our knowledge or awareness of these conflicts depends almost entirely on whether the media take an interest in them, or are allowed to take an interest in them. The break-up of the former Yugoslavia was widely covered, and the searing pictures of the resulting wars are emblazoned on our memories. The conflict in Chechnya, by contrast, is less well documented, as the media have been kept away by the Russians "for security reasons." The genocides in Eastern and Central Africa, which to date are estimated to have cost lives in the millions, not the thousands, have gone vastly underreported. The murder of hundreds of thousands of Rwandan Hutus, while a small UN force stood helplessly by, appalled the world. Since then, sadly, this death toll has been vastly outmatched in continued fighting in eastern Congo, and yet little is said or done about this devastating conflict. There is a UN force there, but its work goes largely unreported in North America.

Darfur gets headlines, but the humanitarian tragedy of Sudan's repeated attacks on its western province has never been matched by an effective international response. The joint UN–African Union force that is in Darfur has never had the military capability that would allow it to do the job that has to be done. How to use international intervention to protect populations whose very survival is at risk is now a central tension at the heart of international politics and the United Nations. The test is pretty clear: those conflicts that strike at the heart of Western security concerns will get much attention, as will those that allow relatively free access to the media. But others do not, and their neglect still makes it hard to talk of a "global village" as if it were a community with a common moral compass.

The break-up of the Soviet Union and of Yugoslavia, and even the peaceful divorce of the Czech Republic and Slovakia, are often cited as examples of "federalism not working." This is, to put it mildly, faulty logic. The one-party dictatorship in place in each country concealed simmering ethnic conflict and national aspiration, and for this reason alone they were federal in name only. The end of communism and the competition for spoils left a vacuum that was filled by ethnic nationalists whose only card in the chaos was an appeal to resentment, at once economic and racial. The result was an ugliness whose destructive power shocked the world. "Federalism" is not to blame, because it was not really tried. Indeed, the countries that have now found independence are coming to realize that sovereignty itself is not absolute, and as they fall into the embrace of the European Union they will discover how insistent these new structures will be for coordination and integration, the very goals of federalism itself.

Neither the United States nor Europe – nor indeed NATO or the United Nations – can take any pride in the time it took to bring former Serbian president Slobodan Milošević and his supporters to ground. After the collapse of Yugoslavia as a single, communist nation, he embroiled the region in civil war in his quest for Serbian primacy. Far too many people died during the war, and there was much hesitation and finger-pointing before the world effectively mobilized itself into action. The UN's International Criminal Tribunal in the Hague has been kept busy in the painstaking exercise of trying to ensure justice and an end to "impunity," but the lesson of how to intervene sooner and with more effectiveness has not yet been learned, except by those involved in the prosecutions of, most notably, Milošević (who died in 2006 before his trial concluded) and former Bosnian president Radovan Karadžić.

Russia's journey toward democracy has been rocky, to say the least. While its natural gas and oil reserves have given the country's finances a boost, its underlying economic development is badly skewed, as the standard of living of millions actually declines while a new wealthy elite reaps the benefits of privatization. Life expectancy has fallen dramatically, alcohol and drug abuse are widespread, and the quality of life and sense of security of the average Russian have taken a major hit. Vladimir Putin's emergence as a strongman has brought back an authoritarianism that has always been beneath the surface. But he enjoys popular support at home for his ability to appeal to the widespread sense that

Russia needs to regain its prestige and place on the world stage. Corruption remains endemic. Power is deeply centralized as it ever was under the tsars and the communists. Russia continues to treat the various nationalities within its borders and within the so-called Commonwealth of Independent States as client peoples, and resents any efforts by the West to embrace human rights issues either inside the country or in countries like Ukraine and Georgia, which Russia insists are in its "zone of influence."

Russia is threatened by domestic conflict and violence, primarily from Muslim Chechnya and other parts of the Caucasus, but thus far its response has been almost exclusively military. Russia's empire is striking back, but an effective response would be a more dramatic reinvention of governance than the appeal to old nationalism and authoritarianism that seems to have captured the popular imagination.

CHAPTER 5

DEMOCRACY AND THE END OF EMPIRE:
China, India, and Africa

S oviet Communism's self-destruction was sharp and dramatic, but the changes in China since 1980 have been equally so. In fact, China moved away from a centralized, command-and-control economy long before the collapse of the Berlin Wall. Mao Tse-tung's death in 1976 and the rapid discrediting of the Gang of Four were followed in 1979 by the ascendancy of Deng Xiaoping and a team of bright technocrats around him, led by Zhao Ziyang, who eventually became premier and later general secretary of the Communist Party of China.

China's shift to a market economy, which was a genuine revolution, was a reflection of both necessity and shrewd leadership. If a different course had not been followed, mass starvation could well have ensued.

Deng understood that China, like Napoleon's army, marched on its belly. Collectivized agriculture had to be destroyed, and farmers had to be allowed to grow food and raise animals for themselves as well as for the market. If prosperity could be brought to the countryside, the rest of the economic transformation would be possible. Without it nothing else could happen. This reform was followed by a series of moves designed to develop a private sector, to allow Hong Kong, Taiwanese, and other foreign investment, especially in manufacturing, and to begin the painful process of modernizing massive state industries and monopolies whose continued dominance threatened to bring down the entire economy.

The contradiction in the rapid modernization of China has been the continued political monopoly of the Chinese Communist Party existing side by side with a liberalized market and an almost libertarian consumer culture. The devastation of China's feudal system in the early twentieth century, followed by the reign of the warlords and the Japanese invasion has, to put it mildly, put a premium on order and political stability. Chinese nationalism has also played its part. The humiliation of the concessions forced by the West in the imperial era had to be followed by a negotiated return of Hong Kong and Macao to the fold. Sovereignty, and Han Chinese settlement, were extended to Xinjiang and Tibet, territories nominally part of the Mongolian and Chinese empires since the thirteenth century. Resistance was brutally put down.

The continuing gap between economic freedom and political repression came to a head during the protests held in Tiananmen Square in Beijing in the spring of 1989, a few short months after the beginning of the end of the Soviet Bloc and the Soviet Union. A rapidly growing student population was insisting that China follow its economic reforms with political change. For a brief few weeks, protests took place in the square every day. In his remarkable book *Prisoner of the State*, which was published after his death in 2009, Zhao Ziyang describes how he tried to persuade the Politburo Standing Committee that the student protesters should not be brutally put down, but rather engaged in a dialogue: "All students, teachers, and intellectuals should be allowed to express themselves freely . . . bloodshed must be avoided, no matter what."

But it was not to be. The leadership of the party, including an elderly Deng himself, swiftly removed Zhao as general secretary, and ordered the army to clear the square, with as much force as necessary. Hundreds were killed and thousands were arrested. The putting down of the revolt was as brutal as it had been in Hungary in 1956 and in Czechoslovakia in 1968. The outside world could only look on. A military response was unthinkable, and an economic boycott would have been unworkable. China is too big, its links to the world economy too deep.

The Communist Party retained its grip, while continuing to allow the privatization and opening up of its economy with the world. Within a few years China joined the World Trade Organization, and it continued with its policy of encouraging joint ventures and dismantling the vast array of state-owned enterprises that had provided cradle-to-grave security to their employees. As these organizations shed hundreds of thousands of jobs, and with the countryside unable to provide jobs to vast numbers of the unemployed, China's challenge was to maintain stability at the same time as it continued to push for change and openness.

Visitors to China seldom see the political repression applied to those who take their political right to dissent seriously and insist on being able to express it. The Internet is blocked and controlled, dissidents are jailed, and some groups, like the spiritual movement Falun Gong, are treated as illegal conspiracies. Nationalists in Tibet and Xinjiang (where the minority Uyghurs live) are thrown in jail, often for years, and the dream of Chinese democrats that their political system will match the openness of their economy remains just that, a dream.

Zhao Ziyang spent the last fifteen years of his life under house arrest. He had climbed to the top of the Chinese Communist Party only to be summarily dismissed and cast aside. He was not killed, but was reduced to a non-person. Remarkably, he secretly made tapes of his experience and views, summarizing his feelings about modernization and democracy as follows:

> If a country wants to modernize, to realize a modern market economy, it must practice parliamentary democracy as its political system . . . otherwise . . . it will run into the situations that have occurred in so many developing countries, including China: commercialization of power, rampant corruption, a society polarized between rich and

poor . . . On the other hand, given the reality in China, we
need a relatively long period of transition. (Zhao, 270-71)

Zhao was not calling for the immediate overthrow of the Communist
Party, even from his isolation under house arrest. Rather he was
insisting on the importance of incremental change, on the need to
avoid chaos. Edmund Burke would have understood.

There are key relationships that will affect China's evolution.
The return of Hong Kong and Macao to the fold was marked by
an important concession by China: both would remain self-
governing, and while their autonomy and level of democracy are
circumscribed, they are allowed a level of freedom and political
diversity unknown on the mainland. But freedom has a way of
spreading, and the level of openness found today in Hong Kong
and Macao, their methods of governance, their political culture,
will inevitably, if slowly, alter the nation around them, starting
with the Pearl Delta. This will be a controlled process, and will
not come without conflict. But it would be a serious mistake to
think that there are no voices for change in China, or that it will
never come; however, the Chinese people's preoccupation with
order will affect its degree and pace.

The other key relationship is with Taiwan. Already there have
been changes that were unimaginable even a decade ago. People
can now travel easily back and forth on scheduled flights, and
ferry traffic is rapidly reconnecting Taiwan to the mainland.
Economic investment had already preceded these changes by
many years. Taiwan's has been steadily evolving into a flourishing
and vigorous democracy since the death of Chiang Kai-shek in
1975. Exactly what form the future discussions between China
and Taiwan will take is unclear. Taiwan itself remains divided on
how to proceed, and there are widespread concerns about political integration without guarantees for freedom and democracy.
But, as with Hong Kong and Macao, the reality of Taiwan's openness and freedom will affect China as times goes on.

Finally, there is the question of how China deals with its diversity. The leadership is currently preoccupied with the lack of growth and investment in many parts of rural China, which stands in stark contrast to the transformation of the coastal regions. When they visited Nanjing, the capital of Jiangsu province, in 1986, members of an Ontario trade delegation stayed in the only international hotel in an undeveloped city. Today, Nanjing is a city transformed, as bustling and sophisticated as any in the West. The pace of development has been extraordinary, but the countryside and many cities in the interior have not seen a similar change.

The ethnic diversity of China is something the regime has difficulty coping with. Religious freedom is also circumscribed – the case of Falun Gong is well known, but Christians of all denominations are met with contempt and persecution from a regime that cannot countenance adherence to values other than the immediate goals of modernization and stability. The question remains whether China can ever feel secure enough to tolerate or even celebrate its diversity.

One thing is clear: that attempts to "punish" China, as some governments have done, by refusing to engage and understand the depth and extent of the country's changes and challenges, are futile. So is the reluctance to recognize that a mature China policy necessarily involves a vigorous commitment to expanding trade, cultural, and educational exchanges, coupled with a steady reminder about the importance of political reform. The great Chinese nationalist leader Sun Yat-sen acknowledged this when he said, "Worldwide trends are enormous and powerful; those who follow them prosper, and those who resist them perish" (quoted in Zhao, 272).

The American journalist and author Thomas Friedman has written eloquently about the pace of globalization and how governments that fail to put on what he calls the "golden harness" will find themselves on the margins of the drive to prosperity and modernization. Both Adam Smith and Karl Marx had a clear sense

that the industrial revolution taking place around them had a powerful global reach that would transform every society, breaking
down old social structures and casting aside traditional economies.
People have a variety of ways of dealing with a pace of change
that is never even, that involves great hardship as well as great
expansions of opportunity. In the last century, we've seen the
gamut of reactions, from the anti-Semitism and xenophobia of the
fascists, to the wars for independence waged by nationalist movements against old colonial structures and regimes, to the appeal
that religious extremism holds for millions of underemployed and
disenfranchised youth. Kant's adage that nothing straight was
ever made out of the crooked timber of mankind is proved true by
each generation.

One vast and densely populated country that has confronted
modernization with an uncommon degree of democracy and
respect for diversity is India. Once the realm of rajahs and poten-
tates, both Muslim and Hindu, India's incorporation into the
modern British Empire took place over many decades. We saw
earlier Edmund Burke's conclusion from the abuses of Warren
Hastings and the East India Company that a private commercial
monopoly had to be converted into a public trust. The consequence of this conversion was a steady expansion of direct British
rule, under the control of a cabinet minister responsible to
Parliament. Benjamin Disraeli called India "the jewel in the
crown" of the British Empire, and noted that "Empress of India"
was Queen Victoria's favourite title. But even at its peak during
her reign, the idea of empire had its opponents and doubters.
There were liberal imperialists, and so-called Little Englanders,
liberals who doubted the permanent legitimacy of rule from afar,
who realized that the young men, and eventually women, of the
colonies who were being trained and educated and asked to read
John Stuart Mill would begin to ask why, if democracy and
freedom were such good things for Englishmen, they were not
good for them.

The movements for independence led by Mohandas Gandhi, Jawaharlal Nehru, and Muhammad Jinnah were among the great democratizing forces of the twentieth century. Independence was fiercely resisted by Churchill because it ran counter to his vision of an empire on which the sun never set. But it proved an irresistible force, and had a powerful appeal well beyond India – the drive for an end to colonial rule, broader economic development, and self-government was not simply about a narrow nationalism, but about the drive for freedom itself.

But this drive was diverted by the conflict between Muslims and Hindus, and the demand by Muslims, led by Jinnah, for their own separate state. Gandhi regarded the partition of India as the great tragedy of his life. He died believing that the notion of two communally based states living side by side was a colossal mistake. Millions died in the fighting over the creation of these two states, and it is hard to avoid the sense that an opportunity was lost in 1948. Two territories were carved out of India, one to the northeast and the other to the northwest, and these formed the new nation of Pakistan, which was to be the homeland for Muslims. India insisted on its own status as a state for both Muslims and Hindus, and its constitution as a federal country affirmed its commitment to diversity. At the same time, the Congress Party, which maintained a strong grip on power, determined that its development would follow the socialist path, and Hindu nationalism was never far from the surface. Jawaharlal Nehru's unequivocal assertion that Kashmir, which has a Muslim majority, had to remain an integral part of India was an effort to control as much territory as possible, and the region has remained a flashpoint between India and Pakistan ever since.

India's remarkable evolution has not been without conflict and violence. Fighting over Kashmir, wars with Pakistan and China, and serious internal battles in the predominantly Sikh state of Punjab and in the eastern part of the country have cost tens of thousands of lives. Some profound underlying issues remain, with Marxist and tribally based guerrilla movements still active in parts of the country, and the deep poverty of both rural and urban areas a dramatic feature of India's uneven development. Nehru died in his bed but the same cannot be said for his daughter, Prime Minister Indira Gandhi, who was murdered by her Sikh bodyguards after a bloody assault by Indian troops on the Golden Temple at Amritsar in Punjab in 1984, and his grandson Prime Minister Rajiv Gandhi, killed by a Tamil Tiger suicide bomber in the middle of a political campaign in 1991.

But India has endured. A significant amendment to its constitution in 2006 redrew several state boundaries so they coincided more closely with language and ethnic realities. Economic growth further empowered the regions, and the digital revolution has allowed tens of millions to flourish through jobs that are integrated into the global economy. States have been granted increased powers and responsibilities; the central government has abandoned its heavy-handed determination to control all aspects of the economy, and while the economic revolution has been slower than in China, it is now in full flight. The changes in governance that Zhao Ziyang at the end of his life argued were essential for China are now largely in place in India. It has a free press, independent courts, a sophisticated legal system, and a multi-party political system. Its federalism is more vibrant and decentralized than ever, and partnerships between the national and local government are stronger than in many other federations.

There are poverty, corruption, and violence in India, but there are also a rapidly growing middle class, a press and court system that fight corruption, and a sense of the importance of the rule of law that remains at the forefront of the political culture of the country. Caste, class, and gender remain barriers to opportunity for millions, but there is an openness and vitality to Indian life that have rightly earned it the characterization of "chaos that works." India is a functioning democracy and federation, not only at election time but between elections.

Its success is in stark contrast to Pakistan, which has been bluntly called "an army in search of a country." The decision of East Pakistan to break away and form an independent Bangladesh in 1971 was definitive proof that Punjabi centralism would not work. Pakistan has been ruled by military dictatorship longer than it has by civilian rule, and its budgets reflect that fact: it has a huge military apparatus, spends very little on public education and health, and has not experienced anywhere near the kind of investment and growth its neighbour has. Madrassas – religious schools, some of them extremist – have filled the gap left by the absence of public education, and the deep poverty of the people in the northwest of the country has been fertile ground for extremism. In Burma and Sri Lanka, two nations in the broader Indian subcontinent once ruled by the British, authoritarianism is still very much in contention with the democratic spirit. Where economic growth is weak, the institutions of civil society are feeble as well. Under the rule of a brutal military regime since 1962, Burma (named Myanmar by the ruling junta) is an isolated place, with much poverty and little investment. What military rule has placed on the country is not the golden harness imagined by Thomas Friedman but a brutal tourniquet.

Nehru and Gandhi both left a profound legacy in the achievements of India, but no leader in our century deserves more credit for revitalizing democracy in his country than Nelson Mandela.

In the nineteenth century, South Africa's Boer settlers imagined themselves a chosen people whose covenant with God gave them the strength to fight the rival British settlers as surely as it did the right to rule the Zulu and other tribes who lived in their millions around them. The battles of subjugation and enslavement of blacks were brutal. South Africa's self-government and status as a dominion within the Empire after the British defeated the Boers in a war for control of the territory in 1910 did not include majority rule, but rather a privileged position for whites that eventually was enshrined as a formal apartheid policy in 1948. Every resident of South Africa was racially identified as either white, black, or coloured. That identification defined all aspects of life: where one could live, whom one could marry, what jobs were available – the lists of separation and repression were endless.

Blacks who were living in vital neighbourhoods in large cities were moved out in the 1950s into suburban townships that were little better than camps. Their homes were razed to the ground. Political dissent was not tolerated. People were thrown in jail for their beliefs as much as for their actions, and as dissent grew so did the repression. In 1948, Nelson Mandela, a young lawyer who grew up as a tribal leader and made his way to Johannesburg's Sophiatown, joined the fledgling (and illegal) African National Congress, later becoming the leader of its armed wing. In 1962 he was arrested and charged with being part of a conspiracy to blow up a power line that had killed a white guard. He was jailed and spent the next twenty-seven years in captivity.

Not all dissent could be silenced in South Africa. It was too diverse. The liberal tradition was too persistent and too deeply rooted. Its internal critics were joined by supporters around the world who found its politics too heinous to let pass. A worldwide Anti-Apartheid Movement pressed governments to boycott South Africa in all respects, ranging from barring cricket and rugby teams from international matches to ending all investment. Canadian Prime Minister John Diefenbaker joined the fight to throw South Africa out of the Commonwealth in 1961, and Brian Mulroney pushed Commonwealth leaders to ignore British Prime Minister Margaret Thatcher's refusal to adopt sanctions against South Africa and make the economic boycott more effective during his tenure in the 1980s. In my two meetings with Mandela, he made a point of emphasizing how much Prime Minister Mulroney had done for the cause of a democratic South Africa.

Mandela's release from prison and his triumphant return to the centre of South African political life in 1990 is one of the great reconciliation stories of our time. By having tea with Betsie Verwoerd, the widow of the man who had presided over his imprisonment, and dining with his former prison warden, Mandela demonstrated a personal generosity that simply puts him in a different class from most political leaders of our time. At a gathering of Rhodes Scholars to commemorate the centenary of the death of Cecil Rhodes and the creation of the Rhodes Trust, Mandela made a point of emphasizing that he was proud to be Rhodes's successor as a South African leader. It was a truly brilliant way of capturing the middle ground, of refusing to accept the notion that he was a militant extremist, or that whites were not as equally South African as he.

South Africa has rightly been called "the world in one country." Here exists great wealth, and even greater poverty; people who are white, black and every shade between; great cities and a vast countryside; the crisis of widespread AIDs infection; competing visions of development; and the challenge of maintaining order in a society and country that remain deeply divided. The dominance of a single party, the African National Congress, poses a challenge to political pluralism, as does the nation's reluctant embrace of its federal reality. Corruption, abuse of power, and crime are endemic. But two transitions of presidential power by popular vote have taken place since Mandela's term in office, and the relatively peaceful replacement of apartheid South Africa by a multiracial state with a black majority remains one of the great miracles of modern times. The end of apartheid was not only a remarkable success for South African democracy, it was also a success for the Commonwealth and the United Nations. International engagement worked. The economic boycott of South Africa was never complete, but over time it forced the South African government to realize that the cost of its isolation was unmanageable. At the same time, the political engagement with South Africa, both public and private, helped pave way to change.

Boycotts and sanctions are effective only if steadily and universally applied and enforced. The bigger the gaps, the less effective they are, and as they become unworkable the pressure from those applying them to be allowed to compete with the non-compliers becomes stronger and stronger. Various countries and international bodies are experiencing this dilemma today in considering how to deal with Iran, Zimbabwe, Sudan, and North Korea – countries currently being boycotted by some but not all nations. These attempts at international isolation have had uneven effects, at best. Zimbabwe, for example, is an economic basket case and a political tyranny. Robert Mugabe's misrule has impoverished his people, enriched himself and his entourage, and made a mockery of democratic principles. The region and the African National Union have remained unable to effect real engagement, let alone change. The United States, Europe, Canada, and Australia have imposed sanctions and forced Mugabe to accept his rival, Morgan Tsvangirai as prime minister, but Mugabe is still in charge.

Africa's emergence from the colonial era has been fraught with pain and great hardship. To this day we underestimate the cost to Africans in human life and suffering of the slave trade and the extent of colonial oppression in the nineteenth century. The race for spoils was such that virtually every square inch of African territory was claimed by one European power or another by the time of the Congress of Berlin in 1875. The boundaries and borders they drew were based on administrative convenience, and had nothing to do with traditional African tribal territories. The various colonial governments invested as little as they could and took whatever resources possible. The idea that colonialism was a "civilizing mission" was a veneer that could scarcely cover the exploitation at the core of imperial rule. There is a tendency in some quarters today to view imperialism as a noble cause that left libraries, learning, and the rule of law behind. But this view ignores the discrimination, the killing, and the abuse of power that have also left their legacies.

Fewer whites settled West Africa, and the end of colonialism was less traumatic there than it was in Algeria, Kenya, Rhodesia, Angola, Mozambique and, of course, South Africa. Algeria's fight for independence from France was bloody, and lasted until the collapse of the Fourth Republic brought General Charles de Gaulle back to power in 1958. The irony is that he was initially supported by the French settlers of Algeria, who believed those who told them that Algeria would always remain "an integral part of France." On his first trip to Algiers, de Gaulle left with words of magnificent ambiguity: "Je vous ai compris" (I have understood you). The settlers took this as an undying commitment to their cause; de Gaulle understood otherwise, and promptly negotiated independence for Algeria.

The rest of French colonial Africa soon followed, albeit under heavy tutelage from France, which has never abandoned its ties or its presence. Over the past fifty years, it has been a common sight to see French paratroopers descending from the skies to attempt to establish a semblance of order, to say nothing of dictators returning from France for a medical visit or a trip to the bank. The economic and social ties are deep, strengthened by the cultural bond of La Francophonie.

Leopold Senghor was a poet of the first rank whose intellectual ties to France were profound. Born in 1906 in Senegal, he went to France to study at the age of twenty-two. Only as he grew older in France did he realize that while his language and culture were profoundly French, his colour and background were not. He joined the struggle for independence and became Senegal's first president after independence in 1960. One of the authors of the concept of *la Négritude*, Senghor was among the most eloquent of those who saw that from the celebration of black identity would come personal pride and emancipation, since the colonial experience was so much about the loss of identity.

Frantz Fanon, whose 1961 book *The Wretched of the Earth* was one of the most widely read books of its time, took this theme even further. Noting that white cultures had been planted in Africa by violence, and that even the minds of black people had been "colonized," Fanon, who was born in Martinique and worked as a psychiatrist in Algeria, concluded that only the purifying effects of violence itself would allow those excluded from power to become truly human again. Drawing on the theories of Marx, Freud, and the writings of the French anarchist Georges Sorel, Fanon painted a grim picture of an excluded and embittered colonized majority, whose personal and political vindication would come from only a violent confrontation with the colonial master.

Fanon's writings were controversial both because of their supposedly "clinical" basis, and the justification they gave to violence, just as Georges Sorel's had done before the First World War. Not until Osama bin Laden spoke forty years later would we see such a clear rationalization of the "cleansing" and "purifying" power of murder and mayhem. But if the prescription was terribly wrong, the diagnosis of the problem was still acute: exclusion and discrimination are the dry grass that can be lit by a demagogic leadership.

Over the past fifty years Africa has time and time again been marked by deep violence, abusive leadership, and a poisonous cocktail of greed and corruption. Adding tragedy to the mix, the AIDS epidemic is being met with much individual courage but grossly insufficient resources. To say that the hopes for democratic self-government have not been realized is a vast understatement. But, as the Bard says, the fault lies not in our stars but in ourselves. From the outset of decolonization, the colonial regimes in Africa left behind constitutions that were poorly thought out, with few social investments or working institutions and little but goodwill to carry the new nations forward. Conflicts within countries, unresolved during the colonial era, soon reached disastrous proportions – for example, the province of Katanga's attempt to secede from the Congo, the Nigerian-Biafran Civil War, the genocide against the Tutsis in Rwanda, and the civil wars in Sudan, Angola, and Somalia.

Nigeria's newfound oil wealth lined the pockets of a few but did little for the public good. A federal country, Nigeria has had longer military than civil rule, and is now wrestling with deep ethnic and religious conflicts that the passage of time has only made worse. When Kenya came close to a flat-out civil war in the winter of 2008, it was a surprise to those who had not been watching. The Mau Mau Rebellion of the 1950s had of course aroused world attention: it became an emblem of wanton violence, a slaughter of the innocent. We now understand it better as a brutal uprising of the landless and the jobless, orchestrated by leaders who themselves were either executed or jailed for their commitment to violence. Frequently forgotten are the estimated 20,000 Kenyans killed by British troops in their efforts to quell the rebellion.

The recent bloodshed in Kenya was yet another wave of brutal tribal violence that revealed the fragility of its political community. UN Secretary-General Kofi Annan was called in to broker a peace between two political parties whose rivalry had spiralled out of control, but only after hundreds died in a wave of killing following a deeply contested election. Kenya was indeed on the precipice.

Decades earlier, Britain's colonial policy in East Africa had for a time attempted to match the successful Anglo settlement of Rhodesia and South Africa by providing direct encouragement to Britons to move to Kenya and take up farming in the area known as the White Highlands. This gave rise to inevitable demands from the settlers for more autonomy and self-government, and increasing rage from native Kenyans that their land was being stolen from under them, and that they would only fare worse under a settlers' government. The brutal repression that followed the Mau Mau Rebellion succeeded in radicalizing young black leaders, and made the demand for independence inevitable.

Harold Macmillan, Britain's Conservative prime minister, travelled to Cape Town, where on February 3, 1960, with an angry South African Prime Minister Verwoerd looking on, he spoke of the "wind of change" that was sweeping through the continent and the wider empire: "Ever since the break-up of the Roman Empire one of the constant facts of political life in Europe has been the emergence of independent nations," he argued (Brandon, 550). The clear implication of his comments was that apartheid and ideas of racial separation and superiority were simply unsustainable, and the forces that would lead to majority rule and decolonization could no longer be resisted. Macmillan's government, like Harold Wilson's after it, came to the firm conclusion that protecting the white community was simply not going to happen, just as de Gaulle had reached the same conclusion about Algeria.

Jomo Kenyatta, the Kenyan leader who led the country's battle for independence, spent several years in jail because of his alleged involvement in the Mau Mau insurrection. He was released by the British, and (like so many before and after) went from being prisoner to president in rapid order. But his ascendancy was not matched by self-restraint. The idea that "it's our turn to eat" became a way of life as each successive government, Kenyatta's and the following one led by Daniel Moi, rewarded itself by appropriating wealth and advantage, with each man's tribal base – first Kikuyu, then Kalenjin – first in line to grab what it could. In recent years, offshore bank accounts, luxury houses, and a vast fleet of E-Class Mercedes-Benzes in Nairobi became the symbols of success and power.

The last fifty years have seen tragedy, corruption, poverty, and profound conflict in Africa, and Kenya has had its share of each. Key leaders, like Tom Mboya and Robert Ouko, have been assassinated. Land that had been seized by the colonial power was transferred to the new generation of political leaders for their personal use. Phony procurement contracts, wholesale looting of the public purse, a political elite isolated from its people by income and wealth, growing urban poverty and deep hardship in a drought-worn countryside – all rampant in Kenya – are symptoms of a country in deepest difficulty.

The election of Mwai Kibaki as president in 2002 was supposed to change all that, but it did not. The corruption continued. The battle for power that followed the next election in 2007 finally produced a Grand Coalition brokered by Kofi Annan with President Kibaki and Prime Minister Raila Odinga, longstanding rivals, finally agreeing on a common agenda. It remains to be seen whether they can deal with the crimes of the past, implement a new constitution, and devise an agenda for sustainable economic growth and social justice. Can the walking match the talking? Africa needs some victories, even small ones, and this is one case where the result depends on the Kenyans themselves.

The new draft constitution contains much that would ordinarily be in regular statutes. It is the product of a lengthy consultation with a mistrustful public, who want better laws, jobs, and a promising future, and who want them now. If an inelegant document were the only consequence, the result might be ignored. But it's more serious than that, because the constitution contains ambitious plans for devolution and power-sharing between the president and the prime minister. Whether these plans are successful will greatly determine the future of the country. As Kenyans debate the fine points of constitutional detail in a new national referendum, much is riding on a successful journey to reform.

Just a few miles from Nairobi is one of the most spectacular and evocative views in the world: the Rift Valley stretching as far as the eye can see. This is the place where primitive man evolved, and a hundred thousand years ago began the slow trek out of Africa to populate the world. Africa is mankind's common home. We can't abandon it now.

Yet the rest of the world's engagement with Africa comes in fits and starts. Much of the West's involvement in the years of the Cold War was a proxy battle with the Russians and other communists (notably the Cubans), which clearly undermined any pretensions to be "working for democracy." During this era, the West supported the dictators Antonio Salazar of Portugal and General Francisco Franco of Spain in their wars against the independence movements in their respective colonies, and went easy on the South African apartheid regime. The collaboration of Western governments with some of the worst offenders against human rights and democratic development, like Mobutu in the Democratic Republic of the Congo (also known then as Zaire), were excused as compromises necessary to maintain strong relationships with those who were at once fighting communism and demonstrating a firm hand on power.

The determination of the West to insist that African countries remain open to international investment, particularly resource exploitation, meant that those governments willing to do business were supported, regardless of their commitment to human rights. While the administration of President Jimmy Carter attempted to add human rights and democracy to the agenda of American foreign policy, and the Commonwealth began to add the language of human rights, democracy, and "capacity building" to its lexicon, their actions were more symbolic than substantive, and were undercut by the willingness of President Reagan and Prime Minister Thatcher to put the promotion of real democracy well behind the protection of Western interests.

But with the end of the Cold War, it became harder for the West to justify its support for corrupt dictatorships that failed every test of acceptable behaviour. No regime better personified this in Africa than that of Joseph Mobutu in the Democratic Republic of the Congo. The Congo's independence in 1960 was marked by a determined separatist group in the province of Katanga, led by Moise Tshombe, who attempted to mobilize Western support against Patrice Lumumba, a Marxist leader whose radical language brought him into immediate conflict with the West. The Secretary-General of the UN, Dag Hammarskjold, lost his life in a plane crash during the conflict, from which Mobutu emerged as a strong-man who would keep the country together.

The West's support for Mobutu was for the better part of three decades unapologetic, despite well-documented evidence of his corruption and brutality. In a continent with few examples of leadership approaching democratic standards, there was no surprise that this backer of "Western values" would receive emphatic support, especially given the depth of the conflicts in surrounding countries, notably Zimbabwe, Uganda, and Angola.

This stance was thrown into question after the Rwandan Tutsi genocide of 1994, which took place despite the presence of an admittedly small UN force, and Mobutu's decision to shelter the fugitive Hutu leadership and their followers, including many who were undoubtedly instigators of the genocide. This decision had disastrous consequences. He was abandoned by the West, which gave tacit support to the Rwandan decision to invade eastern Congo, which in turn set off a conflict that has rightly been called "Africa's world war." In his brilliant book of the same name, Gérard Prunier describes the complex chain of events which led Uganda, Angola, Burundi, Zimbabwe, Chad, Sudan, and Namibia to become directly involved with their armies and air forces, and Zambia, Malawi, South Africa, the Central African Republic, and Libya to be indirectly implicated. Although more than four million have died so far, this vastly under-reported conflict is still going on today, despite agreements and the presence of UN peacekeepers.

The West has three broad geopolitical interests in Africa. The first is to maintain access to oil supplies in Nigeria and Western Africa. The second is to protect access to mining exploration. The third is to monitor Muslim extremism, across North Africa, and in Sudan, Somalia, Kenya, and Tanzania.

Osama bin Laden planned al-Qaeda's attacks on the United States from Afghanistan, but he rose to prominence among extremist Muslims while in Sudan. He joined the cause against the Soviet occupation of Afghanistan and began to assert his authority and develop his ideological foundation in Peshawar, Pakistan, during the late 1980s, whence he used his considerable personal wealth to funnel arms and Arab volunteers to the muja- hideen fighting in Afghanistan. After the Taliban took over Afghanistan in 1989, he moved back to his birthplace of Saudi Arabia, where he was treated as a hero until he broke with local allies over a rejected offer to assist Saddam Hussein in the first Gulf War. He then moved to Sudan where, with fellow Afghan veterans, he was able to fundraise, organize, and develop his network freely, without the interference of any state apparatus or security forces.

It was from Sudan that his organization plotted the deadly attacks on the Khobar Towers in Saudi Arabia and the World Trade Center in 1993. His free ride in Sudan came to an end after his heated rhetoric against Saudi Arabia, an attempted assassination attempt on Egyptian President Hosni Mubarak, and widespread pressure from the United States and other countries prompted President Bashir to strip bin Laden of his passport and return him to Taliban-ruled Afghanistan.

On a trip to Sudan on behalf of the Forum of Federations in 2003, I found a deeply autocratic country emerging from a long civil war between the Islamic north and the predominantly Christian south, and still immersed in conflict in Darfur and else-. where. A vast country south of Egypt that straddles the boundary between the Arab world and Africa, Sudan has been immersed in conflict for the past twenty years. From the late nineteenth century onward, Britain ruled the north and south quite separately. In the south, Christian missionary schools were widespread, and the purpose of public administration was principally to provide a link to Uganda and Kenya. Then came Britain's sudden decision to merge the administrations of north and south and to leave in 1956.

Political forces in the largely black, Christian and animist south first suggested a federal structure for the country in 1947, again in 1953, and consistently thereafter. From the mid to the late 1960s, the Anyanya movement in the south challenged the authorities in Khartoum in a violent conflict, which led in 1971 to limited self-rule for the south. This seemed to bring the conflict to an end, but in 1983 President Gaafar Nimeiri unilaterally created three separate provinces in the south in a crude attempt to divide and rule. Thus was born in earnest the liberation movement in southern Sudan, the SPLA, led by the charismatic John Garang, whose death in an air crash in 2005 deprived his people and the world of an effective leader who could have helped transform the politics of northeast Africa.

The civil war between the north and south was bloody and brutal. An estimated two million people died, with an equal number wounded and displaced. When Omar al-Bashir came to power in 1989 in a coup in Khartoum, an Islamist government with even stronger triumphalist tendencies was born. Indeed Khartoum became an important epicentre of Muslim extremist activity. In 1994 the Sudanese constitution was changed again with the creation of twenty-six states, and the explicit adoption of a federalist model. But in reality this was very limited. The states had no money and even less capacity. Locked in a brutal conflict in the south, the army was dominant throughout the country. And one party, the National Islamic Front, had a monopoly of power throughout the country. Major efforts were made by a number of countries to bring the conflict to an end. Even the oil industry got into the act, insisting that the war was preventing exploration and production. The fact that they were in Sudan at all made them subject to a powerful boycott throughout North America and Europe. The United States imposed significant sanctions on Sudan.

The fight between north and south was eventually brought to a close after major efforts at international mediation. The Nigerian president led a team who eventually persuaded the parties to sign the Machakos Protocol, which provided for some wealth sharing and the joint management of the central bank. They also eventually agreed to a "trial marriage," then a referendum in the south on self-determination, which is due to be held in 2011.

It is now clear that the south is far more interested in self-rule than shared rule. It's hard to be coexist peaceably after a brutal civil war, unless core civic values have changed on both sides. They clearly have not. Islamic triumphalism and revolutionary one-party separatism are equally incompatible with the federal idea, which clearly implies democracy and pluralism.

I spent ten days in Sudan in an effort to see to whether the conclusion of the war between the north and south had led to any lessons learned that could help resolve the burgeoning conflict in Darfur in western Sudan. I was quickly disabused of this notion when I met with the Ministry of Federal Rule, which contrary to its name proved to be a haven of centralist obscurantism. The minister told me solemnly, "Darfur is tribal – and it's solved."

Other political leaders I talked to were critical of the government, but incapable of providing an alternative. Former prime minister Sadiq al-Mahdi was quick to say of the government, "They talk federalism, they do not practise it." But his real grievance was that he resented being excluded from the ceasefire talks.

Recent events would seem to point to some success at bringing the terrible conflict in Darfur to a close, but a there has also been a deep renewal of tensions with the south. The referendum will produce an overwhelming vote for southern independence, because none of the efforts at integrating the warring parts of the country have proved even remotely successful.

Now the central challenge will be not so much knitting together north and south as providing reasonable governance in both countries. Bashir is now an accused man, expected to appear before the International Criminal Court for his role in the genocide in Darfur. The south is already showing signs of falling apart, with more deaths, disappearances, and displaced in 2010 than in Darfur.

Gérard Prunier, whose powerful book *Africa's World War* is the best account of the fighting in Central Africa, gives this tough assessment of democratic progress:

The problem is that democracy as a form of government presupposes a certain degree of social integration, the existence of a political class with some concept of the national interest, and a minimum of economic development. None of these existed. The African political class was largely made up of "tropical gangsters," and the continent's economy was a stagnating swamp. Attempts at democracy, although inherently hopeful, tended to end badly either through violence or, more often, through the deliberate perversion of the new institutions, which were promptly emptied of any democratic content. (xxxii)

There is nothing to be gained by blaming the victim for this diagnosis. The political structures of Africa are largely a colonial inheritance, and it is simply not possible to walk away now. We cannot pretend we do not have a shared interest in building the key components of democracy: education, social solidarity, women's rights, better governance, and political reform. These elements are as important in the fight against AIDS as they are in providing better maternal and child health. This is what makes the West's on-again, off-again interventions in Africa incompatible with our deep knowledge of what works and what doesn't, and of what needs to be done. The time to re-engage, with eyes wide open, is now.

CHAPTER 6

RHETORIC AND REALITY:

Three Presidents, Three Speeches, Three Wars

On a cold January day, a young, vigorous president, whose style and substance seemed to capture the imagination of a generation, spoke these brave words:

> The same revolutionary beliefs for which our forebears fought are still at issue around the globe – the belief that the rights of man come not from the generosity of the state, but from the hand of God. We dare not forget today that we are the heirs of that first revolution. Let the word go forth from this time and place, to friend and foe alike, that the torch has been passed to a new generation of Americans – born in this century, tempered by war, disciplined by a hard and bitter peace, proud of our ancient heritage, and unwilling to witness or permit the slow undoing of those human rights to which this nation has been committed, and to which we are committed today at home and around the world. Let every nation know, whether it wishes us well or ill, that we shall pay any price, bear any burden, meet any hardship, support any friend, oppose any foe, in order to assure the survival and the success of liberty.

The words were, of course, spoken by John Fitzgerald Kennedy, war hero, charismatic senator, and exemplar of a generation that was ready to take its place at the helm of power.

Thomas Paine would have been proud of the rhetoric. Edmund Burke would have taken the last sentence and cross-examined long and hard. Like many rhetorical flourishes, it contained a promise that could not be kept.

The cadences of President Kennedy have been heard and repeated often enough, the finger jabbing the air, the confidence and brio of "the best and the brightest" who were impatient with the desultory ways of an aging administration. His predecessor Dwight Eisenhower, the man who led the Allied troops at D-Day and beyond, had ended his time of office on a suitably Burkean note: "In the councils of government, we must guard against the acquisition of unwarranted influence, whether sought or unsought, by the military industrial complex. The potential for the disastrous rise of misplaced power exists and will persist."

Kennedy's self-confidence, some might say hubris, led to the disaster at the Bay of Pigs, the CIA-financed and organized invasion of Cuba by exiles that ended in humiliation. Bad intelligence, exaggerated claims of what could be done and achieved, a goofball execution, and misleading public diplomacy led to defeat, retreat, and capture. As Kennedy put it bluntly, "Victory has a thousand fathers, but defeat is an orphan." That experience alone should have led to a dramatic reassessment, a different sense of the limits of power, a stronger recognition that words are one thing and execution another. But it was not to be. The Bay of Pigs misadventure was a dry run for the Americans' calamitous engagement in Vietnam. Historians will debate into the distant future whether Kennedy would have reduced the U.S. military commitment had he lived, but the fact remains that the core members of the Kennedy team – Robert McNamara, McGeorge Bundy, Walt Rostow, among others – remained at the heart of American policy in Vietnam throughout the 1960s, and were responsible for advising President Lyndon Johnson on the need to expand troop commitments from a few thousand "advisors" to hundreds of thousands of troops, to go from assisting the South Vietnamese government in countering a Viet Cong guerrilla movement to waging a full-scale war on North Vietnam that was expanded later by Richard Nixon and Henry Kissinger to Cambodia.

Johnson's promise that "we seek no wider war" may have been spoken with sincerity, but a vastly wider war it became, as the bombs followed the movement of fighters and supplies between Ho Chi Minh's government in the north and the guerrilla movements in South Vietnam.

The war was initially resisted by very few Americans, even as the toll of escalation grew steadily. American intervention, the administration argued, was needed to support a fledgling democracy, South Vietnam. The Russian and Chinese were using Ho Chi Minh and the Viet Cong as surrogates. A "line in the sand" had to be drawn to stop the communist tide. If South Vietnam fell then, one by one, all the nations of Southeast Asia would topple to the communists "like dominoes." An alleged attack in international waters on the U.S. destroyers *Maddox* and *C. Turner Joy* in August of 1964 by North Vietnamese torpedoes was the pretext for the Gulf of Tonkin Resolution, which passed 88-2 in the Senate and 416-0 in the House of Representatives. It authorized President Johnson "to take all necessary steps, including the use of armed force," against aggression in Southeast Asia.

The floor manager for the passage of the Gulf of Tonkin resolution was Arkansas Senator J. William Fulbright, chairman of the Senate Foreign Relations Committee. Writing of the speedy passage of the resolution two years later, Fulbright described his own role as "a source of neither pleasure nor pride to me today." A patrician voice of the Old South, Fulbright soon started to speak out against the decision to commit American lives and money in Vietnam.

In his book *The Arrogance of Power*, published in 1966, Fulbright explained that what he meant by "arrogance of power" was "the tendency of great nations to equate power with virtue and major responsibilities with a universal mission." In Fulbright's view this tendency lay at the heart of the great risk America faced: the possibility that, like all great powers before it, it would overreach, confuse its mission with its capacity, and mistake domination for good policy. He cited President McKinley's words when America annexed the Philippines after the Spanish-American War in 1900: "It is America's duty to educate the Filipinos, and uplift and civilize and Christianize them, and by God's grace do the very best we could by them, as our fellowmen, for whom Christ also died." He also cited the words of Senator Albert Beveridge, who said of Americans, "We are a conquering race. We must obey our blood and occupy new markets and if necessary new lands . . . In the Almighty's infinite plan . . . debased civilizations and decaying races [must disappear] before the higher civilization of the nobler and more virile types of man" (Fulbright, 6-7). He also wrote:

> We are now engaged in a war to "defend freedom" in South Vietnam. Unlike the Republic of Korea, South Vietnam has an army which fights without notable success and a weak, dictatorial government which does not command the loyalty of the South Vietnamese people . . . I do not question the power of our weapons and the efficiency of our logistics . . . What I do question is the ability of the United States, or France, or any other Western nation to go into a small, alien, undeveloped Asian nation and create stability where there is chaos, the will to fight where there is defeatism, democracy where there is no tradition of it, and honest government where corruption is almost a way of life. (Fulbright, 15)

Fulbright was calling for nothing less than a change in America's basic assumptions: about itself, about the world around it, about what it would take to create a new partnership between the American people and the rest of the world. He quoted with approval George Kennan, the scholar and diplomat who had been a key advisor to earlier presidents: "There is more respect to be won in the opinion of the world by a resolute and courageous liquidation of unsound positions than in the most stubborn pursuit of extravagant or unpromising objectives" (Fulbright, 17-18).

American welfare imperialism, however well intentioned, was bound to fail, because, he said, "We have intruded on fragile societies, and our intrusion, though successful in uprooting traditional ways of life, has been strikingly unsuccessful in implanting the democracy and advancing the development which are the honest aims of our 'welfare imperialism'" (Fulbright, 19).

Fulbright wanted America to abandon its sense of mission and replace it with a sense of example, to end the overreach and seek a sensible accommodation with a world undergoing a revolution. He argued – years before Nixon – for the recognition of China, for a negotiated withdrawal from Vietnam, and for an acceptance of multilateral obligation rather than an insistence on American exceptionalism. He believed that Americans needed to embrace the complexities of the world and understand that conflict and confrontation could lead to nuclear annihilation unless tempered by the acceptance that "excessive ideological zeal" is as much a risk for Americans as for communists. He closed the book with a powerful reassertion of Burkean faith: America should not get carried away by abstractions: "America . . . can be an intelligent example to the world . . . we have the opportunity to serve as an example of democracy to the world by the way in which we run our own society. America, in the words of John Quincy Adams, should be 'the well-wisher to the freedom and independence of all' but 'the champion and vindicator only of her own'" (Fulbright, 255-57).

Rather than accept the advice of William Fulbright, Americans went through a dark night. The assassinations of Robert Kennedy and Martin Luther King in 1968 shook a nation that hadn't yet come to terms with John F. Kennedy's assassination less than five years earlier. Deeply divided over the war, Americans elected Richard Nixon as president in November that year. On his watch, the war was widened to Cambodia, at great loss of life, before America finally accepted the inevitability of withdrawal. Vietnam became a deeply repressive dictatorship, but it was not an outpost of either the Russian or Chinese empire. Other dominoes did not fall. The horrors that had been paraded by the architects and strategists of the Vietnam enterprise never came to pass, except that a corrupt plutocracy in the guise of Vietnamese communism replaced the puppet regime of the Diems and the Kys in the south. Cambodia's destruction in the years after the end of the war was even more tragic, as the dictator Pol Pot carried out a reign of terror and destruction, a genocide of his own people that came to an end only when Vietnam stepped in. It is only now that those responsible for the deaths of at least a million people are being brought to account.

Fulbright's plea for a decisive rejection of the assumptions that led to the war mostly fell on deaf ears. Administrations rarely allow themselves that much insight. The Carter presidency tried to reassert America's commitment to human rights and democracy around the world, but it went down to defeat because of a stagnating economy and an uncertain response to the capture of American diplomats in Iran. President Carter did succeed in brokering a peace agreement between Egyptian President Anwar Sadat and Prime Minister Menachem Begin of Israel, but this achievement was not matched elsewhere.

President Ronald Reagan offered a return to pride and a sunny America once again. His formula of great confidence, massive military spending, and limited foreign intervention by American troops assured his re-election in 1984 and George Bush Sr.'s election to the White House four years later.

The collapse of the Soviet Union and the end of the Cold War provided ample justification for Reagan's reign of good cheer. What had seemed implausible – especially the tearing down of the Berlin Wall and the reunification of Germany – led some to speak with confidence of "the end of history." They took the disintegration of the Marxist myth of the liberation of mankind through common ownership of the means of production as a sign that modern capitalism was "as good as it gets," and "that's all there is."

Just as the corks were popping and Western governments were busy figuring out how to spend the peace dividend, Saddam Hussein of Iraq invaded Kuwait. It was an act of aggression as clear-cut as can be imagined – he sent his troops into a neighbouring country because he believed he could get away with it – and it was met and repelled by Operation Desert Storm. The United States and its allies were back. The Iraqi military was beaten by overwhelming power, on land, sea, and air. It was not so much a war as a rout. Coalition troops quickly in, quickly out; royal family back on the throne in Kuwait; massive environmental cleanup; Iraqi army in disarray scuttling back to Baghdad; Saddam still in charge but tied down.

But there was a nasty legacy to this "clean war." Believing that the West was serious when it spoke about fighting tyranny, the Shias in the south and the Kurds in the north of Iraq took their cue from the invasion and renewed their own fights against Saddam. A brutal dictator who had dropped chemical bombs on Kurds and Iranians – with impunity and without any reprisal from the international community during Iraq's war with Iran in the 1980s – Saddam mounted a response to these uprisings that was swift and bloody. The Americans and British did what they could to protect the Kurds. Thousands of Iraqi Shias were killed in the aftermath of the coalition's retreat, and not a finger was raised to save them. More was done to protect the Kurds, with the UN banning Iraqi flights over Kurdish territory.

Saddam was hemmed in and tied down by UN sanctions and American and British flyovers intended to ensure he couldn't do much more than oppress his people and enjoy the power he had. He was feared in Iraq and vilified in the West as one of a club of truly bad rulers, dictators like Robert Mugabe of Zimbabwe and Kim Jong-il of North Korea, whose rule had devastated their people.

No leader in modern times has spoken with such emphasis about the connection between freedom, democracy, and foreign policy as President George Walker Bush. It was not a rhetoric he came to immediately. After he took office at the turn of the century, Bush put nation-building on the back burner. His first inaugural address was not memorable, and did not extend beyond the usual bromides. All this changed with al-Qaeda's attack on the Twin Towers, the Pentagon, and United Airlines Flight 93 on September 11, 2001. While al-Qaeda had been linked to several other attacks on American interests – in the basement of the Twin Towers in 1993, the U.S. military headquarters in Saudi Arabia in 1995 and 1996, U.S. embassies in Nairobi and Dar es Salaam in 1998 and a US navy vessel in Yemen in 2000, – the breathtaking scale and execution of the assault, and the subsequent tragic collapse of the iconic towers of the World Trade Center on that infamous day transformed the West's sense of the world. NATO invoked its charter and declared that an attack on a member of the alliance was an attack on all. As soon as it was determined the attack had been carried out by al-Qaeda, an organization whose leader, Osama bin Laden, was using the hospitality of the Taliban government in Afghanistan to recruit and train followers, the next step became clear: demand that the Taliban give up bin Laden and al-Qaeda or face the consequences.

This the Taliban leader, Mullah Mohammed Omar, would not do, and so the die was cast. The joint American and NATO attack on Afghanistan was swift and overwhelming. It was the largest bombing since the Second World War, and of a country that was among the poorest in the world. Afghanistan had been invaded and occupied by the Soviets in 1979, and during the resulting civil war that lasted throughout the 1980s, the mujahideen forces opposing the Soviet troops had been sheltered and encouraged by Pakistan and heavily subsidized by the CIA, which was acting on the principle that "the enemy of my enemy is my friend." Osama bin Laden, as we have seen, was active during this period, recruiting fighters from throughout the Arab world to fight with the mujahi-deen. The retreat of Soviet troops in 1989 saw the Taliban swiftly take control of much of the country and subject it to an extreme and punitive form of Sharia law.

The U.S.-led invasion quickly hounded the Taliban from the cities of Kabul and Kandahar, but tens of thousands of Afghan civilians died, and hundreds of thousands more were added to an already staggering homeless and refugee population in northwestern Pakistan. The infrastructure of much of the country was devastated.

In the early days, the apparent elimination of the Taliban gave the architects of the invasion a false sense of security and optimism. In language worthy of Woodrow Wilson, the Afghanistan Compact, launched at a conference in London in 2006, used these powerful phrases:

> Recognising the courage and determination of Afghans who, by defying violent extremism and hardship, have laid the foundations for a democratic, peaceful, pluralistic and prosperous state based on the principles of Islam; . . . Mindful that Afghanistan's transition to peace and stability is not yet assured, and that strong international engagement will continue to be required to address remaining challenges; Resolved to overcome the legacy of conflict in Afghanistan by setting conditions for sustainable economic growth and development; strengthening state institutions and civil society; removing remaining terrorist threats; meeting the challenge of counter-narcotics; rebuilding capacity and infrastructure; reducing poverty; and meeting basic human needs. (Building on Success)

The world solemnly committed itself to the reconstruction of a stable, democratic Afghanistan where the rights of all would be respected, and where the chaos of the past three decades would be quickly replaced by peace, good governance, and admittance to the family of democratic nations. But there were several things missing in this scenario. The first was that the Taliban had not been defeated. They had made a rapid exit from formal government and from Kabul and Kandahar, but it soon became clear that this had been a strategic retreat, not a rout. The second was that the presence of Western troops on the ground did not suit the geography of the country and the reality of a guerrilla war. The third was that the noble objectives of the compact and the Afghan Constitution that emerged from early political discussions were very far removed from the realities of the country. Three decades of conflict had destroyed any real economy. Agriculture in many parts of the country had been abandoned, and the value of poppy and opium production soon equalled the official GDP. Illiteracy was widespread, and girls and women were denied access to education. The gap between the rhetoric of powerful intentions and the reality on the ground was stark.

An early decision was made to dismantle what little remained of a Taliban civil service and government, and so both local and central governments reverted to the power of local leaders, many of whom had been warlords during the resistance to the Soviets and in the absence of any effective central governance. Ironically, a sudden surge of large of amounts of aid contributed to corruption, as did the burgeoning drug trade.

There were two other critical misjudgments. The first involved Pakistan, then under the military rule of General Pervez Musharraf. The second was the truly cavalier decision by the Bush administration to take its focus away from Afghanistan and to invade Iraq.

On a trip to Pakistan in early 2006 to attend a seminar on federalism sponsored by the National Democratic Institute, I was assured by my local guide on arrival at the airport that Islamabad was completely safe. While I was taking a jet-lag nap a few hours later, I was woken by a large bang nearby. Then came sirens. Then came a phone call from the Canadian high commissioner asking if

I was all right. A suicide bomber had entered the hotel through the back entrance; after being challenged by the security guard he blew himself up, killing the guard and damaging the hotel, but not the lobby or any guest rooms. The hotel was quickly surrounded by police and ambulances, the large crowd that had gathered outside was dispersed, and the management assured all guests that "the danger has been averted." The next day I travelled to Peshawar for a meeting with local political leaders, and discovered on my return to the capital that night that there had been a huge explosion in the centre of that city, killing a popular police chief and many more people who were attending a funeral.

The purpose of that trip was to discuss the nature and meaning of modern federalism with a range of people active in Pakistani politics in both the national parliament and the regions. The Baluchi leaders in northwestern Pakistan were particularly adamant about two things. First, that the Pakistani government was really a Punjabi military government with a colonial attitude to requests from the regions for more autonomy and authority. Fighting in Baluchistan had been going on for a long time and was devastating any capacity for local democracy. The second was that the Taliban were not only tolerated in the northwest of Pakistan but were actively encouraged by the Musharraf government: Mullah Omar was holding press conferences in Quetta at the same time as the Pakistani leadership was assuring the West of its co-operation in the war on terrorism.

Throughout the period immediately after 9/11 the consensus in the West was that President Musharraf was no democrat but that he was the best bulwark against chaos in Pakistan and could be persuaded or cajoled to do more to deal with the Taliban and al-Qaeda. What I heard during that trip convinced me otherwise, and that the porous border between Afghanistan and Pakistan was a critical issue. The Pashtun people straddle the border between the two countries. Pakistan under Musharraf was neither free nor democratic. Its notorious Directorate for Inter-Services Intelligence, or

ISI, functioned as a government within a government, and had deep links with extremist Sunni Muslims in Pakistan and in Afghanistan. The irony that this was the very agency whose work had been so actively assisted in "Charlie Wilson's War" made the situation even more complex. The ISI had played all sides, taking billions over the years from the U.S. intelligence and military establishments, and supporting the mujahideen in Afghanistan and in the impoverished northwest of their own country, as well as in the massive refugee camps established in Pakistan after the Soviet invasion of Afghanistan.

NATO's failure to craft an effective strategy in Pakistan has long been identified as a critical weakness of our efforts in Afghanistan. The support for Musharraf was justified as a critical bulwark in the war on terrorism, much as American support for Cuban dictator Fulgencio Batista was once justified by the idea that "he's a bastard but he's our bastard." The unravelling of public support for Musharraf, a revolt by judges and lawyers, and the eventual return of both main opposition leaders paved the way for an election in 2008 that saw the brief and tragic resurrection of the political career of Benazir Bhutto. Her assassination while campaigning in 2007 was ample demonstration that the forces of zealotry and extremism in Pakistan were on the ascendant and that the security services either could not or would not protect her against them.

If the failure to address Pakistan's role was the first key weakness in the West's effort to stabilize Afghan society, an even bigger problem was the decision by the United States and the United Kingdom to invade Iraq and overthrow Saddam Hussein. Richard Clarke, a senior security advisor to both presidents Clinton and Bush has argued convincingly that this decision had disastrous consequences: the West took its eye off the ball in Afghanistan, neglecting strategic military, political, and development initiatives that had yet to address key problems in that country. Equally important, by destabilizing Iraq, the invasion in fact broadened the playing field for al-Qaeda and a whole host of both home-grown and foreign terrorist groups.

The reasoning behind the invasion was clear and emphatic. Australian Prime Minister John Howard and opposition leader Stephen Harper were categorical in speeches supporting the Iraq invasion delivered in their respective parliaments just two days apart: "There is no doubt that Saddam Hussein operates programs to produce weapons of mass destruction. Experience confirms this. British, Canadian and American intelligence leaves no doubt on the matter," said Harper. The phrase "Canadian intelligence" was thrown in just for effect. In fact, Canada insisted in its communications with the Americans that UN weapons inspectors had not been able to find any such weapons in Iraq. We now know that the speech U.S. Secretary of State Colin Powell gave at the UN, armed with facts, figures and photographs, was plain wrong. The Bush administration was trying to recreate an "Adlai Stevenson moment," when Ambassador Stevenson produced aerial photographs in October 1962 that proved there were indeed Soviet missiles in Cuba. The trouble was that the "facts" Powell presented on stolen uranium from Central Africa and weapons of mass destruction on train tracks in underground bunkers were just not true.

Saddam was a brutal dictator. He had sacrificed hundreds of thousands of lives in a futile war he instigated against Iran in the 1980s, and had gassed and killed his own people. He jailed and tortured thousands of opponents. His was a brutal regime. But the decision to leave him in power after the Iraqi retreat from Kuwait meant that his power was, from an international perspective, limited and curtailed. Hemmed in by sanctions, no-fly zones, aerial monitoring, and UN weapons inspections, he could repress dissent and fulminate about his enemies but he could not invade any neighbour.

It is now well known that the plan to invade Iraq was concocted soon after 9/11, and that its supporters included those who had wanted to "finish the job" in the aftermath of Saddam's invasion of Kuwait. Some in the Bush administration believed that democracy needed a beachhead in the Arab Middle East, and that Iraq would be the best place for it. The war on terror could not be limited to one front, but had to be extended to all those whose purpose was the disruption of the West. Saddam simply had too much power and influence in the region, and offered too much solace to the enemies of the West, to be allowed to stay in power. Getting rid of him would free the world of a new "Hitler," and show for all time that the battle for democracy knew no boundaries. Incidentally, it would also protect the strategic interests of the West in the oil-rich region, just as getting rid of Mossadegh in Iran had done fifty years earlier.

No speech better invokes this spirit than George W. Bush's second inaugural address in January 2004. Evoking President Kennedy's promise to "pay any price, bear any burden, meet any hardship, support any friend, and oppose any foe, in order to assure the survival and success of liberty," George Bush proclaimed:

> The survival of liberty in our land increasingly depends on the success of liberty in other lands. The best hope for peace in our world is the expansion of freedom in all the world. America's vital interests and our deepest beliefs are now one. From the day of our founding, we have proclaimed that every man and woman on this earth has rights and dignity and matchless value because they bear the image of the maker of heaven and earth. Across the generations, we have proclaimed the imperative of self-government, because no one is fit to be a master, and no one deserves to be a slave. Advancing these ideals is the mission that created our nation. It is the honorable achievement of our fathers. Now it is the urgent requirement of our nation's security, and the calling of our time. So it is the policy of the United States to seek and support

the growth of democratic movements and institutions in
every nation and culture, with the ultimate goal of ending
tyranny in our world.

Ignoring the fact that the founders of American democracy
were hardly committed to the proposition that no one should be
a slave, or that Thomas Jefferson might have taken great exception to the notion that the rights of man had anything to do "with
the image of the maker of heaven and earth," Bush's argument is
clear enough. The United States is engaged in a war of good
against evil, of right against wrong, of truth against falsehood, of
liberty against tyranny. No one could question his sincerity. But
some of Edmund Burke's insight would have been in order here,
and ironically it was as absent from Bush's conservatism just as
surely as it did not find its way into the rhetoric of John Kennedy
forty years earlier.

The difficult truth is that there was no justification in international law for the invasion. Kofi Annan, the UN secretary-
general, was right when he called the war "illegal," and no amount
of rhetoric can deny that fact. While international rules may be
unreliable, they are not meaningless. They were sufficient to persuade Canada and a number of other countries that the invasion of
Iraq didn't meet the critical test. The decision by Prime Minister
Jean Chrétien not to commit troops was widely supported in
Canada, although Opposition Leader Stephen Harper expressed
his support for the Bush doctrine: "The time has come to recognize that the U.S. will continue to exercise unprecedented power
in a world where international rules are still unreliable and where
security and advancing of the free democratic order still depend
significantly on the possession and use of military might" (May
2003 speech to the Institute for Research on Public Policy).

The invasion was seriously undermanned. The overreliance
on massive aerial bombing meant there was substantial loss of life
and further devastation of the Iraqi infrastructure, already fragile

from years of war and neglect. Far from being greeted by crowds throwing flowers, as Vice-President Dick Cheney had predicted, American and British troops were met by a fierce resistance whose strength grew after the Coalition Provisional Authority decided to dismantle the entire structure of the Iraqi state. Tens of thousands of mainly Sunni civil servants were fired, as were members of the army and police. The political and administrative vacuum could not be filled by either Iraqis or the coalition, and in the resulting chaos the Sunnis and the majority Shias mobilized militias to battle for control of the formerly secular state. Terrorist groups from all across the Middle East and Central Asia rushed to Iraq to join one side or the other or to conduct their own campaigns.

Just as the collapse of the Soviet Union and Yugoslavia had revealed deep ethnic and religious fissures that dictatorship had papered over, the divides in Iraqi society were laid bare for all to see. The Kurds in the north had taken advantage of their autonomy in the 1990s to establish a functioning regional state, although the geopolitics of the neighbourhood prevented them from proclaiming full-blown sovereignty. The cities of Mosul and Kirkuk remain to this day deeply divided between Turkoman, Arab, and Kurd, with the Christian minority dispersed and in great difficulty.

My first visit to Iraq was to Kurdistan in 2003, where I joined Michael Ignatieff, who at that time was a professor at Harvard, in a discussion with Kurdish leaders about what post-invasion Iraq would be like. There was no open talk of secession, but the focus was far more on building Kurdistan than on building a federal Iraq. The Saddam era was a dark, living memory, although the leaders we met were fully engaged with both Sunni and Shia Iraqi Arabs in efforts to establish the truth of Saddam's massacres and to achieve reconciliation. The Kurds' historic claim to Mosul and Kirkuk as lying firmly within the boundaries of Iraqi Kurdistan was carefully set out, although people seemed prepared to negotiate the claim rather than take up arms to settle it. A generation of children was being educated in Kurdish, not Arabic, and Baghdad (despite its large Kurdish population) seemed far away. An evening I spent with university students in Sulaimaniyah left me with the impression that the younger generation, even more than their elders, was nationalist, outspoken, and focussed on Kurdistan – not Iraq – as the future.

My colleague at the Forum of Federations, David Cameron, had been travelling to Iraq since constitutional discussions began, and I was able to follow his efforts in the summer of 2005 in the company of George Anderson, who succeeded me as president of the Forum. The head of the UN constitutional team was Nick Haysom, a brilliant South African who had been a legal advisor to Nelson Mandela, and who is now a senior advisor to UN Secretary-General Ban Ki-moon. Haysom and I had met many times over the years, and had worked together earlier in Nigeria and Sri Lanka. He combined an extraordinary capacity for hard work with a deeply practical sense of constitution-making as a political, and not an academic, exercise. He had no particular ideological baggage and believed profoundly in getting the parties to see their way to a political resolution, a perspective that had served well in his successful effort to find a constitutional solution to the war between north and south in Sudan.

Our flight into Baghdad from Amman involved the scary "corkscrew manoeuvre," where our DASH plane took a spiral nosedive to present a smaller target for any surface-to-air missiles. The trip from the airport to the Green Zone was equally tense, and my head was full of the security briefing that said the "risk of an incident every day" was "reasonably high." International advisors of all kinds stayed in various places inside the heavily armed Green Zone, and during our stay any travel outside was strictly forbidden, although there were a number of NGO employees and others who lived and worked outside the zone.

Soon after the invasion, U.S. Secretary of State Colin Powell had talked optimistically about how quickly a new government could be formed and democracy proclaimed. "How long can it take to write a constitution?" he was quoted as asking. Well, in the United States, eleven years passed between the Declaration of Independence in 1776 and the adoption of the new Constitution in 1787, years that saw a full-scale war, unsuccessful Articles of Confederation, and a spirited debate about what kind of constitution would work. Deep political debates continued in the country until the bloody Civil War in the 1860s finally resolved the issue of slavery and established a stronger basis for the union. The postwar experiences of Germany and Japan in formulating new constitutions were also those of long, drawn-out debates and procedures, albeit without a continued insurrection. Britain's constitution took hundreds of years to evolve, with much bloodshed along the way. But these experiences were ignored or overlooked by the White House in its optimism that peace and democracy would be rapidly embraced by the Iraqis.

The Iraqi constitutional discussions have been difficult and intense, and as I write the jury is still out as to their success. Any deal that involves the Kurds has to accept a federal structure, but federalism is a house with many rooms. From the outset of our visit, we encountered resistance to the federal idea from the Sunni lawyers and academics who were acting as advisors to the Iraqi Parliament. Federalism in their minds meant division, meant sovereignty existing somewhere other than in a strong centralized state.

By this time I was very familiar with these arguments, as they were similar to the views I'd heard expressed by Sinhalese scholars and advocates in Sri Lanka, to say nothing of naysayers in Sudan and Afghanistan. The notion that sovereignty was something that could be divided, or located within a constitution, was initially incomprehensible at best, and often seen as a notion completely foreign to "Iraqi thinking" (or Sri Lankan thinking, or Sudanese thinking or Arab thinking or . . .). I responded by asking them to describe how a country could be brought together that did not recognize the distinctiveness of Kurdish culture, and that did not find room for other minorities.

Anderson and I used to refer jokingly to federalism as the "F-word." We often made more progress by not using the term (it is only found briefly in the preamble to the British North America Act, for example), but rather by focusing on more practical questions, in the case of Iraq the thorny subject of oil and gas exploration and revenue sharing. The eventual constitution adopted in 2005 left the details of this to further legislative drafting in the Iraqi Parliament, a task which continues to this day, as does the vexing issue of the status of the city of Kirkuk.

The Forum's role was sometimes misunderstood. We were not writing a constitution. We were there to answer questions, and sometimes to ask questions, of those who were making the political compromises that always lie behind any constitutional negotiation. None of us was Thomas Paine, the advocate who thought that being directly involved, as a foreigner, in the writing of a document was all right because constitution writing was an objective exercise. Nor were we there to impose the Canadian model, or any other model for that matter. Indeed, we made a deliberate effort to broaden the awareness of the federal idea as something that was working in Asia and Africa, and not as a colonial import.

Forum-sponsored interveners in the Iraqi constitutional talks came from around the world, and while what we were doing overlapped with the efforts of the aid agencies and democracy endowments of both Britain and the U.S., we understood that the perspective we brought to bear could only take hold if it were seen as a quiet adjunct to the intense political discussion in the Iraqi Parliament.

The advice we offered was often rejected. This made perfect sense, as constitution-making is a political enterprise. For any mediation to work, the two sides have to be in control of the process, and the mediator has to be free to offer candid advice. There is no point in taking offence if that advice is not followed. Nothing is easier than negotiating in front of a mirror, or drafting the ideal scheme for oil-revenue sharing in a library. Seeing the "zone of agreement" with detached ease is one thing; it is quite another to get the two sides to accept it, and another still for them to persuade their supporters that it must be accepted.

Another negotiating dictum I frequently applied in these discussions was "never ask your adversary to accept a position you know he can't defend or implement." Whenever this happens, victories at the bargaining table are invariably followed by bitter disappointment. A weak adversary will often make a concession and then find it impossible to sell. This undercuts his credibility and leads to bitterness all around.

The Forum continued its work after the passage of the Iraqi Constitution, and I attended another week-long session in January of 2006 at a hotel on the Dead Sea in Jordan with Sunni legislators, participants from the United States Institute for Peace, and other experts from around the world. It was a fascinating exercise, because it focused almost exclusively on those who believed the invasion and all of its offspring, including the new constitution, to be illegitimate. It was a tough conversation. The Sunnis were surprised to hear from many of the foreign observers that they shared their view about the legality of the invasion, but felt that constitution-making of some kind was inevitable, and better done with the presence of the UN than not at all.

As the conflict in Iraq continued to take its heavy toll, Americans began to question whether they were in fact ready to "pay any price and bear any burden." At the end of the 2008 American presidential election, Barack Obama – the candidate most critical of the original decision to enter the war, the most troubled by its legality, and the most convinced of its unworkability as a strategy for the country – won. In his inaugural address, President Obama addressed the same subject that both John F. Kennedy and George W. Bush had spoken about in their inaugural speeches. What Obama said is interesting for its similarities to and differences from what his predecessors said:

As for our common defense, we reject as false the choice between our safety and our ideals. Our Founding Fathers, faced with perils we can scarcely imagine, drafted a charter to assure the rule of law and the rights of man, a charter expanded by the blood of generations. Those ideals still light the world, and we will not give them up for expedience's sake. And so to all other peoples and governments who are watching today, from the grandest capitals to the small village where my father was born: know that America is a friend of each nation and every man, woman and child who seeks a future of peace and dignity, and that we are ready to lead once more.

Recall that earlier generations faced down fascism and communism not just with missiles and tanks, but with sturdy alliances and enduring convictions. They understood that our power alone cannot protect us, nor does it entitle us to do as we please. Instead, they knew that our power grows through its prudent use; our security emanates from the justness of our cause, the force of our example, the tempering qualities of humility and restraint . . .

We will begin to responsibly leave Iraq to its people, and forge a hard-earned peace in Afghanistan . . . we will not apologize for our way of life, nor will we waver in its defense, and for those who seek to advance their aims by inducing terror and slaughtering innocents, we say to you know that our spirit is stronger and cannot be broken; you cannot outlast us, and we will defeat you.

The speeches of presidents Kennedy, Bush, and Obama are similar in their reverential reference to the Founding Fathers. The mission of America as the hope of the world and of Americans as an almost chosen people is equally assumed. Each was captured by rhetorical overreach. But there are differences. Obama stresses that power does not entitle America to do as it pleases, and refers to the "tempering qualities of humility and restraint," which neither Kennedy nor Bush referred to, or would have been comfortable mentioning. Obama's explicit reference to the rule of law is something deeply ingrained in his training, teaching, and political thinking. But he cannot appear weak or admit the possibility of defeat, any more than Kennedy could have described the Bay of Pigs in that way, or Johnson or Nixon Vietnam, or Bush Iraq. Hence Obama followed an ambiguous statement about forging a "hard-earned peace in Afghanistan" with the more traditional American boast that "our spirit is stronger and cannot be broken; you cannot outlast us, and we will defeat you."

The powerful military and civilian surge in Iraq that President Bush authorized late in his second term, combined with an Iraqi administration more successful at managing both security and the economy, had begun to create better conditions in that country by the time President Obama took office. What was now widely seen as a "bad war" had the potential to produce a better result than the "good war" in Afghanistan. But conditions in the two countries prior to invasion were vastly different, so different outcomes were always probable. Iraq had oil, better-educated people, and a growing economy. Afghanistan had a devastated economy, half of which was based on narcotics, low rates of literacy, and few traditions of civic order and administrative capacity. Iraq's parliamentary election in March 2010 was marked by challenges to its honesty. Sectarian conflict still runs deep, and violence continues to take many lives, but a federal, reasonably run "government by discussion" at least seems a possibility.

What Obama faced in Afghanistan was the fact that, while the invasion and overthrow of the Taliban had received strong support from the UN and the sanction of international law, this alone had not made the task of bringing peace, stability, and democracy to the country any easier. The United States and NATO had the right to respond to an unwarranted and unjustified attack. But when considering the likelihood of success, one might do well to consider

William Fulbright's warning forty years ago: "What I do question is the ability of the United States or any other Western nation to go into a small, alien, undeveloped Asian nation and create stability where there is chaos, the will to fight where there is defeatism, democracy where there is no tradition of it, and honest govern- ment where corruption is almost a way of life."(Fulbright, 15)

Obama immediately commissioned a study similar to that by the Independent Panel on Canada's Future Role in Afghanistan headed by John Manley, to determine what could be done to devise a more realistic and more successful strategy.

The keys to this new approach, which is now being attempted with some determination, are to transfer as much responsibility as possible to the Afghans themselves, on the understanding that most of the them do not want to return to Taliban rule, and that there is a powerful national majority against extremism. This is supposed to meet the first two of Fulbright's issues – chaos and defeatism. With this goal in mind, the training and development of the Afghan military and police become crucial. The military strategy has to be based on the understanding that an insurgency cannot be defeated in an armed battle.

Counterterrorism is rooted in the British Emergency in Malaya in the 1950s. It was there in the dense forests of what is now Malaysia and Singapore that the concept of winning "hearts and minds" emerged. The British learned that only by winning over the populations that feed and support the insurgents could the war be won. Put simply, if the river is drained, the fish will die.

A purely military campaign is ineffective, because military actions alone do not sway a local population's attitudes. Military retaliations to suicide bombings and other acts of terror have been shown to strengthen the public's support of insurgent groups. The threat of terrorism is complex and cannot be eradicated with large bombs or swift operations. Insurgents are not out in the open wearing uniforms, but are camouflaged in local communi- ties, at once exploiting them and being supported by them.

There is another reality. The American military commentator Edward Luttvak pointed out some years ago in an article in *Harper's* that the dilemma facing the American military was that brutal techniques that were available to other empires at other times could not be used under the terms of the Geneva Convention, signed in the aftermath of the Second World War. The Romans could wipe out a village to teach the region a lesson. The bodies of crucified rebels hanging from crosses were harsh reminders of who was in charge. The conduct of war is subject today to different tests and different rules, as it should be. When carried out in the glare of publicity (as all wars involving the Americans and their allies are), such brutality is no longer possible. Whenever abuse and brutality come to light, as they did after the My Lai massacre during the Vietnam War and at the Abu Ghraib prison in Baghdad in 2004, they are denounced and investigated. None of us should lament this evolution. But we must understand that it means there is now no alternative to a hearts-and-minds strategy, and that policies that have insufficient support in public opinion either at home or in the country where conflict is occurring are simply not sustainable.

In other words, President Obama's statement, "Our spirit is stronger and cannot be broken; you cannot outlast us, and we will defeat you" is only as true as support is deeply entrenched in public opinion in the West (as well as in Afghanistan) for a continued presence and partnership in pursuit of a shared objective. Otherwise it is just another empty promise.

In Afghanistan the West is fighting an opponent with a different value system, whose methods can be as brutal as it chooses to make them, and whose view of the world and the justness of its cause is more immediate. The Taliban and other insurgents are defending their land, their soil, their beliefs, their way of life. President Obama has recently said that the struggle in Afghanistan is not a war of choice but a war of necessity. It is actually both, and there is an ongoing struggle for public support whose challenge cannot be underestimated.

General Stanley McChrystal's description of the strategy now in effect in Afghanistan, which involves a surge in the numbers of both military and civilian personnel, is "clear, hold, and stabilize." The decision to face the enemy head-on where they are currently in strong positions in the southern provinces of Helmand and Kandahar has meant far heavier casualties on both sides, but the West's military superiority seems to assure that the "clear" part of the strategy can be sustained, so long as there is a willingness to accept a large number of deaths of soldiers, and civilian casualties can be kept to a minimum. It is the "hold and stabilize" part that is the more difficult to achieve, because it depends on a relatively honest and open Afghan administration being able to win the struggle for hearts and minds. And that has emerged as a real Achilles heel.

Even the neo-conservative government in Canada (which, in the words of Stephen Harper, sees the American conservative movement "as a light and inspiration to people in this country") had to come to grips with some simple facts. While originally describing the Canadian mission as part of the global war on terrorism and a chance to bring freedom to the Afghan people, the Harper government now talks of the goal in much more modest terms: to create enough stability in the country for it to be able to govern itself. This shift was facilitated by the report of the Independent Panel chaired by John Manley, a former Liberal cabinet minister, which emphasized that "victory" would have to be defined in other than military terms, and that the keys to the future were getting government to work more effectively, getting NATO to coordinate better, and working harder to eliminate corruption and oppressive governance from the heart of Afghanistan politics and administration.

In other words, the war is not just about what the military call "kinetics," (i.e., armed combat) or even, to use General Hillier's unfortunate expression, "beating scumbags." It is about something more difficult and more complex.

The initial operation in Afghanistan was largely military in nature with an extremely light force of peacekeepers and CIA operatives. While foreign troops were initially welcomed by much of the Afghan population, heavy-handed raids that produced large civilian casualties, on top of an insensitivity to local conditions, and reports of torture and prisoner abuse began to turn local sentiment against the West. The country has received over thirty billion dollars of aid, and yet it is still hard to see much if any improvement in the economic life of many Afghans. Much of the financial assistance was fed into corrupt patronage systems, leaving the majority population feeling disenfranchised and frustrated. Little effort was made to understand the relationship between the many local warlords, militia groups, and tribal leaders. Widespread poppy cultivation remains an extraordinary challenge that cannot be fought with tanks and guns.

The challenge still is to engage the Afghan people, to gain their trust and prove that what the government of Afghanistan has to offer is better than Taliban rule. Training the Afghan military and police, and working with them to secure the territory regained from the Taliban, ensuring that it is better governed and better able to respond to the needs of the people, is the only way to go. Electricity, jobs, water, and education – none of which can be supplied by a military force – are the key priorities.

President Hamid Karzai's re-election in 2009 featured at least a million phantom votes – from polling stations where no one actually voted. President Karzai is good at mouthing the words about ending corruption. For example, addressing a conference of village elders on rural development in Kabul in 2007, he said, "All politicians in this system have acquired everything – money, lots of money. God knows it is beyond the limit. The banks of the world are full of the money of our statesmen." But his opponents believe he's part of the problem. A member of the Afghan Parliament said bluntly, "Hamid Karzai is by nature not a strong leader . . . People in his family are involved in corruption, and so are people from his team and some of his allies" (Sultanzoy).

One long-time observer and aid worker in Afghanistan put it this way in a confidential e-mail:

> I believe it [corruption] is at the root of everything that has gone wrong in Afghanistan since 2002 . . . Corruption as it impacts the population is to be found in the everyday conduct of government business. In every department, at every level. The capturing of development projects for the benefit of government cronies. The misappropriation of public land. Huge surcharges for the performance of regular government business like the issuing of passports or death certificates. Shakedowns and ad hoc "taxes" by police and army. Extortion of "bribes" by customs officials. Judicial decisions up for sale. The seating of cronies in all government positions in a given province, so the people have no recourse, no place to bring their complaints. It is this kind of corruption that has entirely turned the Afghan population away from its government, and even more than narcotics, represents a cancer that will kill the state.

Rory Stewart, the British foreign service officer who worked in Iraq and then walked across Afghanistan in the winter of 2001-02 (a trip detailed in his unforgettable book, *The Places in Between*), wrote in *Time* magazine in July 2008: "The government has not established its authority or credibility . . . Afghans increasingly blame us for the problems in the country: the evening news is dominated by stories of wasted development aid. The government claims that in 2007, $1.3 billion out of $3.5 billion of aid was spent on international consultants . . . Our lack of success despite our wealth and technology convinced ordinary Afghans to believe in conspiracy theories. "

But, as we saw earlier, the second half of the challenge lies beyond Afghanistan, in Pakistan, where that government's policy has often seemed closer to that of the old Roman Empire than a modern counter-insurgency effort. This is not simply a matter of ill will. It is all about capacity and training. Amassing a large army and air force, demonstrating superior fire power, destroying infrastructure, and, yes, intimidating a local population are what the Pakistani army has been trained to do in its focus on its number one enemy, India. To create an effective counter-insurgency strategy takes training, time, and money. It means money for development, for education, for health care. It also means a government that can command the support and respect of the people. Foreign soldiers, however well-intentioned, can't do that, nor can colonial administrators. It can only come from a local administration that is reasonably honest and has the ability to encourage economic development and sufficient social solidarity to maintain support in the face of attack. And that is not entirely in the West's hands or control.

President Obama's description of the current objective in the region is to "forge a hard-earned peace in Afghanistan," not to win a war. But even this more modest objective will be hard to achieve, not least because it is not primarily the West's struggle to win or lose. It will depend on the determination of both the Afghan and Pakistani governments to see their writ extend the full length and breadth of their borders, with sufficient support from the people living in all parts of their countries. It will also depend on those two governments ending a long-standing enmity and mistrust. Afghanistan, it is worth recalling, was the only country to vote against Pakistan's admission to the United Nations. No visit to a senior Afghan official is complete without a full account of Pakistani treachery and of their full-blown support for the Taliban. More neutral observers concede that the Pakistani government seems at long last to be serious about the threat to their existence from the internal insurgency. The conflict in the Swat Valley seems evidence of this. They are less certain about Pakistan's real interest in helping the Afghan government overcome the Taliban; hence the delay in getting rid of the Taliban bases in North Waziristan.

Janice Stein and Eugene Lang have called Canada's engagement in Afghanistan "the accidental war." In their book of the same name, they describe how our troops were committed to Afghanistan in good part to offset the criticism that we had not been sufficiently supportive of the U.S. effort in Iraq. NATO's response to an armed attack required participation from Canada. It would have been unconscionable of us not to be part of the NATO effort. But our largely military effort in Kandahar, as marked as it has been by significant casualties and loss of life, has not been effective at seizing land and holding it. That would have required a larger number of troops, which is what the American surge is all about.

The 2008 report of the Manley Commission urged a broader diplomatic effort in both Afghanistan and Pakistan, including the appointment of a special envoy for the region, better focus on aid in Kandahar, and a stronger effort to bolster the training of the Afghan army. Some of this is being done and key priorities have been set (building a dam, establishing schools, fighting polio), but it is hard to say that Canada is leading as effectively as it could in the efforts to "forge a peace." A special envoy has still not been appointed. The best traditions of Canadian military engagement and diplomacy should allow us to do this. We certainly have the people with the skills to be more engaged, at more levels, in what it will take to make a difference in this exceptionally difficult challenge.

Three presidents, three speeches, three wars. America took on Vietnam at the height of the Cold War and survived defeat without losing its pre-eminence, at least in part because the country's economic and technological superiority were not challenged. The collapse of the Soviet Union created a sense in the United States that all was possible, that there was a limitless Pax Americana, and that a resurgent relationship with NATO and other allies would keep the peace and lead to expanding freedom and democracy around the world.

The persistence of ethnic and religious conflict that is now re-emerging even in Europe, grinding poverty and war in Africa; and the dramatic rise of new economies in Asia, Russia, and Latin America all cast a shadow on this happy picture. Two events combined to make the sunny scenario even less plausible: the first was 9/11, the largest terrorist attack launched on American soil. The second was an economic crisis whose origins lay in a decision by American financial institutions to lend billions of dollars in subprime mortgages to people who could not afford them, and to divide the liability among financial instruments sold to other financial institutions around the world, thereby transmitting a virus from which the global economy is still reeling.

The 9/11 attack revealed a vulnerability that any open society has to deep and violent fanaticism, and we are still dealing with its aftermath: a heightened insecurity in every society that is threatened with the possibility of violence and repression. The price has been high: millions of dead, wounded, and displaced in Iraq and Afghanistan, and hundreds of billions of dollars expended in a difficult effort to punish those responsible and remake the societies that produced this zealotry.

The disastrous fallout from the sub-prime mortgage crisis has taken its own toll. Those who doubted that globalization was a reality, or thought that it was just a empty phrase, have been shown how a collapse in one market very quickly became a collapse around the world. Its effects raced from banks and finance houses to real estate to manufacturing; from private finances to galloping public and private deficits and debts. Few countries or regions were immune – from Iceland to Portugal, Greece and Ireland to California, Latvia and Thailand, the effects have been devastating for citizens, financial institutions, and economies.

The extent and depth of these crises brought to light what had been clear to some for many years, but had never completely penetrated the public consciousness: America remains a military superpower, but its superiority cannot reliably be translated into automatic and decisive success. It could remove Saddam Hussein and the Taliban from power, but the next step – stable governments presiding over economies with steady growth and populations grateful for the military intervention, such as were established in Japan and Germany after the Second World War – did not follow, and required more than military power to even get started. There are limits to power, and all the bombs, tanks, and infantry in the world will not successfully extend it.

The second lesson is even more difficult. America's economy is characterized by its innovation and resilience, but it is not alone in the world, and it is no longer the sole dominant one. The ebb and flow of empire does not allow for an American exception. The rise of other economies will affect America as surely as all other economic changes have affected imperial primacy since time immemorial. This reality will in turn require more multilateral collaboration, a strengthening of international institutions, and a willingness to prepare for a century that belongs not to the United States alone, but to a world that includes America yet is not always led by it.

CHAPTER 7

ISRAEL AND THE ARAB WORLD:
Democracy's Fate in the Middle East

N o conflict has proven more intractable than the struggle
between Israelis and Palestinians in the Middle East. What
was, in the early nineteenth century, a quiet corner of the Ottoman
Empire had been the scene of great religious battles in earlier
times: the destruction of the first and second temples in Jerusalem,
the harassment of early Christians, the expulsion and dispersal of
the Jews in the Roman Empire, and the Crusades of the Middle
Ages. Jerusalem is a holy city to the three Abrahamic religions,
and as such has been home to Muslims, Christians, and Jews for
centuries. Then the emergence in nineteenth-century Europe of
modern Zionism as a political, nationalist movement set the stage
for a conflict that has now endured for over a century.

The Jews of the 1800s were a people without a country, living
and working in Europe, Asia, and the Middle East with only
varying degrees of civil rights and acceptance. Expelled from
Spain, Britain, France, and many other countries in the Middle
Ages, subject to pogroms and blood libels in Russia and Eastern
Europe, living in the margins and ghettos of the Ottoman Empire,
the Jews were often forced to leave or assimilate.

The calls for political freedoms that eventually transformed
the old empires of Austria-Hungary, Russia, and Turkey found a
home in the Jewish community as well, and at the turn of the
twentieth century Theodor Herzl became the father of modern
Zionism, when he promoted the idea that the Jews needed a
country of their own, and that it should be in Palestine, the ancient

and original home of the Jewish people. Across Europe, Zionists began to pack up and move to Palestine, an outpost of the Ottoman Empire. There they faced resistance from the predominantly Muslim population. The struggle continued after the British were given the mandate over Palestine by the League of Nations, following the declaration by British Foreign Secretary Arthur Balfour in 1917 that the creation of a homeland for the Jewish people in Palestine was now a principle of British public policy: "His Majesty's government view with favour the establishment in Palestine of a national home for the Jewish people, and will use their best endeavours to facilitate the achievement of this objective, it being clearly understood that nothing shall be done which may prejudice the civil and religious rights of existing non-Jewish communities in Palestine, or the rights and political status enjoyed by Jews in any other country."

Chaim Weizmann, founder of the Democratic Zionist Party, had campaigned hard for *the* rather than *a* national home, but it is hard to see how that would have been possible given the existence of a vibrant, long-standing Palestinian community. The years of the British Mandate were a time of struggle and conflict, with Arabs imploring Britain for an end to Jewish settlement; Jews complaining that immigration was being unfairly restricted, particularly after Hitler's rise to power in Germany; the British caught between competing pressures both at home and abroad, satisfying no one. Two royal commissions were established by the British between the wars, each wrestling with how to cope with the rising demand from Jews to get in, and fierce opposition from Palestinians to keep them out.

Today, all official visitors to Israel are taken first to Yad Vashem, the memorial to the six million killed in the Holocaust. On my most recent visit my guide told me, emphatically, "All Jews – not just the direct survivors and their families – are damaged people. This will explain why."

Canada's own treatment of Jewish immigration into Canada

has been brilliantly chronicled in Irving Abella and Harold Troper's 1983 book, *None Is Too Many* (the title is the notorious comment of an immigration official in 1945 when asked what the quota for Jewish entry should be before the Second World War). Anti-Semitism, the chronic prejudice of Western societies that erupted into its most grotesque form in Hitler's Germany, underlay the decisions made by a variety of governments in the years before the war to discriminate against the Jews and to hope that appeasing Hitler would produce a lasting peace. Writing in his diary after meeting Hitler at his mountain retreat, Prime Minister Mackenzie King allowed that "Hitler might come to triumph as one of the saviours of the world."

The harsh discrimination of the Nazis' Nuremberg Laws, the prewar concentration camps, and German expansion into the Ruhr, Austria, and Czechoslovakia were met almost everywhere with appeasement and the notion that this was Germany's attempt to "make itself whole" after the unjust peace at Versailles. Even as the efforts of Jewish families to get out of Germany became more frantic, doors remained closed. Hitler used this response to show the hypocrisy of his critics. The West might find his racial theories extreme, but it was not prepared to do anything about it.

Hitler's initial goal was to expel Jews, not to kill them. When he wrote *Mein Kampf* in a Munich jail in the 1920s, he concluded that human history was about the struggle between races, with the Aryan race the purest and most in need of protection for its survival and ultimate triumph. Non-Aryan races, like the Slavs of Eastern Europe, were inferior, but the Jews in particular, he claimed, had a subhuman form. He was drawing heavily on the noxious theories of social Darwinism and racial superiority that swirled through Western Europe in the nineteenth century, but also on his intensely unhappy time in cosmopolitan Vienna before the First World War.

Classical anti-Semitism is deeply rooted in Christian cultures that for centuries blamed the Jews for the death of Jesus Christ, despised a culture that permitted money lending and commercial success, and encouraged peasant beliefs that Jews drank the blood of children captured and killed for the purpose of satanic rituals. The ultimate conspiracy theory was the infamous *Protocols of the Elders of Zion*, published in 1903, which purported to be a blueprint for the Jewish takeover of the world. It is depressing to note that the Protocols, today completely discredited in the Western world, except among white supremacists and in the bizarre fringes of the Internet, are widely available in the Muslim world. A soap opera based on theories of primitive blood libels has been shown on Egyptian television and other Arab networks in recent years.

During the Second World War, while Nazi soldiers and their collaborators were meeting at Wannsee in January 1942, Nazi leaders set out in a chillingly brief document what would become known as the Final Solution. Those Jews who survived direct military assaults were to be rounded up and shipped to concentration camps, where they would be killed in gas ovens built for the express purpose of eliminating an entire people from the face of the earth. The Jews, Hitler repeated, were not really people. They were vermin, "subhumans," and a "cancer" that had to be extinguished for all time.

Hundreds of thousands of Jews managed to get out of Europe, many of them fleeing to Palestine. And after the end of the war in 1945, when the horror of the Holocaust became known, extraordinary impetus was given to the creation of the State of Israel in the physical place where so many Jews had already settled.

The UN General Assembly resolution of 1975, which branded Zionism as a form of racism and colonialism, misses the point that the creation of the State of Israel had many origins and many fathers. Herzl's dream was a state that guaranteed Jews the full rights as citizens that they had been denied so long in Europe. After toying with notions of going to Uganda and elsewhere, Herzl settled on Palestine as the logical place. Jews had always lived there and it was their historic homeland. For others, the creation of a Jewish state was a chance to put into practice the principles of socialism and human solidarity. For others still, it was indeed a chance for the Western values of freedom, human rights, and democracy to take root in a land of oppression. Israel would quickly become a vital, diverse and pluralist society.

Israel's commitment to the rule of law and the strength of its institutions remain undiminished despite great challenges. As Jews in postwar refugee and settlement camps came to terms with the devastating reality that there was no real place for them in much of Europe, and only limited access elsewhere, the idea of going to Palestine became more practical and more urgent. By 1947, just two years after the end of the war, the Jews in Palestine comprised roughly a third of the total population. The British by this time were exhausted both financially and politically with the no-win choice between enraging Arab opinion with more open immigration to Palestine, and enflaming both Jewish and much liberal opinion in the rest of the world by barring access. Such a ban seemed inhumane, given the overwhelming price that Jews had just paid for having no homeland. The British turned over the question of what to do to the fledgling United Nations. A specially constituted commission recommended partition, the creation of two states, as the preferred solution. This was firmly rejected by Arab Palestinians and their neighbours, who had never been even remotely reconciled to the idea that the Jewish people had a legitimate claim to found a nation for themselves in Palestine. This rejection of partition would prove to be a disastrous choice for the Arab world.

The day of the declaration of Israeli Independence on May 14, 1948 is commemorated by Palestinians as the Naqba, a day of disaster, because in the war that followed as many as 750,000 Palestinians fled or were expelled from their homes in what was now Israel's territory. Once they left, the door to return was closed, and what began as temporary refugee camps became permanent settlements. My colleague Irwin Cotler has pointed out the existence of a second "Naqba," the heightened persecution of the Jews in the Middle East. What had been centres of Jewish life in Morrocco, Algieria,

Tunisia, Egypt, Syria and Iraq became places of evacuation as Sephardic Jews fled to Israel throughout the next two decades.

It was far more than a battle of opinions and ideas. Both Jews and Arabs created guerrilla armies who fought hard and used the toughest of tactics. Many civilians were killed in efforts to gain the upper hand. Thus began the postwar version of the conflict. The borders and boundaries of partition suggested in 1947 by the UN and expanded in Israel's favour in 1948 as the result of the war that followed, were never recognized by any of Israel's neighbours, although armistice lines were established in January of 1949 (known today as the Green Line).

The steady erosion of both the British and French empires in the face of powerful nationalist movements in the Middle East, Africa, and Asia became the backdrop for one of history's great miscalculations. Gamal Abdel Nasser, a young military officer who seized power in Egypt in a coup against the corrupt King Farouk in 1952, spoke to the younger generation of Egyptians and Arabs in a new language of socialist planning and nationalist pride. There were four steps to his campaign to bring Egypt into the modern world, a campaign that he believed could be adapted and adopted throughout the Middle East. Ending a puppet monarchy sustained by an aging empire was the first step. Maintaining a fierce opposition to the State of Israel as an illegitimate Zionist outpost was the second. Building the dam across the Nile at Aswan was third. And nationalizing the Suez Canal was fourth.

"Nasserism" had its counterpart in many countries, and still does today. It is characterized by big, centralized, and bureaucratic states; public ownership of most enterprises; a strident secularism; and a heavy reliance on police and security institutions to maintain power and quell dissent. Nasser was hardly the first modern "man on horseback" who used the military to consolidate power, promote change, and enforce control. Nor will he be the last.

It was Nasser's decision in 1956 to nationalize the Suez Canal that prompted prime ministers Anthony Eden of Britain, Guy

Mollet of France, and David Ben Gurion of Israel (whose young defence minister was Shimon Peres) to concoct a scheme whose real nature was quickly exposed. The plan was for Israel to move its troops across the Sinai to the banks of the Suez Canal and for British and French troops to descend on Egyptian territory, ostensibly as "peacekeepers," but in reality in defence of their imperial interests as shareholders of the canal.

Eden regarded Nasser as a modern Hitler who had to be stopped at all costs, but he also saw a military confrontation with Egypt as a way to restore British prestige in the region and, on a personal level, as an antidote to Britain's prewar appeasement policy, which he had opposed by resigning as foreign secretary in 1938.

It was a terrible misread. The Americans, furious at not being consulted, denounced the raids as unjustifiable. As the pretext of the clumsily orchestrated scheme became clear, Nasser, a master of radio communication in a language Arab opinion could readily understand, inflamed opinion in the Middle East against the foreign invaders.

The Suez Crisis was one of the earliest and most series tests for the young United Nations – and for Canadian Secretary of State for External Affairs Lester "Mike" Pearson, who was one of the architects of the new international institutions of the postwar world: the United Nations, created at San Francisco in 1945; the General Agreement on Tariffs and Trade, signed in 1947; the UN Declaration of Human Rights, approved in 1948; and the NATO military alliance, founded in 1949.

Canada had emerged from the war as a powerhouse of talent and ideas. Our infrastructure had not been destroyed. Our public finances quickly rebounded as prosperity and effective management took hold strongly after 1945. Our disproportionately large role in the fighting in Europe had won us prestige internationally.

Pearson was key to the San Francisco negotiations over the United Nations, and other Canadians were no less involved. Dana

Wilgress was central to the negotiation of the GATT, John Humphrey crafted the Declaration of Human Rights, and Pearson and his team were at the centre of the negotiations that led to the creation of NATO.

These were all institutions to which the Americans were deeply committed, in stark contrast to the stance of an isolationist Senate that in 1920 had dismissed the League of Nations as an expensive European plot. Pearson had watched with pain and embarrassment as Prime Minister Mackenzie King publicly undermined Canada's representative to the League of Nations, Walter Riddell, over the issue of sanctions against Italy after the invasion of Ethiopia in 1935.

Canada had been emphatic in its support of the UN effort to stop communist expansion in Korea in 1950, and endorsed wholeheartedly the creation of NATO a year earlier, insisting on adding Article 2 to the NATO Treaty, which broadened the political and economic purpose of the association from being a purely military alliance.

It was this emphasis on the legality and morality of international political behaviour that drove Prime Minister Louis St. Laurent and Pearson to action over Suez. Pearson's gift for mediation, his knack as an unabashed helpful fixer, allowed the first reaction to be channelled in a positive way. On a recent trip to Cairo, I happened to meet a retired Egyptian diplomat whose first posting had been as the most junior member of his country's UN delegation in 1956. He remembered Pearson well. "He was everywhere, smiling, showing drafts, listening, very approachable. When I think of Canada, I think of him. What has happened to that Canada?" We shall come to that question shortly.

Canada's goal was to get the British, French, and Israelis out of a difficult situation without a total humiliation. Pearson's first idea was to allow the British and French peacekeepers to change uniforms and work for the UN. Nasser would have none of that, and so Pearson proposed the creation of a separate peacekeeping force that would allow the complete withdrawal of British and

French troops. His proposal was accepted, and war over the Suez was averted. It was for this achievement that Pearson won the Nobel Prize for Peace in 1957

General E.L.M Burns, known alternatively as "Tommy" and "Smiler" (because he didn't), wrote a first-hand account of his years as commander of the United Nations Emergency Force in the years after Suez. *Between Arab and Israeli* is a sobering book. The conflict has been marked by three wars (1956, 1967, 1973); two intifadas (Arab uprisings inside Israel and the occupied territories); the dramatic visit by President Sadat to the Israeli Knesset in 1977; the Camp David Accords that returned occupied lands in the Sinai Peninsula to Egypt; the Oslo Accord that marked the first agreement between Israel and the PLO; tens of thousands of deaths among both Israelis and Palestinians and other neighbouring countries; refugee towns that have become cauldrons of poverty, resentment and extremism; Jewish settlements far from any borders contemplated in 1948; terrorism, suicide bombings, occupation, and a dispute that continues to dominate the political landscape of the Middle East.

Canadian recognition of Israel as a full member of the family of nations has rightly been clear, emphatic, and unambiguous. Canada supported the partition of Palestine even before 1948 because it saw the need for a separate Jewish state. But the logic of accepting partition should also mean the recognition of a second state, for Palestinians, on land ruled by Jordan and Egypt until 1967, then captured by Israel in a six-day war that year. But this acceptance has taken considerable time.

Canada needs to be as clear an ally to the peace process and to the birth of modern Palestine as we have been and will continue to be to the State of Israel. This is not about balance for its own sake. It is about doing the right thing: right for peace and stability, right for the interests of the people in the region, and right for Canada's role as a country whose international focus must once again become what it was in Pearson's day – the prevention and resolution of conflict, and the support of democratic and human values.

Israel's military victory in 1967 seemed a triumph at the time, but it was a victory that has come with a price. All of Jerusalem fell into Israeli hands, as did the West Bank, the Golan, Gaza and Sinai. Those Israelis with a vision of a Greater Israel, a homeland not just *in* Palestine but *of* Palestine, saw the military victory as the basis to expand settlement into all corners of the occupied territory. This view is still supported by some influential politicians. The recently appointed foreign minister, Avigdor Lieberman, refers to the occupied territories as Judea and Samaria, historical names whose modern use was popularized by Menachem Begin.

The most famous face of modern Zionism was presented by David Ben Gurion, whose Labour Party promoted the idea of Israel as a secular, social democratic state distinguished by solidarity and fellowship. Ben Gurion and most of his colleagues were kibbutzniks, dedicated to building communities where everyone would share the work and even the raising of children would be a communal activity. It was Ben Gurion who insisted on compromise and a ceasefire in 1948, and who rejected calls at that time for an expansionist policy.

A voice less known in the West, but deeply revered in Israel, was that of Ze'ev Jabotinsky, Ben Gurion's fierce opponent, whose vision of Zionism was more expansionist and less compromising. When Winston Churchill, as colonial secretary, barred Jewish settlement on the eastern bank of the Jordan River in 1921, Jabotinsky was thrown in jail for insisting that living on both sides of the Jordan was an integral part of the Jewish birthright. The argument Jabotinsky set out a pamphlet presciently entitled "The Iron Wall" was crystal clear: Palestine would always have two peoples, Jewish and Arab, and there should never be a question of expelling or oppressing Arabs. But neither should the Jews be surprised that the Arabs were resisting the presence of the Jews, because "there has never been an indigenous inhabitant anywhere who has ever accepted the settlement of others in his country." Jabotinsky went on to say, "Arab nationalism sets itself the same aims as those set by Italian nationalism before 1870 and Polish nationalism before 1918: unity and independence. These aspirations mean the eradication of every trace of British influence in Egypt and Iraq, the expulsion of the Italians from Libya, the removal of French domination from Syria, Tunis, Algiers and Morocco. For us to support such a movement would be suicide."

His conclusion was stark. There would have to be an "iron wall" that "the natives cannot break." The "colonizers" could not and should not compromise, and only once their complete determination was understood would a political compromise be possible.

Jabotinsky died in 1940, but his ideas were kept vibrant and alive by the Irgun movement he founded, and by its successor organizations, Herut and, more recently, Likud. His intellectual and political disciples Menachem Begin and Yitzhak Shamir in turn have their successors today, most notably Benjamin Netanyahu, the current prime minister of Israel. The post-1967 settler movement has an additional, religious component as well.

I have spent much time in recent years trying to determine whether, after the collapse of the Oslo Process in 1996, the subsequent brutal wave of suicide bombings and military excursions into the West Bank, Gaza, and Lebanon, and the recent attempts (first the Annapolis process then the Mitchell effort) to get peace talks back on track, there is any real prospect of negotiations that would get beyond the iron wall.

There are challenges as well as opportunities. Let's start with a better sense of the opportunities. All mediators like to talk of a "zone of agreement." On the face of it, that zone seems pretty clear. In the last days of the Clinton administration an agreement (the Camp David Peace Proposal) was close at hand – not done, but certainly closer than ever before or since. It would have involved each side's recognition of two states, borders and boundaries that would grant Israel land settled close to the 1948 Green

Line, and other land given to the Palestinians in exchange; a new governance arrangement in Jerusalem; a limited right of return and compensation to refugees; and generous financial assistance to the new Palestinian state.

The Palestinians insist there was no unambiguous deal "rejected" by Arafat in 2001. The Israelis and Americans are equally insistent that this is precisely what happened. We'll let historians argue about it. The point is that the peace proposal demonstrated that the two parties, at their best, are not irretrievably far apart.

The question today is whether either the Israeli and Palestinian leadership has the political will or capacity or support to continue and to conclude peace negotiations along similar lines. Right now, officials exchange maps and there are "proximity talks." Israeli conservatives talk not of "resolving" the conflict, but of "managing" it. Their attention now is focused more on Iran's nuclear intentions, and that government's relationship with the two militant Palestinian organizations, the Sunni Hamas in Gaza and the Shia Hezbollah.

History teaches us that breakthrough agreements happen only when a deep consensus emerges that the cost of continuing a conflict is too high. But this kind of consensus rarely emerges on its own. A visionary and decisive leadership on both sides is almost always required to drive the consensus. What is troubling about the policy of "managing the conflict" is that it ignores the claim of Palestinians to be full citizens in their own country. It also makes light of how difficult living conditions are for many Palestinians in the West Bank and Gaza, and that it will take much more than the cessation of hostilities to make their prosperity possible. The Netanyahu government insists that these conditions can be improved, and points to the reduction of the number of roadblocks in the West Bank and evidence of improving civilian and economic life in Ramallah and other Palestinian cities. Some Israelis say that settlements are not an issue, meaning they will be resolved at the bargaining table, but continued building of exclusively Jewish communities on occupied land is seen as both a provocation and an obstacle to peace by even the most moderate of Palestinians.

The challenge remains to find solutions to the barriers between the parties. The daily life of Palestinians in the occupied territories and their deeper political aspirations currently depend in good measure on the goodwill of the occupying power. This is a no-win situation for Israel, because democracy necessarily implies that the people living within the borders and boundaries of a defined state have equal rights and freedoms, including the right to vote. The Arabs living in the occupied territories can vote for the Palestinian Parliament, but the Palestinian Parliament is not sovereign. An indefinite occupation corrodes Israeli democracy. Political support in Gaza and the West Bank is divided between Fatah, which has finally endorsed a two-state solution based on the borders of 1967, with East Jerusalem as its capital, and Hamas, an offshoot of the Islamist Muslim Brotherhood, which is committed to armed resistance to what it calls the "Zionist occupation," i.e., Israel itself. It shares this position with Hezbollah, the military and political organization of Shiite Muslims that led guerrilla fighters against the Israeli invasion and occupation of South Lebanon from 1982 to 2000, and again in 2006. The first invasion – the Long War – was based on Israel's notion that it could recraft the divisive confessional politics of Lebanon, and ensure security on its northern border.

This ended in 2000 with the grim recognition that the original purpose of the invasion had not been met. It would be wrong to blame Israel for Lebanon's own brutal civil war, but Israel's lengthy presence in South Lebanon did allow Hezbollah to achieve significant public support as the effective voice of the resistance. In particular, it helped build Hassan Nasrallah's reputation as a decisive leader at a decisive time. Israel's original purpose in invading Lebanon was to tilt the balance of power away from Shiite extremism and to end the support and protection Hezbollah receives from Syria. Exactly the opposite ended up happening. Confessional politics remained as brutal as ever, assassinations remained the order of the day, Nasrallah became a revered figure in his community, and Israel's moral and strategic reputation was severely tarnished.

This was the situation in the summer of 2006 when Hezbollah fighters attacked an Israeli military station, killing four soldiers and capturing two others. Israeli public opinion was inflamed; the decision was made to engage once more, with Israel feeling justified in responding to a clear breach of the northern border with a full-scale assault on Hezbollah in South Lebanon. But feeling that a response is justified does not mean the response will be successful. It was not in 2006. The conduct of the Israeli military and the management of the invasion were both deeply flawed, as a public inquiry later confirmed.

Israel's challenge is that it faces two enemies, Hamas and Hezbollah, who are engaged in a guerrilla fight against Israel's conventional army and air force. In Gaza, Hamas fighters place rocket launchers on the rooftops of schools and apartment buildings to discourage retaliation. Its military headquarters are buried deep beneath a hospital. Guerrillas are often indistinguishable from the rest of the population. This makes fighting these wars painfully difficult for Israel. Its rockets and bombs go astray, innocent men, women and children are killed, and the world is watching.

If the United States lost the Vietnam War on the television sets of America in the 1970s, Israel's war faces the challenge of the Internet. The effective use of hand-held video cameras and the rapid dissemination of pictures on the Internet can create a climate of opinion worldwide that is intensely difficult to overcome.

The invasion of Lebanon in 2006 was detrimental to Israel from a public relations perspective, but ironically its conclusion has enhanced security on the Israeli–Lebanese border. There are now international troops patrolling the region, and Hezbollah leader Nasrallah will have much difficulty convincing his supporters and the broader Lebanese public that what the country needs is another war. It is significant that during the Gaza conflict of 2008–09 he made many eloquent speeches denouncing Israel, and criticizing Egypt for "doing nothing" to help the population of Gaza, while he was stymied himself. The world rightly worries about Hezbollah's links to Iran and Syria, as well as its implacable hatred of Israel and its effective veto power over the divided government of Lebanon. But circumstance has becalmed its military wing, as its political wing is weighed down by the need to court opinion and maintain support.

Gaza is another story. A narrow strip of land along the Mediterranean surrounded on the north and east by Israel and in the south by Egypt, Gaza is a densely populated, deeply impoverished enclave of 1.5 million people. Governed by the Egyptians from 1948 to 1967, it is still seen with suspicion as a hotbed of radicalism by the Mubarak government. Eight thousand Israelis settlers built prosperous walled communities in Gaza in the years after 1977. Unlike the Golan Heights and East Jerusalem, which have been annexed by Israel, Gaza's legal and political status is unclear.

Fatah leader Yasser Arafat welcomed President Clinton there in 1994, and it became the focus of some efforts to encourage development, but the first and second intifadas led Israel to drastically curtail access in and out of Gaza, which in turn led to more violence and resentment and to tighter restrictions on movement.

In a dramatic turnaround before his incapacitating stroke, Ariel Sharon ordered the withdrawl of all settlements from Gaza. This decision was met by rocket fire from Hamas and in the winter of 2008-2009 by an Israeli invasion that left 1,300 killed. There is now an uneasy ceasefire and a relaxation of border restrictions on goods entering Gaza. But it is not a sustainable situation.

On the West Bank, events have unfolded differently. Arafat's decision to authorize armed struggle and suicide bombings led to Israel's armed entry into Ramallah. The massive destruction of property and loss of life resulted in a dramatic deterioration in the overall security situation for both Palestinians and Israelis. It also had a profoundly disillusioning effect on the Israeli centre and left. The period of quiet engagement up to Oslo saw hugely heightened expectations for peace among both Israelis and Palestinians. I led a delegation of Canadian business leaders to Israel, the West Bank, and Jordan in the winter of 1993-94. Euphoria is too strong a word – but there was a sense that an enduring peace, a real political settlement, was possible.

That hope was shattered when the negotiations failed. Yitzhak Rabin, the Israeli prime minister who had gone to Washington to sign the Oslo Accords, was assassinated in 1995. The dramatic failure of Arafat's and Rabin's successors to reach a conclusion led to more resistance, suicide bombings, and a heightened military response from Israel. The escalation of hostilities was ignored by President Clinton's successor, George W. Bush, who only turned his attention to the Middle East after 9/11, and then only fitfully. This failure of leadership has fortunately not been imitated by President Obama, who on taking office immediately appointed George Mitchell as his special Middle East envoy. Today, strenuous efforts are being made to get the two sides back on track.

The gap in leadership on both sides is deepened by divisions in public opinion. Every taking of the public pulse says that both Israelis and Palestinians want peace, but it is not clear that either side is yet prepared for the wrenching change such a peace will require. Nor is there the level of trust that is a precondition of peace. Israelis feel themselves surrounded by neighbours who are unfriendly – a Hezbollah-dominated Lebanon and a Hamas-led Gaza – or who are not yet ready to accept Israel as a partner in the region. This inevitably means an Israel preoccupied by security, and profoundly skeptical of the possibilities of a lasting peace. Every Palestinian leader I have met has felt that Israel was not really prepared to make the painful withdrawals and concessions that will make a Palestinian state viable. "We all know sovereignty isn't an absolute, but it has to mean something" was the way one Palestinian spokesman put it to me. The agreement on the two-state solution has to get to the next step: outlining the borders of the two states and planning the route to a viable Palestinian economy.

It is often said of Northern Ireland that what made peace possible was the decision by the vast majority that peace would bring more benefits than war, that enough people had a stake in prosperity. The same cannot yet be said in Palestine. There are still far too many people who feel they have nothing much to lose and nothing apparently to gain. Most people who visit the Middle East are struck by the differences in the narratives of history and politics. Nowhere is this divide clearer than in Israel's decision to build a security barrier right through the heart of Jerusalem and the West Bank. Israeli officials point to the dramatic reduction in suicide bombings; Palestinians see a nine-foot wall dividing neighbourhoods, making movement arduous, and having the potential of becoming the ipso facto border. It is impossible not to think back to Jabotinsky's "iron wall," which "the native population" cannot break, to use his words. But, it is important not to get mesmerized by historical parallels. I have travelled up and down the length of fence, the wall, the barrier, whatever name it is given, in the company of both Palestinians and Israelis. The bluntest comment I heard came from one of the Israeli designers of the project: "It will be a great day when we don't need it, and taking it down will have to be part of a real political settlement."

Where is Canada in all this? Our role never has been, nor should it ever be, one of simple neutrality, because we are committed to values and interests about which there should be no doubt. We were advocates of partition in 1947 and 1948. Our commitment to an Israel with secure and recognized borders, free from terrorism and violence, is not something about which any Canadian government will be neutral.

We are also deep supporters of the rule of law. We helped to craft UN Resolution 242 in 1967, which still remains at the heart of any long-term settlement. It is worth remembering what that resolution says:

1. Affirms that the fulfillment of Charter principles requires the establishment of a just and lasting peace in the Middle East which should include the application of both the following principles:
   (i) Withdrawal of Israeli armed forces from territories occupied in the recent conflict.
   (ii) Termination of all claims or states of belligerency and respect for and acknowledgement of the sovereignty, territorial integrity and political independence of every State in the area and their right to live in peace within secure and recognized boundaries free from threats of act of force.
2. Affirms further the necessity
   (a) For guaranteeing freedom of navigation through international waterways in the area;
   (b) For achieving a just settlement of the refugee problem;
   (c) For guaranteeing the territorial inviolability and political independence of every State in the area through measures including the establishment of de-militarized zones.

A note here on the importance of pronouns. We saw earlier that the Balfour Declaration talked about "a" homeland, not "the" homeland. Resolution 242 also has a missing "the" before the word "territories." It is not without significance.

Canada must be more engaged than we have been recently. Our friendship with Israel is deep and permanent, and transcends partisan differences. But it in no way means we can be indifferent to the Palestinian claim to a viable state. A new State of Palestine is on the verge of being formed. We should be supporting it, and showing more leadership in facilitating it. All of our allies, including the United States, have shown a willingness to do so. Canada so far has not.

———

The Madrid Conference of 1991 gave Canada the chairmanship of the committee looking at the Palestinian refugee situation. This is a critical responsibility, but little has happened in the last few years.

The Annapolis Conference in 2007 set in motion a crucial effort to help the Palestinian Authority take greater responsibility for security matters. An American general, Keith Dayton, has become a key figure in assisting the Authority to train six thousand members of the National Security Force as well as the two-thousand-strong strong Presidential Guard. In addition, the European Union is helping train local police. There are eighteen Canadians deeply involved in what is called the Dayton Process. Canadians on the ground say that the Authority is ready to take on more administrative responsibility, that there is reason now to dismantle checkpoints and roadblocks throughout the West Bank. A wizened Fatah commander, who is now in charge of the Authority's National Security Force, was emphatic about it going further, saying, "Give us the tools to do the job and we shall do it." An old fedayeen fighter, he is ready to embrace the two-state solution, but he sees no real willingness in Israel to do so.

On the difficult issues of Israel's settlements and the governance of Jerusalem and its holy sites, which were so close to resolution at Camp David and the Taba Summit in 2001, Canada, should be as deeply engaged as we were in 1948, 1956, 1967, 1973, and at so many other critical points along the way.

Michael Bell, a former Canadian ambassador to most of the countries of the region, has been doing just that. The Jerusalem Project is his brainchild. It is a good-faith effort to look at the tough question of effective governance of the Old City. His approach is to get people to focus on the details of what it will take to resolve the conflict in daily life. It is not enough to draft broad formulas, or to leave the details to later. As every negotiator knows, the devil is in the details. That's where we could be usefully engaged right now, that is where Canada can be a vital part of what we all hope will become known as the Mitchell Process.

The Oslo negotiations were successful in breaking down the barriers to communication, which led to an agreement that, for all its imperfections, is still the basis for future talks. The weaknesses of Oslo are threefold. First of all, it was an agreement between people who wanted to agree, and did not include those who were opposed to or skeptical of the process. In Northern Ireland, progress was finally made only when the real hardliners were in the room. They were brought in only after many talks about talks persuaded the IRA and some extremist Protestant groups to abandon violence as the alternative to peace. That will be true in the Middle East as well.

The second weakness is what might be called the Oslo method, which I also saw at work in Sri Lanka. Agreement is found on some principles, resulting in a ceasefire, but more difficult issues are put off. The risk with this approach is that it creates the illusion of agreement, when in fact the parties remain deeply divided and at loggerheads. A ceasefire is better than no ceasefire, but if the parties, or at least one of them, are only buying time or marking time, there is no momentum toward a lasting peace.

The third weakness is the most important, and this has to do with the nature of the Palestinian condition itself. From the time of the partition decision by the United Nations, the Palestinians have been unable to accept the loss of part of their homeland and the need to create a democratic state in what remains. They believed in 1947 that resistance would reverse the migration of Jews, but it did not. Instead it led to the war of 1948 and, from their perspective, a worse result: hundreds of thousands of refugees and lost territory. A twenty-year unresolved conflict led to another war in 1967, and more lost territory. Then the leadership chose to take resistance to another level – the extremism of the 1970s, with Arafat being forced from Beirut, leading a kind of guerrilla movement in exile, taking on the Jordanians, and travelling the world looking for support, money, and arms.

All of this was antithetical to democracy and to Palestinian self-interest. It was what prompted Israeli Foreign Minister Abba Ebam to say that the Palestinians "never missed an opportunity to miss an opportunity." Political and military power was concentrated in the hands of a clever, charismatic leader. Finances were hardly transparent. Differences of opinion were met with death. Nothing changed when Arafat finally "came home" and took office in Ramallah. The culture of exile and extremism remains dominant and it has proven resistant to change. The PLO and Fatah make up a secular, political movement with a rhetoric and ideology that owe more to Marx than to Allah. It is a creature of the same ideology of a secular, one-party state that the Baathist Party enforced in Iraq and that still prevails today in Egypt and Syria. But the stasis and oppression of these states has led to the flourishing of militant, extremist, and retrograde religious movements throughout the Muslim world. This extremism has had a profound effect in Gaza and the West Bank, as surely as it had in Jordan, Lebanon, and elsewhere. Hamas and Hezbollah are proponents of this Islamist ascendancy, and have to be understood as part of that wider revival.

As will be clear from this book, I am a great believer in looking at what people actually say. To understand the goals of Hamas, Likud, the PLO, and Hezbollah, let's look at their words. The Hamas Charter makes it clear that all of Palestine is holy to Muslims, and will always be so, and that "nothing is loftier or deeper in Nationalism than waging Jihad against the enemy and confronting him when he sets foot on the land of the Muslims . . . There is no solution to the Palestinian problem except by Jihad. The initiatives, proposals and International Conferences are but a waste of time, an exercise in futility. The Palestinian people are too noble to have their future, their right and their destiny submitted to a vain game."

Article 7 of the Hamas Charter states that Hamas is

one of the links in the Chain of Jihad in the confrontation with the Zionist invasion. It links up with the setting
out of the Martyr Izz a-din al-Qassam and his brothers
in the Muslim Brotherhood who fought the Holy War
in 1936; it further relates to another link of the
Palestinian Jihad and the Jihad and efforts of the Muslim
Brothers during the 1948 War, and to the Jihad operations of the Muslim Brothers in 1968 and thereafter. . . .
the Hamas has been looking forward to implement
Allah's promise whatever time it might take. The
prophet, prayer and peace be upon him, said: "The time
will not come until Muslims will fight the Jews (and kill
them); until the Jews hide behind rocks and trees, which
will cry: 'O Muslim! there is a Jew hiding behind me,
come on and kill him.'"

Article 22 is a restatement of the Protocols of the Elders of Zion:

This wealth [meaning the Jews'] permitted them to take
over control of the world media such as news agencies, the
press, publication houses, broadcasting and the like. [They
also used this] wealth to stir revolutions in various parts of
the globe in order to fulfill their interests and pick the
fruits. They stood behind the French and the Communist
Revolutions and behind most of the revolutions we hear
about here and there. They also used the money to establish clandestine organizations which are spreading around
the world, in order to destroy societies and carry out
Zionist interests. Such organizations are: the Freemasons,
Rotary Clubs, Lions Clubs, B'nai B'rith and the like. All
of them are destructive spying organizations. They also
used the money to take over control of the Imperialist
states and made them colonize many countries in order to
exploit the wealth of those countries and spread their

corruption therein . . . They also stood behind World War II, where they collected immense benefits from trading with war materials and prepared for the establishment of their state. They inspired the establishment of the United Nations and the Security Council to replace the League of Nations, in order to rule the world by their intermediary.

Article 28 repeats this same anti-Semitic diatribe and states categorically: "Israel, by virtue of its being Jewish and having a Jewish population, defies Islam and the Muslims." "Nazi Zionism" is the enemy, and resistance to it is a religious, political and personal obligation of every Muslim.

The Hamas Charter makes it clear that the Palestinian Liberation Organization and all other Arab states risk being brought into the "Zionist orbit" because of their secularism and willingness to negotiate a peace that would accept Israel's right to exist. It is the refusal to accept this right that is the working premise, the *raison d'être* of Hamas. This is what makes it so difficult to imagine achieving a working dialogue with them.

The Likud Party platform doesn't provide much help in seeing a way clear to a solution either. It states categorically:

The Jewish communities in Judea, Samaria and Gaza are the realization of Zionist values. Settlement of the land is a clear expression of the unassailable right of the Jewish people to the Land of Israel . . . Israel rejects out of hand ideas raised by Labor Party leaders concerning the relinquishment of parts of the Negev to the Palestinians . . . The Government of Israel flatly rejects the establishment of a Palestinian Arab state west of the Jordan river. The Palestinians can run their lives freely in the framework of self-rule, but not as an independent and sovereign state. Thus, for example, in matters of foreign affairs, security, immigration and ecology, their activity shall be limited in accordance with imperatives of Israel's existence, security and national needs . . . The Jordan Valley and the territories that dominate it shall be under Israeli sovereignty. The Jordan river will be the permanent eastern border of the State of Israel. (http://www.knesset.gov.il/elections/knesset15/elikud_m.htm)

Hezbollah was born as a result of the Israeli invasion of Lebanon. Its focus is the establishment of an Islamist government in Lebanon, and it has called for the destruction of Israel, which it refers to as "the Zionist entity . . . built on lands wrested from their owners." The document "Hizbullah: Views and Concepts" states:

> Hizbullah views the Zionist Jews' occupation of Palestine, displacing its people and establishing the entity of Israel on its usurped land, as the living materialization of the most hideous kinds of aggression and organized terrorism that is supported by the USA, the sponsor of international terrorism, and some other states that claim to be democratic and protecting human rights whilst they support Israel that was founded on invasion, killing and blood-shed, besides its daily violations of human rights in Lebanon and Palestine.
>
> Hizbullah does not believe it is right for some people in the world to view the Zionist Jewish occupation as accepted violence and terrorism, while they condemn the counter-violence, which is a natural human reaction to the Zionist violence and terrorism.

It is interesting to note the difference in tone and language between Hamas and Hezbollah. Hezbollah is insistent in its determination to enter into a dialogue with other religions and perspectives: "It should be clear that the kind of Islam we want is a civilized endeavour that rejects injustice, humiliation, slavery, subjugation, colonialism and blackmail while we stretch out our arms for communication among nations on the basis of mutual respect . . . The Islam we mean is the religion that recommends communication among civilization[s] and rejects divisive collision between those civilizations" (Hizbullah).

Many consider Hassan Nasrallah, the leader of Hezbollah, to be the most eloquent speaker in the Arab world since Nasser. He walks a fine line between being a religious and political leader, and Hezbollah's provision of a broad range of services to Muslims in South Lebanon has had the inevitable effect of tempering its political ideology. In many statements, he has shown some respect for Palestinians to reach their own solutions to the conflict, but in others has made it clear that suicide bombings are fully justified, and that resistance to the State of Israel is a core belief of the organization he leads. Despite much insistence that it draws a firm line between Judaism and Zionism, Hezbollah has done its share of spreading anti-Semitic propaganda.

In an article written for the *Guardian* newspaper, Benny Morris, a leading Israeli academic known as a friend of the peace process, concluded that the fundamental differences between Israelis and Palestinians cannot be bridged. "The minor problems are Israeli Prime Minister Benjamin Netanyahu's unwillingness to partition Jerusalem and enable the Palestinians to constitute the eastern half of the city as their capital, and his reluctance to freeze the settlement enterprise in the West Bank. The major problem is that the two-headed Palestinian national movement is averse to sharing Palestine with the Jews and endorsing a solution based on two states for two peoples."

There is a deep pessimism in Morris's analysis: that there is simply too much resistance to the idea of two states on both sides to make it a workable proposition, and that to push it as a solution at this point will only lead to disappointment. In other words, Morris is arguing that the zone of agreement simply isn't there. The question of Jerusalem, the right of return, all these issues are, in this view, too divisive and emotional to permit real negotiation. But the current leader of the Palestinian Authority, Mohammed Abbas, strongly disagrees. He emphatically embraces a two-state solution and sees the resistance as coming from the other side, with settlers and fundamentalists still set on "greater Israel." The view that the Arab world will never accept two states and the legitimate existence of Israel is also challenged by the Arab Peace Initiative. This effort was launched in 2002 by the Saudis, and it was ultimately adopted by the Arab League. Its thrust is "back to 1967 and all will be well." It has been called "disingenuous" by Israeli governments, and comes late in the day. But it is an important step beyond the pure and simple rejectionism that marked Arab and Palestinian opinion from the beginning of the twentieth century.

When I met Israeli Foreign Minister Avigdor Lieberman in 2009, he emphasized that he did not believe there were "insurmountable issues" with the Palestinians, and he insisted that the settlements were not the obstacle to peace. There was war before 1948, after 1948, before and after 1967. "There has always been terror, pogrom, and friction," Lieberman asserted. Israel evacuated twenty-four settlements and ten thousand Jews out of Gaza and in return, "we got Hamas and bombs and terror." The borders and the boundaries have to allow for "natural growth; dovish governments brought us nothing. I am a settler and I know the Palestinians – they want security, economy, and stability. This we can discuss."

He suggested that while Israel was prepared to deal with roadblocks and outposts, and to help General Dayton, as well as to invest more in Judea and Samaria, it would be wise to avoid "emotional issues like refugees, Jerusalem, a few final issues" which he sees as a dangerous abstraction no one is ready to confront.

We are at a difficult moment in any potential discussions. Public opinion on both sides wants peace, is prepared to accept the need for territorial compromise, and understands that it won't be easy. The difficulty is that any conclusive negotiation will require unusual courage from the leadership on both sides, and a willingness to confront the "impossibilists" who exist among Israelis as well as among Palestinians. On this is certain: the failure to reach a peace settlement that recognizes the claims of both Israelis and Palestinians comes with a high price. Democracy is undermined, and extremism is encouraged. In each generation the attacks could become more brutal and extreme. There is no alternative to reconciliation, as difficult as this is to imagine today.

Finally, it is not possible to discuss the Middle East without also considering the role of Iran, whose current president is a Holocaust denier. He has made a point of describing Israel in the most repugnant terms. As the largest Shiite state in the region, Iran provides assistance to both Hamas and Hezbollah. Up until now Iran has refused to comply with UN resolutions on the development of its nuclear program, and continues with an extensive military buildup as well as uranium enrichment. Iran claims it is developing its nuclear capability for the generation of electricity, but the West rightly fears that the real goal is warheads that would be aimed at Israel.

Can Iran be persuaded to change course? Will sanctions and negotiations work? That, of course, should be the West's hope. But no one should underestimate the risks that Iran is taking with its current rhetoric and approach.

Democracy is hardly flourishing in the wider Arab world. While there are non-government groups that press strongly for broader human rights and freedom of expression, most governments in the region are autocratic, with varying degrees of tolerance for dissent. Part of the challenge facing countries from Morocco to the Gulf States is that many of the groups and individuals subject to severe repression are themselves deeply antagonistic to democracy and more open societies, and if elected would simply turn the tables and put their opponents in jail, at best. Algeria's violent civil war,

the strength of the Muslim Brotherhood in Egypt, and the continuing resonance of the ideas of the Islamist revival all point to the
dilemma that many of the victims of government repression themselves hold extremist positions. The viciousness with which Hamas
treats its internal enemies illustrates the extent of the problem.

The Middle East is a region replete with ironies and contradictions. Syria, a predominantly Shiite state, is a dictatorship
under the grip of the Assad family, who are members of the Alawi
sect, which many Sunnis see as heretical, and not a legitimate
expression of Islam. The Kurds who were placed within the Syrian
state by the Sykes-Picot Agreement feel excluded from full political participation, as do many Christians who have been departing
the region steadily for the last thirty years. Syria's regime is
secular, and determinedly so, yet it is a source of care, money and
arms to Hamas and Hezbollah, both deeply religious and extremist Shiite organizations. If the Hamas leadership dared speak a
word against the Syrian regime it would be shut down in the blink
of an eye. But under the age-old proviso that "the enemy of my
enemy is my friend," the flow of finance and weapons continues.

Egypt is now facing an eventual change in leadership –
Mubarak is older and ailing – while beset with profound tensions.
The state socialism of the Nasser era is a thing of the distant past,
and Egypt's economy is opening up. Its business and economic
leaders are looking to the West for support. The most powerful
opposition to Mubarak comes from the Muslim Brotherhood,
which initiated the Islamist revival and provided its intellectual
underpinnings. In the 1950s and 1960s, Sayyid Qutb was one of
the most powerful intellectual voices of the Islamic resistance,
beginning with his rejection of American materialism, which so
disgusted him while studying in the United States in the 1950s.
He became a fierce advocate of the legitimacy, even the obligation, of violence in fighting the jihad, or holy war, against Zionism
and the West, and the repressive secular regimes that in no way
represented the "true Islamic spirit."

His execution by the Nasser regime in 1966 naturally made him a martyr, and in the years since his death his declaration that Muslims should submit only to the rule of religious leaders and Sharia law has been taken up by Sunni extremists throughout the Arab world, among them Osama bin Laden. Ayman al-Zawahiri, widely seen as bin Laden's right hand, was a student and follower of Qutb's brother, and the Muslim Brotherhood's fierce opposition to the Egyptian government has its parallel in the determined attacks by jihadists on the governments of Saudi Arabia and Jordan.

The rule of secular law, an independent judiciary, equality between men and women, the notion of political power being subject to the will of the people, these are all ideas that are contrary to many other deeply held beliefs in the Arab and Muslim worlds. But public opinion is not completely ignored either, and legitimacy cannot simply depend on the rule of the gun.

There is a genuine battle underway for hearts and minds. Democratic voices do exist, and they should be encouraged. The states of the region are not failed states, and they are not completely closed societies. I have described before how Canada's foreign policy should be based on a knowledgeable, constructive, and engaged approach to the world. The Harper government's current approach is dominated by domestic political considerations and has been fitful and erratic. There is an alarming superficiality, as if the Middle East matters only to a few people. Canada, whose population increasingly reflects the whole world, deserves better, especially when we are dealing with issues that are so vital to peace.

For the longest time, Canadian foreign policy on the Middle East has been bedevilled by the notion that it must be either pro-Israel or pro-Arab. It should be both. Our positions should be founded on international law and universal values and principles. Our ties of emotion and friendship with many countries are deep, and we must be proud of our own history, of our diplomatic achievements and commitments to human rights and the rule of law. Canada diminishes itself when it is less than it could be, when it chooses to see the world through a narrow lens, when it treats every foreign issue as a partisan frolic instead of an opportunity for statesmanship. Our foreign policy needs to be clearly based on the need to reduce, and eventually eliminate, absolute poverty and disease; to prevent conflict and war and to be more effective in doing so; to end nuclear and non-nuclear weapons proliferation; and to bring countries together in an effective plan to fight climate change and environmental degradation.

We can only achieve these goals together. They require a world order firmly based on extending the rule of law. They will be assisted by a world commerce marked by ever freer and fairer trade with clear rules applied on an international basis. Above all they will require a Canada that is fully engaged. We are proudest as Canadians when we are setting the highest standards and seen to be applying them.

CHAPTER 8

THE TEARDROP IN THE INDIAN OCEAN:
Sri Lanka's Civil War

O n the evening of Tuesday June 9, 2009, I arrived at Bandaranaike International Airport, north of Colombo, the capital of Sri Lanka, on a flight from Delhi. I had taken this flight many times before, and I landed as always with a keen anticipation. As chairman of the Forum of Federations, an organization dedicated to sharing ideas of federal governance around the world, I had attended most of the negotiating sessions of the peace talks between the government and the Liberation Tigers of Tamil Eelam in 2002 and 2003, and had met many times with leaders of all political parties and senior officials of the LTTE. I had been back many times since. With my friends and colleagues at the Forum, I had travelled to every corner of the country.

The Forum's involvement with Sri Lanka began in 1999 when we were contacted by G.L. Peiris, the minister for constitutional affairs in the government of the day, asking if he could participate in the first international conference on federalism to be held at Mont Tremblant in the fall of that year. We were happy to invite him, and Peiris presented a paper to a workshop on the possibilities of federal-type solutions to the conflict between the Sinhalese government and the separatist Tamils. The Forum in turn was invited to attend two roundtables held in Locarno and Murten, Switzerland, organized by the Institute for Federal Studies in Neuchâtel just before and after the 2001 ceasefire.

After my election as a member of Parliament in 2008 and appointment as foreign affairs critic of the Liberal Party, I made regular interventions in the House of Commons about Sri Lanka as the civil war there took its final painful course. Once the conflict had reached its terrible end and the conquest of the LTTE had occurred, I wanted to go back to see for myself what had happened. I had successfully applied to the Sri Lankan High Commission for a visa and discussed my visit with the Sri Lankan high commissioner, with the Canadian high commissioner to Sri Lanka, and with officials from the Department of Foreign Affairs. I arranged to travel first to Kabul for a couple of days of discussions about the conflict there, and after a brief stop in Delhi I made my way once again to Sri Lanka. Or so I thought.

When I arrived at the immigration desk at Bandaranaike International Airport close to midnight in the company of two Canadian High Commission officials, I was told there was a problem. Trips back and forth to superiors by the desk officer eventually produced the statement that I was being refused entry "on the grounds of national intelligence." After spending more than twelve hours at the airport trying to find the reason for this decision, I was put on a plane to London.

The Foreign Office in Sri Lanka told me they had no objection to my visit, but the army and the defence secretary made the absurd assertion that I was an LTTE supporter and a "security risk." I was told I would be allowed in if I signed a statement with these words: "The statements attributed to me on the situation in Sri Lanka have been made without full awareness of the true facts of the ground situation, which I regret," but I was never told which "facts" or "statements" they were referring to. I refused to sign. To describe me as an LTTE supporter was a lie, pure and simple. Over the years, I had frequently criticized the Tamil Tigers, so much so that, ironically, my position became a matter of contention at the Liberal Party convention in 2006 where I competed unsuccessfully for the leadership of the party.

In 1839, Lord Durham described Canada as "two nations warring in the bosom of a single state." Those words are even more true of Sri Lanka. The rebellions in Lower and Upper Canada in 1837, which Durham had been sent by Britain to report on, were child's play compared to the life-and-death combat, the killings, torture, kidnappings, forced departures, rapes and catastrophic destruction that marked the Sri Lankan civil war. Unfortunately this war went largely unnoticed and unheralded in the West for its full thirty years.

A brief digression: what is "news" depends mostly on where journalists can go. The conflict between Israelis and Palestinians has been front and centre for sixty years. Every news outlet in the world has had access to seemingly every incidence of violence in Israel. What happens in Darfur, or eastern Congo, does not make the news every day, because it's not covered. It's all about where the cameras and the feeds are, where editors think their scant budgets for foreign reporting are best spent, and where reporters are allowed in. There were no live feeds from the camps in Sri Lanka where a quarter of a million refugees lived in dire conditions, and there was no live coverage of the final days of the civil war, in which the estimates of the number of civilian casualties ranges from none (the government of Sri Lanka) to twenty thousand (*Times* of London) to forty thousand (former UN employees).

Eight years ago there was a window on this terrible tragedy, a ceasefire brokered by Norway in the wake of unprecedented bombings in the southern part of the island and a dramatic toughening of world opinion after 9/11. That is when I attended the peace talks between the government and the LTTE, which took place not only in Sri Lanka but on also on neutral soil in Berlin, Bangkok, and Tokyo. The early discussions were marked by two features that are preconditions for an end to any conflict and the beginning of reconciliation: exhaustion and goodwill. An LTTE attack on the international airport in Colombo, repeated suicide attacks in the capital, a lack of military breakthroughs, and high casualties among soldiers had persuaded the government to seek a political solution. The LTTE side was also feeling hard pressed:

the 9/11 attacks had led to bans in the West of organizations in their midst that supported terrorism, and the fundraising that was the lifeline for the Tiger organization in the Vanni, their base of operations in northeastern Sri Lanka, had largely dried up.

The Norwegian government decided to put international conflict resolution at the heart of its foreign policy. Their determination to help end the Israel–Palestine conflict resulted in the 1993 Oslo Accords. They devoted considerable resources, from the prime minister's office on down, to winning the trust and confidence of both parties, including formal and informal lines of communication, financial support, and, in the case of Sri Lanka, medical support for Anton Balasingham, a senior LTTE official living in London who received a life-saving kidney transplant in an Oslo hospital.

What is the Sri Lankan conflict about? The majority Sinhalese population is Buddhist and traces its ancestry on the island back several thousands of years. The Sinhalese, who comprise close to 80 percent of the population, see themselves as a minority in the Indian subcontinent, and there is much in their culture that claims Sri Lanka as "their island." The channel between the Jaffna peninsula in the north of the island and the south Indian state of Tamil Nadu is only a few miles wide. The Jaffna Tamils of the north and others in the eastern part of Sri Lanka share their language and Hindu religion with the tens of millions of fellow Tamils in India. Enriching the ethnic mix of the island is the presence of European Sri Lankans (known as Burghers), Muslims – both Tamil- and Sinhala-speaking – Christians, and the "Hill Tamils" who were brought to work in the tea country northeast of Colombo by the British in the nineteenth century. When I met with the leadership of the Hill Tamils, I discovered they are a well-organized but deeply marginalized group – many still stateless and looked down upon by the Jaffna Tamils and seen as intruders by the Sinhalese.

Both Tamil and Sinhalese can trace their inheritance to civilizations of thousands of years standing, and link either their separateness or the essentially unitary character of the island to their view of the ancient past. Any observer who attempts to enter these historic conflicts will find himself locked in controversy.

The arrival of the British following the exploits of the East India Company on the continent led to a full-scale takeover by the middle of the nineteenth century. The island the British called Ceylon became yet another pink area on the wall maps that adorned every classroom in the British Empire, and district commissioners ruled the country until the British left the subcontinent in 1949. As in India (and in Canada a century earlier), British rule in Ceylon saw a number of commissions and reports on the evolution of government. The best known of these, the Donoughmore Commission, sat in 1926 and dealt with the question of self-government and relations between the Tamil and Sinhalese communities. The commission fell far short of recommending a full federal structure, something which would have been met with strong support from the minority Tamils and even stronger opposition from the Sinhalese majority. Instead, it argued that only by abolishing communal representation would it be possible for real unity to emerge.

As in so many former British colonies, issues of nation, ethnicity, tribe, identity, borders, and power sharing still remained to be resolved when the British wound down the empire and got out. Despite many Tamil entreaties, minority protections were not built into the first constitution of an independent Ceylon. At the time of independence, the Tamils were seen by the Sinhalese as a privileged group who had been favoured by the British, were more likely to be educated and to have a government job or a profession, and were more urban and simply better off. The ruling families who made up the Sinhalese elite realized that their hold on power could be assured by exploiting the populist resentment against both the British Empire and Tamil "privilege." During the

1950s the governments of Solomon Bandaranaike and John Kotelawala made the disastrous decision to impose Sinhala as the only official language and Buddhism as the only official religion of the country. They also limited access to universities and the civil service by the Tamil community, and refused to broaden the country's politics to allow the effective expression of Tamil opinion. Repeated attempts by moderate Tamils to win a degree of autonomy were met by half-hearted accommodations that were promptly ripped up as the stonewall of resistance among the Sinhalese became clear.

Sinhalese nationalism runs deep. It is closely linked to a Buddhist revival that drew on its strength for the anti-colonial struggle. The Buddhist leader of the early twentieth century, Anagarika Dharmapala, blamed the "decadence" of Ceylonese society on the failure of Buddhists to respond effectively to the presence of the foreigner, and made this sharp distinction between the Sinhalese majority and "the rest":

> Ethnologically the Sinhalese are a unique race. Inasmuch as they can boast they have no slave blood in them, and never were conquered by either the pagan Tamils or European vandals who for three centuries devastated the land, destroyed ancient temples, burnt valuable libraries and nearly annihilated the historic race . . . The Sinhalese are the sweet, tender, gentle Aryan children of an ancient historic race sacrificed at the altar of the whisky-drinking beef-eating, belly-god of heathenism. (DeVotta, 31)

Sir Ivor Jennings, a constitutional and education adviser in Sri Lanka, wrote in the 1950s about the undercurrent of opinion: "It is aggressively nationalist and aggressively Buddhist. In language policy it is anti-English; in religion it is anti-Christian; in foreign policy it is anti-western; and in economic policy it is both anti-capitalist and anti-socialist." (DeVotta, 61)

The language policy was not just anti-English, it was also anti-Tamil. All grievances have a narrative. Ceylon at independence was the most prosperous country in South Asia, with the highest rates of literacy and the highest income per capita. But this comparative advantage was short-lived. The Sinhalese nationalism that insisted on one language deliberately discriminated against both English as the language of colonialism and Tamil as the language of the minority. Socialist economic policies broadened the hold of state and private monopolies, discouraging foreign investment, yet Sri Lanka's small population could not sustain real growth in the economy. Members of the urban elite from all backgrounds began to leave the country for Europe and North America. There was an exodus of professional talent on a massive scale in the 1960s as the country turned increasingly inward and the economy stagnated.

The political pattern in the Sinhalese south began to take on a depressing shape. Ruling families and elites, locked in age-old rivalries, became almost indistinguishable in ideology: after making an attempt at national reconciliation, the "outs" would mobilize dissent, and the "ins" would be out. So it was that the Bandaranaikes, Jayawardenes and Wickremasinghes changed places, each marked by a discouraging turn to violence among their supporters. Solomon Bandaranaike was killed by an assassin in 1959, and was succeeded in office by his wife, Sirimavo. His rival Ranasinghe Premadasa was killed some years later after presiding over the bloodiest period to that point in Sri Lanka's modern history. He faced not only the Tamil uprising and war with the LTTE, but also an insurrection led by the group known as the JVP, a Marxist-Leninist party rooted among poor rural Sinhalese.

The outbreaks of violence in the 1950s and 1960s evolved into a far more violent struggle in the 1970s, when the Tamil Tigers emerged as the most powerful force in the north and east, and the JVP, fuelled by an extreme Sinhalese nationalism, adopted guerrilla tactics in its uprising in the centre and south.

Each in turn was met by brutal repression by a government set on its heels.

The Tigers, who insisted that they and they alone represented the Tamil people, were equally ruthless at killing their opponents in their own community. Their goal was a Tamil state in the north and northeast dominated by the Tigers alone. The notion of multi-party pluralism was anathema to them, and they gunned down their opponents and drove the Muslim minority in the north from their homes.

Two events in the 1980s marked the conflict in ways that are felt to this day. The pattern of repression became deeper. In the 1982 election, the presidential candidate Junius Jayawardene said, "We are contesting the election to win and at a time most favourable to us. We intend to demolish and completely destroy the opposition politically. After that I say to you, roll up the electoral map of Sri Lanka. You will not need it for another ten years" (DeVotta, 147).

Jayawardene won the election. Anti-Tamil riots in 1977, 1981, and 1983 were widespread, brutal, and condoned by the government. Tamil property and homes were burned and destroyed, and by the summer of 1983 the riots had become what can only be described as a pogrom. The government refused to impose a curfew, and Tamil prisoners were summarily executed by prison guards. As many as two thousand Tamils were murdered and seventy thousand were made homeless.

The exodus of Tamils began in earnest – to Tamil Nadu in India, to Europe, to Canada, and to the United States. The guerrilla conflict in the north intensified, and India became increasingly concerned, eventually deciding to intervene. They kept the Tamil Tiger leader Velupillai Prabhakaran locked up in a hotel room until he agreed to a ceasefire and a negotiated solution, or so the story goes. The Indo-Lanka Accord was born, and thousands of Indian troops were sent to the island to keep the peace in 1987.

There was no peace to keep. Prabhakaran had agreed to the limited autonomy imposed by the agreement, but neither he nor the Sri Lankan government were really prepared to compromise. Soon after the Tamil population greeted the Indian troops with garlands, the LTTE turned its guns on the Indian army, killing hundreds of soldiers. The Sri Lankan government insisted the Indians leave, which they did. The impact of the departure was more devastating than first thought possible.

The civil war resumed in earnest, and Prabhakaran then made the fateful decision to authorize the assassination of Indian Prime Minister Rajiv Gandhi. On May 21, 1991, a young woman with explosives strapped around her waist walked into a crowd during a political rally in Tamil Nadu. She touched Gandhi's feet in a gesture of respect and detonated the bomb. She, Gandhi, and at least fourteen others died. The assassination earned Prabhakaran the undying enmity of the Indian government. He was convicted in absentia of the murder and made an international pariah.

At this time, it was impossible to walk into a Tamil-owned convenience store in Toronto or London and not see a reverential picture of Prabhakaran. The flood of refugees in these years included many who actively supported the Tamil Tigers, and they quickly gained control of community organizations in the Tamil diaspora. Tamils abroad were expected to contribute to various funds used to support the war in Sri Lanka, as well as to provide help for friends and relatives in deep need back home. The persuasion used to "encourage" contributions was often heavy-handed, and anyone in the community who objected was told to stay quiet. People who refused to make payments were told, "We know where your relatives are." It was only after 2001 that governments in the Western world began to realize the risks of allowing these international networks free rein. During the ceasefire, the Canadian government decided to hold off listing the LTTE as a designated terrorist group, at the request of the government of Sri Lanka, which had taken a similar step. But when it became apparent in 2006 (and after a change of government in Canada) that the war was resuming, the LTTE was officially banned, and any donations to them were declared illegal.

Diaspora politics are complex and feel very urgent, and have always been so. Thomas D'Arcy McGee, the golden-voiced Irishman who came to Canada in 1857 and was almost immediately elected to political office, was assassinated by the Fenians in 1868 when he broke company with them and insisted that his loyalty to Canada trumped any association with the radical nationalism that was taking hold of the Irish community in North America. To the Fenians, McGee was a turncoat who used his support within the Irish community for his own purposes. To his fellow Canadians, McGee was the one speaker who brought poetry to the dream of Confederation. He was Canada's first modern martyr, and his funeral was attended by one hundred thousand mourners.

It's human nature to look for good guys and bad guys in a dispute. The Sri Lankan government insisted that the Tigers were thugs and terrorists and had to be eliminated. End of story. The Tigers and their supporters insisted that a corrupt and chauvinistic government intended to annihilate the Tamils, and that all the violence should be ascribed to the government. End of story.

The Tigers were indeed ruthless, and they never attempted to make the transition from a guerrilla army to a democratic force. Their sole tactic was violence, and they attacked both civilian and military targets. But as blunt and brutal as their actions were, they continued to receive support from Tamils in Sri Lanka and around the world, who believed them to be the only force that could make the Sinhalese listen.

During the peace talks it proved impossible to get the government to lay out an approach to federal governance (even without calling it that), and equally impossible to get the Tigers to commit to making the transition from guerrilla army to political force. While many leaders privately admitted that change was needed, they were not prepared to admit as much publicly to each other, and were certainly unable to persuade hardliners in their own camp. Anton Balasingham, for example, often spoke of the need for a "breakthrough," but I have no doubt that Prabhakaran, who was never at any negotiation table and who rarely met with foreigners, was never really willing to move off the demand for a separate state, Tamil Eelam, whose sovereignty, independence, and borders could not be compromised.

The Forum's work in Sri Lanka took up much of my time from the end of 2001 to the fall of 2003. The Norwegian effort at mediation was led by Erik Solheim, who had been intimately involved in the years-long process of winning the confidence of both sides and negotiating the ceasefire. The ceasefire itself was not universally accepted in Colombo, which was then in a tense time of "cohabitation" between long-time rivals, President Chandrika Bandaranaike Kumaratunga and Prime Minister Ranil Wickremasinghe. The prime minister's party at that time controlled Parliament, but the president, the daughter of one of the founders of the country, was determined to show her political command of the situation. Public opinion was initially supportive of the ceasefire and an end to the fighting, so she could not come out flat against the arrangement. But she expressed strong scepticism about the recognition and power being given to the LTTE.

My colleague throughout the discussions was David Cameron, a professor at the University of Toronto and a constitutional advisor to different governments, including the one I, as Premier of Ontario, led through the Charlottetown round of negotiations. David is one of nature's wise souls, and his work was outstanding. We were ably assisted by many at the Forum, in particular Priya Sood and Rupak Chattopadhyay, whose appetite for detail and hard work made the Forum's contributions even more valuable.

The ceasefire agreement (known as the CFA) relied for its monitoring on troops and officials from Scandinavian countries. The plan was to move immediately from the ceasefire talks to direct negotiations between the two sides. The CFA designated the LTTE as the sole legitimate spokesman for the Tamil people, which while perhaps necessary to get the agreement, presented the negotiations with a deep contradiction. There is a profound difference between military talks to end hostilities and the constitutional discussions to create a new political direction for an entire country. The LTTE had engaged in vicious fighting within the Tamil community to achieve its monopoly in the armed conflict, and it would not admit alternative Tamil views to be articulated during the constitutional discussions. The making of a constitution requires many voices to be heard. This was a concept completely foreign to the Tigers, and pointed to another central difficulty in the talks. The Sinhalese government representatives kept asking what precisely they were being asked to devolve to. Would a Tamil state be democratic, with multiple parties and many voices? The LTTE's track record was hardly encouraging, and when its targeted assassinations resumed after the end of negotiations the answer was clear. Their goal of a separate Tamil state ruled by military dictatorship was hardly an exercise in sustainable nation building, nor was it federalism in any sense of the term.

Anton Balasingham, a college teacher living in London, led the LTTE team of senior strategist Thambi Thamilchelvan, Vinayagamoorthy Muralitharan (whom we knew as Colonel Karuna) and New York immigration lawyer Visvanathan Rudrakumaran, known as Rudra. The group was joined by a Peace Secretariat headed up by Seevaratnam Puleedevan, whose non-stop jokes and laughter were an odd counterpoint to the overwhelming seriousness of the enterprise.

Cameron and I met frequently with this group, and other advisors, and came to know them well. We never met Prabhakaran, the LTTE leader who was clearly feared and just as clearly the person in complete control of Tiger strategy. Three members of that LTTE team at that time are now dead. Only Karuna, who defected to the other (government) side, and Rudrakumaran, who continues to practise law in New York, have survived.

Prabhakaran's power was enhanced by his mystique, which in turn was enhanced by his elusiveness. He was obviously an organizational genius, as well as a man of ruthless toughness. He managed, with a relatively small army, and a dedicated group around him, to wage a twenty-five-year war against the government of Sri Lanka. For two years in the 1980s, he kept the Indian army pinned down and inflicted hundreds of casualties on troops that had come to the island as peacekeepers. All his Tamil rivals he killed, drove into exile, or co-opted. The Vanni territory that was the heartland of the Tamil community in the north was well organized, with its own police force, and judicial, health, and education systems. It was sustained by massive donations from the Tamil diaspora, as well as by grants from some foreign governments, such as Norway. Prabhakaran's picture was everywhere – a short, pudgy man with a large moustache, wearing military fatigues. The personal devotion to the leader gave the movement an eerie, cultish quality.

He was, as I've said, an organizational genius, who made soldiers out of children and brainwashed young women into becoming Black Tigers – suicide bombers – who waded into crowded markets, police stations, the offices of cabinet ministers, and the Colombo Stock Exchange with bombs strapped around their waists. But he was hardly a master of strategy. At critical moments Prabhakaran demonstrated a fatal inflexibility. This was demonstrated when he rejected the Indo-Lanka Accord of 1987, a deal for partial autonomy that had strong Indian support, and again with the decision to assassinate Rajiv Gandhi. That decision, as time would tell, sealed his fate and, because of the extraordinary control he exercised over the Tiger organization, effectively ended any hope of a political solution.

I found working on this project to be at once a fascinating and deeply frustrating experience. G.L. Peiris, our main government interlocutor, was a decent man, a scholar who seemed genuinely committed to reaching an understanding. Throughout the negotiations, the government side was not so much intransigent as vague, and in the end unable to put forward any proposal that might have broken the logjam. This failure was, as we have seen, a successor to any number of efforts over the past fifty years to go beyond the majoritarian centralism that had become such an ingrained part of Sinhalese political culture.

Dealing with the Tamil Tiger side was also difficult, but in a different way. We met several times alone with Anton Balasingham, both in London and in the Vanni. He was thoughtful and good humoured but inscrutable. We never learned what his real bottom line was. For him, the federal idea was just that, a concept whose varied institutional forms made it seem infinitely malleable and perhaps not relevant. The struggle on both sides was about nation building and not province making or country rebuilding.

Our meetings in the Vanni had their moments. A few scenes will always stand out in my mind. We stayed in a hotel guesthouse called Tankview – it overlooked a reservoir where in the early morning men and women, boys and girls, washed very discreetly, wearing bathing suits and saris – a very peaceful scene. Breakfast was some kind of fish on toast, the inevitable small banana, and tea of course – very strong. We were served at our table in the main dining hall by very young men wearing white shirts, black pants, and no shoes. They had no English at all, just big smiles. Education is deeply treasured by the Tamils, and even late at night we could see children studying by candlelight. The schools were in the open air, but compulsory and well attended by both girls and boys.

My favourite encounter was with a retired international civil servant from the World Bank whose nom de guerre was Kanulsavan. When we met in March of 2003, he started talking at length about Jane Austen and the Brontë sisters, then turned his attention to Pierre Trudeau and what he thought was Canada's failure to realize its true potential as an international player. Then he turned to me and asked where I had gone to university. I said, "Toronto, and a time at Oxford." "Which college?" "Balliol." He smiled. "Shake hands with another Balliol man." We then chatted about teachers, favourite pubs, and a world that seemed far away.

I have told the story of this incongruous meeting many times, but it now has a poignant ending. I never heard again from Kanulsavan, until the war was in its final torturous days in the spring of 2009, when the leadership of the LTTE had been pushed out of the Vanni into an enclosed space near the village of Mullaitivu on the northeast coast. Coming home late one night in Toronto I found an envelope on my doorstep with a handwritten note from Kanulsavan. He was writing to ask me to intervene, saying a ceasefire was essential, that the killing had to stop, that conditions were terrible, and they were running out of food and water. He said he had no regrets about having left Washington for the "struggle," and that all the Tamils were seeking was "justice." He wished me and my family well and ended with the Latin words *floreat domus* (may the house flourish). This is the motto of Balliol College. The British Empire has a strange resonance.

Thanks to the good offices of Valerie Raymond, Canada's high commissioner to Sri Lanka, Cameron and I had good access and discussions with several ambassadors, high commissioners, and think tank members in Colombo. Our access to the LTTE and ability to travel throughout the country, including the Vanni, which few other foreigners had, put us in a good position to share impressions and views with them. One particularly blunt exchange with the Indian high commissioner and the American ambassador made it clear that, while they were not prepared to say anything publicly, the lack of progress was leading them to believe that the LTTE might simply be using the talks to build up strength for another military confrontation. In the event of another military conflict, they said, there would be co-operation between their countries, and the government of Sri Lanka would not be on its own. It was a sobering discussion, as a result of which Cameron and I made one last trip to the Vanni and to talk with Thamilchelvan, Prabhakaran's second in command in the region. It was a long discussion, but ultimately fruitless. Thamilchelvan never went beyond reciting yet again the grievances and the historic claims of the Tamil people. He could not or would not hear what we had to say. The ideology of the struggle completely trumped any assessment of what was actually happening, and new information could not get past the barrier of zealotry.

Cameron and I grew increasingly frustrated with the slowness of the discussions, and with their lack of traction. We drew up a memorandum that we shared in the late spring of 2003 with G.L. Peiris, and we shared its main points with Anton Balasingham as well. In it, we pointed out that while each session of the peace talks had been marked by civility and modest progress, the parties were not engaged in what we would call bargaining. Yes, they had agreed to allow UNICEF to review allegations that the LTTE was recruiting children and had asked Ian Martin, who had worked earlier with the United Nations on human rights issues in East Timor, Ethiopia, and Rwanda, to look at human rights more broadly. Yes, they had agreed in Oslo six months before to consider federalism as the framework for a longer-term solution. But that was it.

In any successful negotiation each party has a clear sense of its bottom line, even if this is not communicated to the other side or to other interlocutors. Then each side knows what would make it walk away from negotiations and what the consequences of doing that will likely be. Both sides have to constantly appraise the relative balance of forces, and consider the prospect of failure, and what its next steps would be. Without all that in mind, the bargaining and leverage that each side brings to the discussion are considerably weaker.

From our first encounter with the negotiations in Sri Lanka, we identified two major obstacles to the prospect that the discussion would result in an accord. The first was the nature of the

LTTE. It was a guerrilla army, not the military wing of a well-defined political movement. It was not hard to see that the transition to any kind of federalism could not possibly be successful without the LTTE itself becoming transformed. This could not happen overnight, but every effort would be made to help make it happen. It was still not clear what the acceptance of the federalism framework by the LTTE at Oslo in December 2002 really meant. The parties needed to make more progress in defining confidence-building measures that would irrevocably solidify peace, but that never happened.

The second obstacle was the difficult political situation in the south resulting from the rivalry between Prime Minister Wickremasinghe and President Kumaratunga. The fact that there was no supra-political understanding between them about constitutional change beyond the ceasefire made it impossible for the government to lay out a clear road map for peace. Yet just such a broad strategy was necessary to convince the LTTE that the political community in the south was fully committed to a peaceful resolution of the conflict, on a basis that would meet the needs of the Tamil community for a considerable degree of self-government and autonomy.

The memo was politely received and the talks meandered on, Then, in April 2003, the LTTE said the talks were suspended. The Norwegians tried to get them back to the table, but to no avail. They exchanged pieces of paper, but the divisions were too fundamental. Direct discussions between the two sides were over.

At a meeting in Oslo in December 2002, the two sides had agreed to explore federalism as the basis for a long-term solution, but neither side had been serious about what that would entail. For the government, it would have meant shifting away from a deep-seated centralism, recognizing the distinctiveness of the Tamil community, and agreeing on its geographical borders and constitutional powers. While the Wickremasinghe government might have been prepared to do that, the momentum for such a major shift quickly waned in the face of stiff resistance from the official opposition, the army, and the Sinhalese community. The government's eventual proposals for devolution were absurdly modest and nowhere near close to meeting the need for self-rule and shared rule, which, we kept pointing out, were what the federal idea was all about.

The LTTE was no better. While their negotiators travelled widely across Europe in 2003, a group of academics and lawyers were advising them that the claim for real sovereignty was strong in international law, that the dream of a separate Tamil Eelam should never be abandoned, and that the government of Sri Lanka would never get serious about heading in the right direction. In October that year, the LTTE produced its own constitutional proposal, which called for an interim authority in the north completely controlled by the LTTE. It was rejected by the government, of course, after alarming hardliners in the south.

The two sides were proverbial ships passing in the night, far apart and never signalling mutual recognition.

In 2004 the LTTE suffered a major body blow. At all our earlier discussions with the rebels, the tough, silent military leader Colonel Karuna had been present. He was from the east of the country, and was commander of the territory around Trincomalee and Batticaloa.

Notwithstanding protestations of unity between Tamils in the north and the east, there were real tensions, with easterners feeling they were taking the brunt of the battle and getting little relief. Then, in March, Karuna split from the LTTE, inflicting heavy military losses on the organization before capitulating and fleeing the country. He has since returned to Sri Lanka and is now a minister in the current government.

There was a brief hope that the horrific impact of the tsunami at the end of 2004 would bring the government and the LTTE back to the table. The entire coastal area of the east and south was swamped by a massive tidal wave, killing tens of thousands, Tamil and Sinhalese alike. Whole seaside villages disappeared in the devastation. More than thirty thousand lives were lost, more than had died during the civil conflict. The international community tried to encourage both sides to see the disaster as an opportunity for unprecedented co-operation. It was not to be. Each side insisted on complete autonomy. The government of Sri Lanka refused to direct any funds to any institutions controlled by the LTTE. The LTTE refused to allow any outside agencies to distribute relief in their territory.

The result was more hardship and even more loss of life. Heavily mined areas (land mines were planted in the thousands by both sides throughout the north and east) were flooded, which meant that the mines moved from known locations, maiming people indiscriminately. Access to food and shelter was limited, and while international disaster relief agencies complained about what was happening, nothing was done.

From 2005 onward, breaches of the ceasefire became more numerous. Foreign Minister Lakshman Kadirgamar became increasingly disturbed by the growing violence and the presence of the LTTE in sleeper cells in Colombo. In our last conversation in the spring of 2005, he reminded me that Westerners did not understand the threat, declaring, "I could be killed getting out of my swimming pool." It was an eerie premonition. That is exactly how he died, shot by a sniper's bullet from a window of a nearby house that August. Every Tamil working for the government was now a target. The next friend to die was Kethesh Loganathan, whom David Cameron and I had come to know during our time in Sri Lanka. He had given us valuable advice. The last time we met he asked us to help a friend, a Tamil dissident whose life was being threatened by the LTTE and who was able to flee to safety.

Kethesh himself was not so lucky. He took a job with the Sri Lankan government's Peace Secretariat, and late one evening in the spring of 2006 responded to a knock at his door. He was gunned down by an LTTE assassin in front of his wife and children. He had joined a long line of Tamil dissidents who did not share the LTTE ideology. Some were in opposition to the government, like Neelan Tiruchelvam, one of the most formidable advocates of liberal federalism in modern Sri Lanka. By 2006, Sri Lanka had become a killing field of violence and destruction. Military jets bombed orphanages, villages, and hospitals; soldiers killed soldiers; and political leaders were gunned down in their homes and in their offices. Children were killed in school buses; teenagers were recruited as suicide bombers. The world watched and wrung its hands.

The parties in Sri Lanka had become addicted to violence. The outside world had accepted the addiction and fed the habit. The arms trade supplied both sides – illicitly in the case of the LTTE, entirely legally in the case of the Sri Lankan government. As the ambassadors had promised in that discussion in 2003, when a Sri Lankan government was ready to "finish the job," it would do so with the full complicity of its neighbour, India, and the rest of the world.

The election in November 2005 of a new president, Mahinda Rajapaksa, had put the Sri Lankan government on a decidedly different course. I had occasion to meet Rajapaksa in the company of Foreign Minister Kadirgamar. He was generally underestimated by the international community, and not seen as a particularly sophisticated figure. The smart money was that Ranil Wickremasinghe would prevail in the election, and he lost only because Prabhakaran ordered the Tamil community to abstain from voting, on the grounds that they had no interest in which Sinhalese would win. Another in a long line of blunders by the supreme tactician.

President Rajapaksa proved himself a wily populist in office, quickly calculating that the continual breaches of the ceasefire by the LTTE had eroded the public's enthusiasm for peace at any price. The ceasefire agreement was formally abandoned by the government in January 2008. Despite many promises that it was not simply seeking a military solution, it was readily apparent that this was indeed the government's firm intention.

The Sri Lankan military was well armed and equipped with the latest in technology. Its planes bombed heavily from the air. The casual use of a cellphone by Thamilchelvan led to a targeted fatal attack in Killinochi.

Anton Balasingham, who had been chief negotiator and our main interlocutor during the negotiations, died in London in December 2006. His funeral was attended by tens of thousands. Bala remained to me a man of mystery, agreeing to things he could not really deliver, falling back on tried and true rhetorical formulas, but unfailingly courteous and eloquent. His ill health, among other things, had prevented him from taking a more vigorous role. It is said he was criticized heavily by Prabhakaran for having agreed to "explore federalism" in 2002. I had the sense that he understood even in 2002 that the tactic of belligerence was not achieving the LTTE's ends, and realized that the dream of a Tamil Eelam won by violent conflict was impossible.

The LTTE badly miscalculated both its strength and what the international community could or would do to intervene. The one government that could possibly help, India, was not prepared to do anything. It had been too badly burned by its intervention in the 1980s, and the assassination of Gandhi had made the LTTE an enemy.

The Sri Lankan government positioned its military campaign as part of the "war on terror." It received support from China, Pakistan, and Iran, and made it clear to Western donors, who had been so supportive of the peace process, that their comments on peace, human rights, and dialogue were no longer appreciated, and that if they pushed the issue, they would have even less influence.

The Bush administration and the Harper government were not about to discourage an all-out assault on the LTTE. Both countries had closed loopholes in their ban on any financial assistance from the Tamil diaspora. Meanwhile, the Sri Lankan military slowly tightened the knot around the Tamils in the north. As the international media were largely shut out of the region by the army, there were few witnesses to report on the devastation of a community.

The final assault on the LTTE in early 2009 was brutal. The LTTE kept tight control of civilian Tamils who had nowhere to go, nowhere to hide, as the Sri Lankan army pushed its forces northeast through the Vanni to the ocean. Eyewitness reports have all been dismissed by the Sri Lankan government as the work of "LTTE operatives" and "special pleaders," but the sheer weight of the evidence provided by representatives of the Red Cross and others leaves little doubt that tens of thousands died in those last few months. We will never know how many. The Sri Lankan government expelled not only journalists but also UN officials, and has not allowed any kind of objective assessment of exactly what happened. The UN Human Rights Council, in a decision that indicates how deeply biased and politicized a body it is, declined to review what took place, unlike its speedy intervention after the Israeli 2009 campaign against Gaza, in which thirteen hundred people lost their lives.

What we do know is that the entire LTTE leadership, including Prabhakaran, were killed. News of his death and pictures of his body were still not enough to convince true believers, but rational people quickly accepted that, with his death, the fight was over. There were frantic phone calls, similar to the letter I received, begging for intervention, but as long as Prabhakaran was alive, full-scale surrender was out of the question, and only a surrender would have stopped a massacre. In the last days in May 2009 two senior officials whom I knew well, Puleedevan and Nadesan, and their families, approached government troops waving a white flag. They were mowed down. We also know that countless civilians must have been killed, as the shelling and bombardment of the beach at Mullaitivu continued relentlessly for weeks on end, and there was precious little chance for anyone to escape the war zone. We also know the government refused countless entreaties to allow for a humanitarian ceasefire that would have permitted . surrender and allowed some international protection for the LTTE leaders. The government of Sri Lanka wanted to wipe them out.

There were approximately three hundred thousand refugees from the conflict, and they remained huddled in camps for months. UN Secretary-General Ban Ki-moon was one of the few outsiders allowed to see the camps in the early days. He said, "I have travelled round the world and visited similar places, but these are by far the most appalling scenes I have seen." *New York Times* reporter Lydia Polgreen wrote in August that severe rains "sent rivers of muck cascading between tightly packed rows of flimsy shelters, overflowed latrines and sent hundreds of families scurrying for higher ground." Lakhdar Brahimi and Edward Mortimer, of the Sri Lanka Campaign for Peace and Justice, wrote in September 2009: "People who question [the deaths] inside Sri Lanka are accused of being traitors in the pay of 'the LTTE diaspora,' while outsiders are accused of using humanitarian concerns as an excuse for neo-imperialist intervention. Sri Lankan journalists who criticized the government have been arrested, beaten, jailed, and, in some cases, murdered. Some foreign journalists and UN officials have been kicked out; Human Rights Watch and Amnesty International are not allowed in."

President Rajapaksa's first post-victory visit abroad was to Burma, where the generals asked his advice on how to deal with the insurgency on the Thai frontier – ethnic groups that have been fighting for years for recognition of their distinct status. The military regime in Burma is one of the most repressive in the world.

My own most recent effort to get to Sri Lanka in June 2009 ended at the Colombo Airport.

My conclusion was that if this was how they treated me, imagine how they treated people who couldn't speak out or make public statements. The Sri Lankan government was afraid of dialogue, afraid of discussion, afraid of engagement.

What lessons are we to draw from the Sri Lankan conflict? Something deep in the culture of antagonism that pervades modern Sri Lanka made it impossible for a peace process leading toward genuine reconciliation to be accepted. It is often easy for outsiders to see "a zone of agreement" – just as we think we can in the Middle East and other parts of the world. But we must not make the mistake of assuming that everyone thinks like us.

The hold of religious zealotry and political extremism in Sri Lanka was strong and depressingly persistent. The stubbornness of the Sinhalese majority created the conditions for a turn to violence by the Tamil minority in the 1970s, and a militant cult of personality and exclusionary nationalism on the part of the LTTE set the country on a course of conflict that proved irreversible. The elimination of the voices of moderation, the assassination of Rajiv Gandhi, the split with Karuna, the decision to seek a military victory after the collapse of the ceasefire, the rejection of any further advice from the international community: these decisions by the LTTE proved to be disastrous for it and for the entire Tamil community in whose name the LTTE was allegedly fighting. The degeneration of a militant cadre into a death cult is not unique to Sri Lanka, but partly explains why the end was so destructive.

Prabhakaran's decision to order the assassination of Rajiv Gandhi summed up his ruthlessness and fatal hubris. As Talleyrand might have said, it was worse than wrong, it was stupid. Gandhi's death earned Prabhakaran the eternal enmity of the Indian government, particularly the Congress Party government. It led to his death sentence in absentia and his status as an international criminal. It meant that he could not lead a movement from armed struggle to sincere political negotiation. A high-ranking Indian diplomat told me emphatically that whatever political course was charted, "Prabhakaran is a dead man. Is that understood?" Prabhakaran would have known this. He could never become a Nelson Mandela or even a Yasser Arafat. His endgame was martyrdom. A very different man might have separated himself from the movement in order to save it. Prabhakaran did no such thing – he used the personality cult right to the bitter end, leading thousands of women, men and children to the slaughter with him.

Sri Lanka has now fallen into a dangerous authoritarianism with the Rajapaksa brothers and their government fully in control. They can point to elections as the source of their legitimacy, but the evidence of a politicized judiciary, widespread corruption, and a deeply repressed and partisan media is a troubling reflection of a political agenda that is leaning far away from the respect for rights and diversity that lies at the heart of the democratic idea. The dilemma has been put forcefully by Neil DeVotta: "Sri Lanka represents a classic case of how a state may eschew constitutional liberalism, which incorporates the rule of law, limited government, free and fair elections, impartial interactions with all ethnic groups, and the freedom of assembly, speech, and religion, and yet appear to be a functioning democracy . . . the ethnic particularism and outbidding that had dominated the country's politics . . . had undermined democratic consolidation" (145).

This is the terrible irony today. President Rajapaksa won a massive majority in the presidential election in 2010, defeating General Sarath Fonseka, who had led the government forces to victory. He then promptly threw Fonseka in jail. Opinion is behind him. There are courts that sit, judges that go to work every day, and newspapers written and sold throughout the country, but none of them dare challenge the government. Anyone who does is threatened, harassed, and told they are not welcome. Dozens of journalists have been killed, and many more have left the country. Democracy is much more than who can win an election. It is how a country is governed between elections. It is government by discussion, not by diktat and decree.

Sri Lanka was at war for half a century, and the end of the war has not reduced the demand for more money and more arms. Instead, military spending and related racketeering have sky-rocketed. Defence now accounts for over a fifth of all government spending and shows no signs of going down. This militarization has far-reaching implications for democracy. But while the West worries, no one is prepared to do anything about it. Sri Lanka's closest allies – China, Pakistan, Burma, and Iran – are not going to criticize the government for its authoritarian ways or its democratic deficit. The decision by the International Monetary Fund in 2009 to authorize US $2.6 billion in credit to Sri Lanka – with Canada's support but abstentions from many Western governments – plus Sri Lanka's success at convincing the United Nations Human Rights Council that there was no merit in an international review of its conduct of the war, is a clear sign that severe repression can take place with impunity.

In 2009, the Worldwide Press Freedom Index placed Sri Lanka between the United Arab Emirates and Bahrain. Today it would be even lower. Transparency International consistently reports corruption at the highest echelons of both the executive and legislative levels of government. A Sri Lanka where mutual respect, some autonomy for Tamils, shared governance, and an abandonment of extremist ideologies are all possible is, tragically, just a dream for now.

Becoming involved in the politics of Sri Lanka has affected me deeply. I could see from the outset that peace and reconciliation were an unlikely result, but the extent of the failure, and the full dimensions of the violence involved have forced me to recognize the difficulty of "sharing experiences." The resolution of deep conflicts isn't a matter of good ideas beating bad ones. It requires far more consistent international pressure, a willingness to punish recalcitrant bad behaviour on both sides, and awareness amongst the parties that the costs of a conflict far outweigh the price of compromise. By the time of the ceasefire in 2001, the suspicion between the parties was so deep and so entrenched that bridging the gap would have taken extraordinary acts of leadership on both sides as well as real engagement from the outside world. But all those who might have been able to steer the talks toward a new workable constitution for the country had been silenced.

If we compare the situation in Sri Lanka to, say, Northern Ireland or South Africa, or even Canada, we begin to understand what is missing. A constitution is not just a piece of paper, crafted after a few weeks of tough discussion. It doesn't flow from rhetoric about democracy and understanding. The real constitution of any country depends on its political culture and institutions, and while those two things are not immutable, they have to be recognized for the forces they represent.

Successful constitutional change requires that the political leaders of the country set aside partisan differences in the understanding that building the framework of the country is an act of statesmanship that goes beyond day-to-day politics. In Northern Ireland it meant that Ian Paisley of the Democratic Unionist Party and Gerry Adams of Sinn Féin had to shake hands. In South Africa, it meant that Nelson Mandela and National Party leader Frederik de Klerk had to come to terms. In Canada, the partisanship and ethnic bickering that marked the young colonies for decades had to be set aside for the greater good at the Charlottetown meetings in 1867, just to get the framework right. Every colonial delegation had leaders of every party present, and that made all the difference.

That didn't happen in Sri Lanka. The two main political parties in the south were at each other's throats the whole time of the ceasefire, which left the LTTE unsure whether any agreement reached could be sustained. The LTTE's artificial status as the sole representative of the Tamils meant that no alternative voices were heard at the table. Other Tamil parties and views were stifled, and the Muslims were on the margins, trying to get to the table. Partisan politics never left the room. But it has to for sound constitutional change to happen.

The fundamental values of a country have to be shared, or at least shared sufficiently so that it can survive changes in government and political leadership. For Thomas Hobbes this might be simply a matter of superior firepower ending debate. But that isn't enough, there has to be a moral basis to the consensus. The Sri Lankan majority insists that there is and that if only troublesome agitators and meddlesome outsiders would leave the game everything would be all right. But reconciliation entails accepting the legitimacy of the other, their religion, their language, their personality. The genius of federalism is that it allows institutions to develop in a country that expresses this acceptance of diversity and difference. As Thomas D'Arcy McGee put it so eloquently in 1865, "It [federalism] is a principle that has produced a wise and true spirit of statesmanship in all countries in which it has ever been applied . . . It is a principle eminently favourable to liberty, because local affairs are left to be dealt with by local bodies, and cannot be interfered with by those who have no local interest in them, while matters of a general character are left exclusively to a General Government."

The Sinhalese majority saw it very differently. They needed the ceasefire in 2001 because the level of violence was threatening the economy, and the entire country felt at risk. But the federal idea, although widely discussed, was never accepted or even properly understood. It was always seen as a foreign idea, and the fact that the LTTE had abandoned the notion of shared sovereignty gave the Sinhalese community the opportunity to say that it was pointless to discuss a federal solution. In their view, federalism was only a halfway house to the breakup of the country.

This is not an argument to be dismissed out of hand. The American Civil War was fought over the integrity of the union, and there are federations that have broken up. But there are also many countries, like Canada, that have stayed together precisely because they are federations, and there are many others that are exploring the federal option.

Sri Lanka is not a failed state but it is now a deeply repressive one, and it faces some clear choices in the years ahead. There is much talk of a closer relationship between all the countries of the Indian subcontinent, of free trade zones, of sharing experience on governance and so on. Now that the LTTE has been defeated, India will become more engaged, and will continue to have concerns about both stability and the recognition of diversity by its smaller neighbour. Sri Lanka will try to encourage China, Pakistan, and even Iran to remain interested in the development of the country (it is unlikely they will be much interested in issues of governance and democracy), but India, if it chooses, can play a central role.

Meanwhile, monitoring by international institutions, public, private, and non-governmental, will continue. Democracy and human rights are not just the idle dreams of Western radicals; they speak to the aspirations of ordinary Sri Lankans in both communities, which I have seen and heard expressed. The institutions that are necessary to nurture and express these aspirations do not yet exist, but in the long term the government cannot avoid pressure from both domestic and international communities. Nor can President Rajapaksa avoid the reality that he remains the leader of an ethnically diverse country, and that oppression can work for a time but it cannot work forever.

CHAPTER 9

CANADA:

Who We Are and Why It Matters

Michael Kinsley, the editor of the *New Republic*, once ran a contest for the most boring headline, and the winner was "Worthwhile Canadian Initiative," from a story in the *New York Times*. Few outside its borders pay attention to Canada, in good part because we are a "peaceable kingdom." War and conflict are interesting and give rise to international scrutiny. Peaceable countries are dull.

And yet Canada has known great conflict. The encounter between settlers and aboriginal people was neither peaceful nor easy. Its scars are still visible today. Two empires fought on our land, and kept an uneasy truce. Today Canada is in the world and the world is in Canada. We are not an ideal showcase, but there is much in what we have learned from our history that makes our experience matter. As the world gets more connected and attempts to reconcile conflicting concepts of war, peace, international law and sovereignty continue, our example becomes increasingly relevant.

The Forum of Federations began in 1997 as a centre for dialogue and research where federal countries could bring their experiences to a discussion of what works and doesn't work in the current federal arrangements. We were soon contacted by representatives of a great many countries that weren't federal at all. We heard from countries that were experiencing conflicts and countries with a unitary constitutional structure that wasn't working. Some gurus had argued world history came to an end when the Berlin Wall was torn down. We found that history was really just beginning.

No two federations are alike. Canada is a country where European settlers met an indigenous population, and the country's origins were ridden with colonialism, racism, disease, and conflict. It is only recently (2008) that we've established a Commission on Truth and Reconciliation, in an attempt to come to grips with the consequences of the colonial subjugation of First Nations people.

Canada's aboriginal population is now close to one million and it is growing at a rapid rate, double that of the rest of Canada. The birth rate is almost exactly that of the Third World. All statistics, including life expectancy, family outcomes, health, and income distribution are significantly worse for aboriginals than they are for the rest of the population. On northern reserves, more than half the population is under the age of twenty-five, and most families are living in quite dire conditions and facing difficult social problems.

As is happening in Australia, New Zealand, and the United States, and indeed all across Latin America, Canada's native population is moving off traditional lands to the city. This trend poses a significant challenge for Canadians, one that most have largely ignored. When the aboriginal population lived far from urban centres, they were outside the orbit of mass attention. Now we face them close up, and their demands and grievances must be heard and addressed.

If a federal constitution for Canada had not been adopted in 1867, the country simply would not exist. Federalism shatters the myth of sovereignty, the notion that an organized monopoly of power in a central structure and the nation state necessarily go together. Federalism is about self-rule and shared rule. It sanctions autonomy and requires co-operation. It constitutes the foundation of every institution and structure in Canada.

This is not to say Canada's constitution was an easy compromise. Federalism, like marriage, does not promise a world without conflict. And from all the crises the country has weathered so far, a pattern has emerged: national parties that have based their beliefs and structures firmly behind the notion that there is a Canadian identity that transcends language, race, religion, colour, and sectarianism of any kind succeed. These parties are critical institutions of accommodation, without which the country would not be able to stay together.

Of course, those advocating the secession of Quebec would never accept the notion that in federalism Canada has found a magic formula. Their narrative points to long and systematic discrimination against the French majority in Quebec and the French minority elsewhere, the residue of imperial and triumphalist thinking that has been a continuing factor in the life of English Canada. They insist that Quebec being itself can only happen if Quebec is a nation state or, as a former premier of Quebec once put it, "a normal country."

The Parti Québécois and the Bloc Québécois continue to stand for the proposition that Quebec should separate from the rest of the country, and Canada has seen two difficult referenda in Quebec where the Quebec government sought a mandate from the people to negotiate separation. The first was defeated handily; the second came very close to passing. There has been a flurry of legal cases and legislation attempting to set the ground rules for future referenda, if such is the political will of an elected government.

Many times during discussions with representatives from other countries about their internal challenges, I have heard Quebec separatism cited as a cause for concern and a defect in our system, as if frank difference and thoughtful jurisprudence were signs of weakness. But far better this than civil war, or the pretence that one's country has no divisions.

The recognition of the distinctiveness of "the other" in Canada did not come easily or evolve automatically. It took the Quiet Revolution in Quebec, with its persistent demands for more autonomy and greater recognition, to force change in the rest of the country. The Royal Commission on Bilingualism and Biculturalism in the 1960s documented the extent of the underlying crisis. Federal institutions were almost exclusively English. French Canadians had great difficulty receiving services in their own language. The wall of discrimination that many Quebeckers faced inside and outside their own province had created a profound sense of alienation and frustration. Real and determined change was needed, change that was not always popular or easily accepted, to strengthen the argument that sharing a country did not mean assimilation, and that there was sufficient vitality in the federation to allow for autonomy and co-operation to co-exist. Official language laws, changes in hiring and recruitment at the national level, a willingness to live with even deeper changes in legislation in Quebec itself, plus a steady shift in patterns of opportunity in employment and the economy, have resulted in the atrophy of the discrimination and prejudice that so preoccupied the Royal Commission fifty years ago.

The seemingly endless round of constitutional discussions of the past half a century led to the patriation of the Constitution and the entrenchment of a Charter of Rights and Freedoms in 1982. While the Supreme Court of Canada had issued decisions that confirmed a common-law right to freedom of speech and assembly and due process, Canadian jurisprudence on the whole had not distinguished itself with a clear defence of the rights of the citizen. In its first twenty-five years, the Charter has played an almost iconic role in forcing judges and legislatures to engage in a real debate about rights and responsibilities, about aboriginal issues, about identity, about the rights of the accused and the rights of those knocking on Canada's doors to get in. Moreover, the Charter has played a critical role in helping to forge a stronger sense of a Canadian identity that is not based on ethnicity or religion or language, but rather on a set of common values that are secular and civil, and that transcend, in the best of times, our other powerful differences.

The Canadian Supreme Court has ruled that immigrants applying for landed status are entitled to due process; that evidence gathered improperly can't be used to convict an accused; that collective bargaining is a right that provincial governments can't ignore; that any province has the right to decide its future and the obligation to ask a clear question and expect a determined and civil negotiation about that future; that a French-language hospital in Ontario could not be closed and treated as if this were just an administrative act by the province without consequences for rights; that French-language communities have the right to their own school boards; that gays and lesbians cannot be discriminated against and have the right to marry; and that aboriginal people have rights that are protected by the treaties they and we have signed.

Some have accused the courts of being too activist, but in fact, they have simply accepted their responsibilities once Parliament and the provinces decided that Canada needed a charter. There were those who warned in 1980 that the consequence of an entrenched charter would be a court that takes power away from Parliament and the provincial legislatures. That has proven partly true, but this is also in good measure because legislatures and parliaments have not always been sensitive to the rights and freedoms of groups and individuals. Courts can and do resist the enthusiasm of majorities. That is what living in a constitutional democracy is all about.

At several moments in Canadian history, the country made decisions to encourage newcomers to come here. We opened the doors for Loyalists during and after the American Revolution, for the veterans of the Napoleonic Wars, and for the victims of the Irish Famine. At the beginning of the twentieth century, the West was opened to newcomers from beyond France and the British Isles to come and make the country grow. Ukrainians, Russians, Poles, and Eastern Europeans arrived by the boatload and become a vibrant new element of our culture and identity. The postwar period saw the country open once again to large European migrations, first of the homeless, and then of economic refugees from Mediterranean countries. In the 1960s the doors were opened wider, and Canada became equally accessible to people in all parts of the world. Each year, Canada hosts on average six migrants per one thousand people, a figure nearly double that of the United States and almost five times that of Switzerland. Almost one-fifth of Canada's population is foreign born.

In the 1960s Canada abandoned the quota system, which favoured immigrants from European countries, for a points system that meant immigrants could come from anywhere depending on their level of education and on the level of demand for their skills. It was a revolutionary decision, made in the interest of fairness. Canada went remarkably quickly from being a multicultural country to being multinational and multiracial. It has vast Chinese, Caribbean, and Sikh communities, and a diverse and growing Muslim population from many different countries. Today there are mosques, temples, synagogues, and churches in the same neighbourhood and sometimes on the same street.

Issues of identity, race, affirmative action, policing, opportunity, conflict resolution, and crime are neither purely local nor international. When some people complain that "these people" bring their disputes with them to Canada they are ignoring that this has been a Canadian habit since the beginning. There is not a conflict in the world to which this country is immune. The world is not just "out there," it is also "in here."

The cliché is that America is a melting pot and Canada is a mosaic. The reality is that in North America, indeed in any society, there is and will always be pressure to be both. Canada allows immigrants and their descendants to be themselves within Canadian society. It encourages the retention of heritage languages and cultures. This means the creation of a common citizenship is at times difficult, although it is undeniably necessary. The simple fact is that individual identity and a commitment to the common good are both required.

The diversity of Canadian society, the jagged and uneven quality of our mosaic, has meant that pragmatism and compromise have been Canada's mainstays. The America of Paine and Jefferson was all about the mission of an exceptional country that could renew itself and be "born again," but it is difficult to find a similar manifesto in Canada. "Peace, order, and good government" is a different call to action from "life, liberty and the pursuit of happiness," let alone "liberty, equality, and fraternity." Canadian experience has taught that ideological enthusiasm is best avoided, and that a principled engagement with the world requires more listening and less preaching.

In response to the *New Republic* competition, CBC *Morningside* host Peter Gzowski asked listeners some years ago for the Canadian equivalent to the phrase "as American as apple pie." The winner was "as Canadian as possible under the circumstances." Not such a bad thing.

Jennifer Welsh, author of *At Home in the World*, suggests that Canada's history of division and subsequent unification once forced its people to think about why we exist and what defines us as a people. But she also argues that Canadians can't watch passively as world events pass us by, merely to comment on the world around us. Principled engagement means making a contribution.

> We need to update the old image of international relations as a game played by centralized states. In reality, the game is much more disaggregated; Canadian "foreign policy" is being made by a whole host of individual Canadians in their roles as businesspeople, professionals, scholars, advocates, and artists. (Welsh, 28)

Canada took a long time to grow up as a country. Our trade service began before the First World War, but our foreign service only came to life at Versailles in 1919. After joining the League of Nations in 1918, Canada began to send ministers and ambassadors around the globe, but the country's instincts remained cautious and isolationist. The Second World War changed the country profoundly and, as we have seen, a new generation of Canadians was present at the creation of the UN and other international institutions. More recently Canada has been instrumental in the creation of the International Criminal Court and in the passing of the Mine Ban Treaty, also known as the Ottawa Treaty. The ICC would not have happened without Canada's consistent and persistent leadership, without our determination to move ahead in creating this new institution.

Our country was one of the founders of the GATT and one of the designers of international trade law, for the simple reason that it was one of the key trading countries in the world at the end of the war and remains so today. More than half of Canada's GDP depends on trade. Canada has one massive trade partner, which means it requires multilateral institutions as well as bilateral trade agreements to deal with the power of the American neighbour and ensure that law, and not sheer power, sets the rules.

As with all countries, Canada's foreign policy is about both values and interests. These values and interests clearly point to three goals: a sustainable and socially just prosperity at home and abroad that is deeply shared; effective ways to prevent, reduce, and resolve conflict; and the steady, practical, and peaceful extension of the rule of law, democracy, and freedom. The means to pursue these objectives will vary according to circumstance and opportunity, and will require a far more effective deployment of resources than is being done at the present time. Foreign policy is about far more than politics and diplomacy: it is about economics and business; war, terrorism and security; ecology and the environment; human rights; the reduction of poverty and disease; and humanitarian assistance in the face of catastrophe. It is about interventions, both military and non-military, increasing religious and cultural understanding, effective policing, as well as about extending the hands of friendship and peacemaking.

Canada has shown in the past that effective international engagement requires both hard and soft power. From Korea to

Suez, from Cyprus to conflicts in Africa and the former Yugoslavia, Canadian troops and diplomats have worked side by side, as they are in Afghanistan today.

Our military effort in Afghanistan is still not matched by our diplomatic effort, not because our public servants in Ottawa, Kabul, Kandahar, Islamabad, Delhi, and other capitals don't have talent and dedication, but because the leadership is missing. Mr. Harper finally made it to China in 2009, but only after four years of lost effort and opportunity. He still hasn't made it to the Middle East.

When it was suggested to Winston Churchill that London's theatres be closed during the war he replied, "Why? What else are we fighting for?" John F. Kennedy said, "Art is the great democrat, calling forth creative genius from every sector of society, disregarding race or religion or wealth or color. If art is to nourish the roots of our culture, society must set the artist free to follow his vision wherever it takes him. We must never forget that art is not a form of propaganda; it is a form of truth." Mr. Harper and his party don't get that.

We need to rethink the connection between diplomacy, politics, economics, and military intervention. One diplomat has called for a new style. A "guerrilla diplomacy," one that is flexible, nimble, close to the ground, and links up all of government far more effectively.

But it is all of Canada that needs to be connected to our various activities abroad. The thousands of Canadians working in NGOs around the world need to know that their government is listening, that it supports their efforts and wants to make sure their policies are going to be effective. The British Foreign Office and the American State Department are now using their websites and significant cultural and public diplomacy budgets to transform how foreign policy is implemented on the ground. Canada has slashed all such budgets to smithereens.

There are in Ottawa today four separate task forces on

Afghanistan – in Foreign Affairs, the Canadian International Development Agency, National Defence, and the Privy Council Office. Literally hundreds of officials are trying to micromanage the work on the ground in Afghanistan, and the authority of our diplomats in Kabul and Kandahar is dangerously diminished. This pattern is repeated throughout the bureaucracy, and Canada now has fewer people overseas than other Western aid agencies or foreign ministries.

The tragedy of September 11, 2001, brought in its wake a different sensibility on domestic security in the United States, which has affected Canada's reputation at home and abroad. While we can take some pride that serious work was done to repair the damage to the lives and reputations of several Canadians of Muslim and Arab origin who were appallingly treated by the governments of Syria and Sudan, the individuals involved paid an appalling price for official neglect. The government's reluctance to uphold the principles of the Charter have led to a series of legal battles where the government has used "executive privilege" as an all-in excuse to deny the Charter's relevance and even the jurisdiction of the courts.

Omar Khadr has been imprisoned at Guantanamo Bay since 2001. He was detained in Afghanistan at the age of fifteen after allegedly throwing a grenade at an American soldier on behalf of Taliban forces. In the summer of 2008, the Supreme Court of Canada ruled that the conditions of Omar Khadr's detention at Guantanamo "constituted a clear violation of fundamental human rights protected by international law." Even John McCain, presidential candidate for the Republican Party in 2009, said he would repatriate Khadr if asked by Canada. The only barrier to this happening is Stephen Harper, who to this point won't recognize that Omar Khadr was a child soldier or Canada's obligations as a signatory to the UN convention on child soldiers.

As happened in the years after the French and Russian revolutions, and indeed in the McCarthy era, a preoccupation with security has led to repression. And the consequences of Canada's failure to fight the death penalty at the United Nations or defend the Charter rights of people the government deems difficult or unpopular has its consequences for foreign policy. Governments from Sri Lanka to Burma, from Russia to Syria, can point to Canadian intransigence and accuse us of hypocrisy. It becomes a vicious circle.

An executive that prorogues Parliament twice, first to avoid a vote of confidence and then to avoid a difficult debate on the treatment of Afghan detainees, hardly does a democracy proud, which is why thousands of Canadians took to the street to voice their protest.

Canadian federalism, its democracy, its Charter, and how its institutions actually work are deeply relevant to the debate about foreign policy. Both Thomas Paine and Edmund Burke would have understood that.

CHAPTER 10

IS GLOBAL DEMOCRACY IMAGINABLE?

A survey of the world in 1939, as we saw at the end of Chapter 3, showed that democracy was then a fragile flower, one that had not taken root in most of the world. Its bastions in North America and Europe were themselves less than perfect examples of states that granted full human rights. A survey conducted today would show a different picture. Many international NGOs, such as Amnesty International and Freedom House, as well as the *Economist* magazine produce comparative indices of the health of rights and democracy worldwide, and they all indicate that either democracy as the West knows it or some form of government by discussion is a widely shared objective. There are tensions and contradictions in the world debate, but it is framed by at least a desire to appear democratic and to conform to shared values and a commitment to respect the rule of law.

Democracy is in decidedly better shape today in Latin America, where the military dictatorships and guerrilla wars of the 1960s to 1980s have, in most nations, been replaced by serious and sometimes contentious debates about equality, sovereignty, and the best path to peaceful development. International response to the 2009 crisis in Honduras, where the military with the support of the Congress and the Supreme Court removed a sitting president, shows how much the world has changed. The coup was denounced by the United States and most of the members of the Organization of American States; major efforts were made to effect the president's return to office before elections. That these did not succeed, and as a result the subsequent election had its share of critics, hardly puts this in the category of the coups and dictatorships of the past.

The OAS spends considerable time and resources on promoting democracy and the rule of law, and the debate between left and right in the Western hemisphere, as harsh as it sometimes can be, is now largely happening within an electoral framework. No one can take this stability for granted, but it is worlds apart from the Latin America of a half-century ago.

Of the two largest countries in Asia, India can be called a federal democracy, albeit one with significant internal challenges. Its economy is now more open, and its federalism is far more real, China is out of the democratic column, but it has at least embraced a rules-based economy, which, it could be argued, will be a major source of pressure for a rules-based political system. This will not happen automatically, but one should not underestimate the contradiction between open markets and closed governments.

The battle for democracy in South Asia is a lively one. In recent years, Indonesia, a presidential republic, has rewritten its constitution to prevent a return to the years of dictatorship under President Suharto (1965-98). Vietnam is a communist dictatorship, which, like China, faces the contradiction of opening its economy to international trade and investment while keeping its political system centralized and closed. Cambodia and Laos are still struggling with poverty and the devastation of the aftermath of the Vietnam War, and Cambodia is also still recovering from the horror of the Pol Pot years, when more than 20 percent of Cambodians died from malnutrition or were executed by the state. The process of reconciliation is proving slow and difficult. In Burma (called Myanmar by its rulers), the military dictatorship, which took power in a 1962 coup, is intransigent in the face of unrest in regions of the country that have never accepted central rule and opposition from a civil society that continues to fight for free elections. The country remains largely closed to the rest of the world and we have yet to see the impact of sanctions against the regime. Aung San Suu Kyi, a redoubtable champion of democracy and human rights, and the most popular political figure in the country, remains under house arrest.

Democratic forces in the Middle East continue to struggle against deep-seated systems of authoritarianism, corruption, misogyny, and a genuine difficulty in coming to terms with the forces of modernity. Throughout the Arab world, governments' overreliance on revenues from oil and other non-renewable resources, and their failure to invest in education, have meant that great wealth has accumulated in few hands, which has contributed to the emergence of religious extremism. It is commonly thought that if the Palestine–Israel problem in the Middle East could be solved, all the other security and political issues in the region would become much easier to tackle. Yet, while there is no doubt that the conflict has taken on a huge symbolic meaning in the region, it is implausible to suggest that resolving it would somehow magically lead to peaceful development. The two-state solution that most of the West promotes is not acceptable to extremists on either side. The agreements contemplated in the 1990s, if implemented, would still mean the vast majority of Palestinians currently in camps outside Israel would not return to the homes they left more than sixty years ago; they would settle in the state of Palestine, split between Gaza and the West Bank, leave for other countries, or be integrated into the countries currently hosting the camps. Again, this solution will be a very hard sell to those in the Arab world, who have never accepted Israel's right to exist. In Israel, it will be equally hard to sell the necessary abandonment of Jewish settlements in the occupied West Bank. We have no choice but to try, because the other alternatives are even more difficult and unpalatable, but we should do so with our eyes wide open.

Beyond the Israel–Palestine conflict, the issues of democracy, women's rights, and competing visions of the relationship between religion and the secular world will continue to dominate debate in the Middle East. But perhaps one important lesson has been learned from the American invasion of Iraq: that the resolution of these tensions and conflicts lies in the hands of the people of the region; they cannot be imposed by force by the West.

Similarly, while many of Africa's problems stem from its devastating colonial experience, it is also true that the solutions for the challenges facing the people of Africa have to come from among themselves. Yes, the developed countries need to share more of their wealth through foreign assistance, responsible private investment, and significantly enhanced trade, even during their own economic hard times. But unless African governments themselves invest substantially in education, make an unequivocal commitment to women's equality, better governance, fighting AIDS, and adherence to the rule of law, development and trade dollars will continue to end up, not in the villages where they are desperately needed, but in foreign bank accounts. This shared commitment from African leaders and Western powers is decidedly a two-way street, in which democracy itself has a critical role to play. The millions dead in the Congo in what has rightly been called Africa's world war, is proof that the West's commitment to peace and democracy on the continent has again stopped short of the people.

Russia's drive to empire in the nineteenth century was as powerful as Britain's, with the notable difference that it was land-based. A visit to the Russian Museum in St. Petersburg introduces the visitor to huge tableaux of warriors in battle, "peace treaties" where the victor claims the spoils, and celebrations of the spirit of expansion. The Putin era has a sense of restoration about it, a return of "Russian pride," to counteract the dramatic decline in life expectancy and well-being that has accompanied the collapse of communism and all its ensuing confusion. The decline in Russia's manufacturing and service economy has been matched by a dramatic rise in oil and natural resources, which strengthens her foreign currency reserves but does little for employment.

Russia has discovered the painful truth that empires have a

way of striking back. Consider the explosions in the Moscow subway, in which young Chechen women indoctrinated in an ideology of resentful extremism strapped themselves with bombs and blew themselves and dozens of others to kingdom come as an example. The bombings will have the inevitable effect of strengthening Putin's hand, leading to demands for more crackdowns and more security. Whether this will produce the desired result is doubtful because, while the battle cry of "fighting terrorism" no doubt has popular appeal, it does not deal with the symptoms and causes of terrorism, which are deeply imbedded in a powerful sense of grievance and alienation in the peoples of the Caucasus.

The federalism of the Soviet Union was completely fake, since whatever formal structures were put in place were belied by the stranglehold of the Communist Party. The gap between the apparent and the real was overpowering, although many observers in the sixty-year history of the regime allowed themselves to believe that all was well.

Putinism's commitment to devolution and diversity is not real, either. The "strong Russia" thesis has meant arguments with Belarus, Ukraine, Georgia, and the Baltic nations, all based on the fact that Russia has not really accepted the notion of their independence. The same is even truer of the nationalities deemed too small or troublesome to be allowed to drift away from Russian sovereignty. Russia's military pre-eminence would seem to settle the issue, but this ignores the reality that brute force by itself does not convey legitimacy. The extent of continuing democratic dissent in Russia is an indication of the problem. True, the demonstrations and denunciations of "Putinism" are hardly a movement of the Russian majority, but they are nevertheless based on a profound and principled belief that authoritarianism continues to infect the soul of Russian political power.

The "national question," and the connected issues of the "immigrant question" and the "Islam question," are a profound challenge for European liberal democracy as well. In Eastern

Europe the borders and boundaries decisions of 1919 and 1945 created problems just as they seemed to settle them. The presence of significant minorities within many countries was submerged during the Cold War but could no longer be contained once the grip of communism was released. The same ethnic national tensions that were such a feature of the buildup to 1914 re-emerged within states that had great difficulty moving beyond the notion of ethnicity as the basis for civic engagement.

While experienced most intensely in Eastern Europe, these issues have their parallels in Western Europe. The communist parties of Italy and France managed to gain a solid block of support during the Cold War. Their hold on the imagination of a quarter of the population dissolved after 1989, and with the collapse of orthodoxy came a bewildering tilt to the right – particularly in France – from the same socio-economic group who had supported communism in the decades before.

The arrival of millions of "others" – some from the old empire, some from an expanding Europe – meant that national narratives about what it means to be French, or Italian, or German, or English were suddenly confronted with a different reality.

In making these assessments of the state of democracy, there will be huge ups and downs, successes and failures. What has changed since 1939 is the extent to which a world in which human rights and democracy are shared objectives. Democracies that respect human rights, the rule of law, and open markets are not universal. But their ideas and advantages are widely understood in a way that was inconceivable even twenty or thirty years ago.

We cannot avoid the realities of power today: the pre-eminent role that is played on the world stage by the United States, both economically and militarily, reinforced by the power of its "organizing ideas" on the universality of freedom. But the lessons of the wars in Iraq and Afghanistan are that there are limits to power, and that legitimacy and authority are engines of persuasion at least as important as military power. Democracy cannot be exported like so many refrigerators or computers. To think that it can be flies in the face of the democratic idea itself. It is the equivalent of forcing someone to be autonomous. The Atlantic Charter that Churchill and Roosevelt signed talks of the sovereign right of nations to choose their governments and their systems of government, which clearly implies that people will often choose a system and a government that are not necessarily of our liking. This is a likelihood not often contemplated in the West, where we tend to assume that a truly democratic election will result in a truly democratic government.

We live in an era where newly powerful economies – like China, India, Brazil, Russia, Indonesia, and other rapidly growing industrial countries – have different visions and ideas. These nations will play significant roles in regimes where their influence is powerful. In Africa, for example, Chinese development assistance is a huge presence. China's aid is not accompanied by a preoccupation about democracy or human rights. One might conclude that the future prospects for the democratic idea are dim, that as the world becomes more multipolar, and as American power wanes, the appeal of liberal democracy will decline as well. For many reasons, this seems too pessimistic a conclusion, not least of which is that the dream of human liberty and equality are deeply rooted in human nature. It is a dream that we shouldn't let go, for all of its setbacks.

Equally important, there are powerful forces at work in the world that are forcing us to face problems together, to spearhead international governance and to allow for greater flexibility within countries. This trend has been called "globalization" – and it is real.

The foundations of the world order today are independent nation states. Yet nation states do not live in isolation and their sovereignty is limited both by forces in their countries and from outside. Some of these limitations are made by us and our governments: treaties are signed, constitutions are made, governments are not as powerful. But some are the inevitable consequence of our being inhabitants of a shared planet, whose environmental health knows nothing of boundaries and borders. Still others are the product of far-reaching technological, social, and economic forces that are less impersonal but nevertheless deeply pervasive and hard to resist and change.

The idea that the nation state is limited reflects the inherent tension between promoting the values of democracy, human rights, and the prevention of poverty, and maintaining hard-won independence and sovereign authority. Many governments that have gained their independence from imperial authority within living memory are loath to be told that international law is now going to prevail over their plans for economic development and sovereign control. These challenges appear more frequently as we realize that the daunting tasks of managing global epidemics, defeating terrorism, and dealing with climate change (just to name a few) require the work of all. Organizations such as the United Nations, the International Monetary Fund, and the World Bank attempt to coordinate a global response to some of these issues, but it falls to the individual nation to implement any changes.

There has been a resurgence in interest in the federal idea in the last two decades. I use the phrase "federal idea" here because the -*ism* in "federalism" has a way of limiting debate and understanding. In Spain, the central government is reluctant to use the word because it seems to connote the dissolution of its sovereign authority in favour of the autonomous regions, including Catalonia; conversely the Catalonians won't use it because in their view it does not sufficiently represent their claim to self-government. In South Africa, the word fell into disrepute because it had some official approval from the apartheid government. As well, the African National Congress's vision of one South Africa made the party reluctant to describe any new constitution as federalist.

These are hardly new debates: the Jeffersonian tradition in

American politics was proud to call itself "anti-federalist" because it concluded that the forces behind John Adams and Alexander Hamilton that wanted a stronger centralized authority had branded the "F-word." Yet both Thomas Jefferson and John Adams were clearly federalists who shared far more key assumptions than their actions might lead some to believe.

What is happening today in South Africa, Spain, Mexico, Nigeria, the United Kingdom, Russia, Brazil, Indonesia, India, Pakistan, Cyprus, Iraq, to mention just a few countries where the debate about federal governance is intense, is a reflection of some important common tendencies that need to be understood. There is certainly more than one way to be a federalist; it is the common idea that matters.

Many ancient societies had political arrangements of co-operation and association, but the modern federal idea is first and foremost a democratic idea. It implies the state's respect for people's identities and their political choices. It is incompatible with populist concepts of democracy that are not based on a respect for individual rights, constitutional process, and the rule of law. It also runs against demagogues who believe they have a pipeline to the "real" or "best" interests of the people. Ideologies that express a certain knowledge of political truth (or religious truths as made manifest in the world) are implacable enemies of the federal idea.

The federal idea, therefore, accounts for the vitality of politics and rival notions of the public interest. It also speaks to a common concern about limiting the sphere of government. Successful federal constitutions are inevitably about the limits of popular sovereignty and the protection of both group and individual rights. They set out which level of government does what, they guarantee rights and freedoms, and in order to keep these two forces in balance they mandate the top courts to interpret the balance – and to enforce that interpretation.

This is the defining element of the federal idea, namely that a federal nation is one where power is both divided and coordinated.

That, of course, is the central tension in federalism: it is not just one idea. It requires an agreement to do certain things separately and other things together. It is about more than just devolution, because the premise is that state or provincial governments have as much sovereignty in their sphere as the national or federal government has in its. There are no higher or lower governments, no senior or junior governments, just different governments doing different things within a common framework. Nor is the national government a mere creature of the provinces, delegated by them to do certain tasks. It too has its own sovereignty, its own direct connection to the people.

The federal idea implies an ongoing dialogue about who does what. There are significant issues in each federation about fiscal matters: how money is raised, how it is shared, how it is spent. In Canada, natural resources are provincially owned and the income from them flows to the provincial governments. In Nigeria, the issue of how oil revenue should be divided is now being argued in court, but the central government claims all oil revenue and is expected to divide it between the regions according to a formula. Australia's revenue-sharing formula between the national and state governments is so complicated that it brings to mind the British statesman's comment, "There are only three people who know the causes of the Crimean War. Two of them are dead, and I can't remember."

There is a growing consensus among economists and governance experts that local and state governments need to be able to raise the money to spend on their own programs: this increases both transparency and accountability. Where this is not possible, central revenue sharing needs to be both transparent and not simply decreed by the national government. When this doesn't happen, as is often the case, conflicts arise.

Those opposed to federalism point to these conflicts, the sometimes bewildering complexity of federal institutions, and the cost of many governments as reasons either for simply abolishing regional governments altogether, or for separatism. We should be skeptical of these claims, as they have little basis in fact. It would be hard to point to the "efficiency" of a one-party Mexico or Nigeria under military dictatorship. Switzerland, a federation, is geographically small and politically complex, yet it has remained for decades a symbol of balance between domestic language groups.

The federal idea is indeed about complexity, but better the give and take of an endless negotiation – isn't that what much of life itself is, anyway? – than the simple world of the Jacobin, the Leninist, the militarist, the religious fanatic, or even the old-fashioned ethnic nationalist who has difficulty with any kind of pluralism.

The resurgence of the federal idea has many different causes. The vitality of the values of democracy, the revolutions in the politics of identity and human rights, the twin collapse of apartheid and bureaucratic communism, the impact of the technological revolution, the economic changes we associate with globalization – all these have made their contribution. In Mexico, for example, one-party rule for most of the twentieth century meant that while the constitution spoke of the federal nature of the country, the government ignored it. The same was true for the Soviet Union, supposedly a federation of equal states. The federal idea is also quite incompatible with the command-and-control mentality of the military dictatorship that until recently ruled in Nigeria.

The renewal of interest is not at all confined to countries that have a federalist tradition. All countries have long had to struggle with the simple truth that their borders rarely define or encompass a homogeneous population. Ethnic, linguistic, racial, and religious conflicts that know no borders have become the dominant issue facing the world order today. Wars since 1945 have been as much within nations as between them, with disastrous consequences for peace and security. It is no longer soldiers who are dying in the millions, but civilians. From Rwanda to Cambodia, from the Balkans to East Timor, the battleground is within countries that are unable to resolve the conflicts of what Michael Ignatieff has called "blood and belonging."

The painful back and forth of negotiations over the governance of Northern Ireland – where thousands died – depends for its resolution on a willingness on the part of each side to recognize the legitimacy of the other, a capacity for political and administrative flexibility, and an ability to bring terrorism to an end. This is all easier to say than to do, but it is hard to see how the federal idea won't be part of the solution – if one is to be found.

Similarly, in Iraq, the existence of a self-governing Kurdistan clearly puts some form of federalism at the centre of discussions about new constitutional arrangements for a unified, but not unitary, Iraq. Indeed, issues of federal governance are at the centre of active political and legal discussions in every part of the globe, particularly in areas where conflict resolution is a critical necessity.

Those responsible for the most recent Afghan constitution created a highly centralized state on the French model, with governors being sent out from the centre to do Kabul's bidding. The trouble with this arrangement is that it ignores traditional power structures in the regions, and there is less scope for local involvement than there needs to be. There is now a painful recognition that both in Afghanistan and outside that this constitutional structure may not be the right one for the country.

The federal idea is part of another trend as well. European cooperation since the 1950s has led to an elected European Parliament, a common court, freedom of movement, as well as free trade and a common currency. National sovereignty is not dead and the age of the nation-state is not over, but the notion that these are exclusive or all-defining is clearly outmoded. Within Europe, the peaceful breakup of Czechoslovakia was facilitated by the existence of the wider European Union around it. Similarly, the progress to resolve the conflict in Northern Ireland was made much easier because both Ireland and the United Kingdom were now part of a broader political formation – the European Union. At the conclusion of the Mont Tremblant Conference on federalism in 1999, President Bill Clinton remarked, "Maybe the federal idea isn't such a bad idea after all." He was right. The collapse of one-party states, the demands of identity, the urge to local empowerment, the insistence on greater openness and transparency in government, and the recognition that in a smaller and much more interdependent world "sovereignty" is no longer an absolute have all brought the federal idea to the fore again.

The Millennium Development Goals were set in 2001 by the United Nations in an effort to tackle eight key international development objectives by the year 2015. They are perhaps the most ambitious and widely supported objectives in recent memory. They include eradicating extreme poverty and hunger; achieving universal primary education; promoting gender equality and empowering women; reducing child mortality; improving maternal health; combatting HIV/AIDS and other serious diseases; ensuring environmental sustainability, and developing a global partnership for development. None of these issues is particular to one country or ethnic group, as they transcend boundaries, oceans, and cultural barriers. And not all of the world's citizens are equally focused or engaged in rising to the challenges they present. This is why a coordinated global response is needed.

The 2009 annual report on these goals stresses that international objectives in such areas as poverty reduction, climate change, health, and education are and will continue to be hampered by the new global recession. The progress that has been realized in the past decade is at risk of being lost. And yet these development goals don't come first to Western minds immediately when thoughts turn to the damage of a global recession.

While climate change has captured the world's imagination most powerfully, it is far from being the only global environmental issue. The destruction of the world's fishery, the despoliation of our land and forests, the assault on limited and finite resources, these are all critical problems. Dealing with them effectively can't stop at a local or national border. The fate of life on the planet forces us to look beyond ourselves, obliges us to make treaties, to find effective methods of enforcement, and to share regulation and governance. The agreement most of the world achieved at Kyoto to deal with climate change was not a socialist plot, as some have charged. It was an act of necessity. That it was not followed up effectively by enough action by nation-states is no cause for derision or despair, but a call to action in the future.

Climate change is already happening, and it will continue to dominate our lives. Arctic people coping with heaving permafrost and disappearing wildlife, nomadic people dealing with lost grazing land and spreading desert, coastal people facing rising seas and dramatic weather – the list of present dangers is endless. The health of the planet is not an abstraction or a question to deal with tomorrow – it is about how we live now.

Environmental scarcity is already playing, and will continue to play, a role in many conflicts around the world, as fighting breaks out over dwindling resources. Scarcity will become more serious as global warming continues, and we must be prepared to address its environmental, social, and economic fallout. Canada must be a leader in environmental preservation and lowering our greenhouse gas output. We know that the biggest cuts have to come from developed and developing countries alike, and until we lead by example we cannot expect our international friends to do the same. We should be supporting energy research and development, and creating incentives for new energy alternatives. Dependence on foreign resources of any kind leaves us vulnerable to local conflicts far away, to fluctuating markets and to other variables beyond our control. We will all be better off with a safe and sustainable supply of energy production.

But it is not just the health of the planetary environment we share that brings the world together, that reinforces the need for awareness and action that extends beyond the nation-state. The irony of 1918 was that, just as the war was ending, a worldwide influenza outbreak killed more people, an estimated 50 million, than had died during the war. Today the success of an anti-polio campaign in Afghanistan depends on the co-operation of neighbouring Pakistan and Tajikistan, and eradicating H1N1, AIDS, malaria, you name it, depends on effective international action. Bugs and viruses travel. As the world shrinks and more and more people move rapidly around, there is no such thing as a local outbreak. National firewalls won't stop a pandemic. Our personal survival forces us to become globally active.

When Roosevelt and Churchill met in the middle of a world war in which millions were dying and killing each other, they reaffirmed that war is a terrible scourge, and that the race for armaments to achieve security can be self-defeating. Yet this did not stop the United States from using the atomic bomb to destroy Hiroshima and Nagasaki, and the Soviet Union quickly thereafter developed its own nuclear weapons system. A new and terrible arms race had begun, far worse than the quest for bigger navies before the First World War or new weaponry and firepower before the Second World War.

President John F. Kennedy referred to the buildup of nuclear weapons in the 1950s as a "sword of Damocles" hanging over the planet, and a generation of popular protest and diplomacy attempted to ban nuclear testing and stop new entrants to the nuclear club. But while the lessening of tension between the U.S. and Russia has led a modest cutback in nuclear arms, Israel, Pakistan, India, and North Korea have all joined the nuclear club. The threat of nuclear destruction, while feeling less urgent in the West since the dissolution of the Soviet Union, has grown, not diminished.

Today, Iran is preparing to join the nuclear fraternity, and to this point the West has not figured out how to stop it. The Iranian regime is a religious dictatorship, which claims it is developing nuclear generation, not arms. But the West does not trust either President Ahmadinejad or the ayatollocracy behind him, viewing them as theocratic, adventurist, cynical, anti-Semitic and anti-humanist. Iran arms Hezbollah, does deals with President Chavez in Venezuela, and is widely believed to be behind attacks on security forces in Iraq and Afghanistan. It represses and tortures its people and steals elections. It ignores UN resolutions and Security Council sanctions.

Many observers have noted that Israel appears to be obsessed with Iran. On my trips to the Middle East, I found that it was not alone. I asked the leaders of several Arab countries two questions: Is Iran's path to becoming a nuclear power clear to you? And should Iran be trusted with a nuclear weapon? The answers were categorical: Yes to the first and No to the second. Sunni versus Shia rivalry ensures such a position. In the event Iran gets the bomb and the capability to use it, others – Egypt and Saudi Arabia, to mention just two – may feel forced to follow suit. But there is no consensus as to how to stop Iran from building a weapon. There is talk of engagement, but it less clear how to get there.

The Arab world remains deeply mistrustful of Israel, and certainly doesn't want it to take a military lead. Israel itself is caught in a bind. Iran's bad behaviour in feeding tensions in the region is not a far-off threat. It is a daily reality. But if it takes military action alone it would face universal condemnation, and risk alienating American and Western support.

Looking outside the Middle East, North Korea's bomb and missile testing is taking place with impunity in the face of universal condemnation. Pakistan's political instability and the ongoing conflicts in the region are a profound concern, because they pose a dual threat – of the bomb falling into the hands of zealots and of the half-century battle between Pakistan and India over Kashmir going nuclear.

There is a further nuclear threat, and that is the risk of a dirty bomb or home made nuclear device falling into the hands of what political scientists call "non-state actors." The father of Pakistan's nuclear bomb, Dr. Abdul Qadeer Khan, is a hero there and has openly admitted to sharing information with a number of other countries. The "how-to" is now available on the Internet, but nuclear states can go further – they can sell the technology and the weapons.

This is as serious an issue as any the world faces, but the phrase "the threat of nuclear proliferation" or even "nuclear disarmament" had virtually disappeared from the political lexicon until the election of President Obama. It has still not fully re-emerged in Canada, despite the fact that disarmament has traditionally been a foreign policy priority since the 1940s, and Canada was a leader in the movement at the UN against nuclear proliferation.

The issue now is not just an uncontrolled buildup of nuclear weapons. Competition in amassing weapons of all kinds from pistols to land mines to bombs of every size and variety is a tragic fact of the world order. Virtually every country has a thriving arms industry, and a world trade of approximately $21 billion a year is unregulated apart from domestic efforts at gun control. From sovereign states to guerrilla groups, organized crime to youth gangs, the trade is thriving, and the consequent death and destruction are entirely predictable.

Canada took an important lead in the push for a land mines treaty, but the existence of the Ottawa Treaty, signed in 1997, has not stopped the manufacture and trade of these deadly weapons. In Colombia and Sri Lanka, their use in the hundreds of thousands prevents resettlement efforts and has cost countless people their lives or limbs. The same is true in East Africa.

Efforts at reducing armaments are often dismissed by hawks as meaningless exercises in do-goodery, but truth be told we need the vision of a world without guns and bombs to inspire our daily steps. The adage "guns don't kill people, people kill people" misses the point that weaponry expands exponentially the destruction caused by the uncontrolled instinct for violence.

Just because it's difficult doesn't mean we should stop trying. Change starts with a willingness to accept gun and weapons control within national borders, and goes on from there. The failure to insist on this necessary first step makes a mockery of any national effort to control and stop violent crime. While the United States focuses on border security and illegal immigrants, its neighbours rightly worry about the cross-border trade in illegal guns that makes gang warfare more violent than it ever has been, and gives organized crime the firepower it needs to control and intimidate.

Crime of all kinds – drug trafficking, the sex trade, financial fraud, virtually every human activity proscribed in any national criminal code – has an international dimension. This means that foreign policy has as much to do with strengthening international institutions as it does with reinforcing governance at the local and national level. The credibility of well-meaning codes, treaties, and policies depends on capacity and enforcement.

The causes of conflict in the world today are many and vast. If the devastation of the first half of the twentieth century can largely be traced to imperial ambition, brutal, if failed exercises in collectivization (in Russia and China), and the clash of competing ideologies, more recent conflicts have arisen from differences of tribe, race, religion, class, and power. Some, like the devastating impact of the so-called Great Leap Forward and the Cultural Revolution imposed by the Maoist government in China, went largely unreported and unacknowledged, although the dead may have numbered in the millions. The creation of India and Pakistan caused a river of blood to flow, and East Africa and the Congo have seen carnage on a mammoth scale for a generation. Intense internal conflict in countries as diverse as Colombia, Nicaragua, Sri Lanka, the former Yugoslavia, the Caucasus and Chechnya, Sudan, Iraq, Iran, and many others has cost millions of lives.

The prevention and resolution of these conflicts needs to be at the heart of foreign policy. A focus instead on the so-called war on terror has meant we have avoided having to understand the roots of conflict and the range of methods needed to reduce tension and create the opportunity for stability. Without question, the attack on the Twin Towers, the culmination of a decade of attacks on Western interests in the Persian Gulf, Saudi Arabia, and East Africa, required a concerted response. Some observers refer to these terrorists as "cowards" and "nihilists," but this is a misunderstanding. They have a political objective, which is to eliminate foreign presence from the "Caliphate," the Muslim world of old, and to restore religious power to its proper place – at the top and centre of every aspect of life. Al-Qaeda's objective in attacking the U.S., some observers have claimed, was to provoke an American-led intervention by the West into the Middle East that would topple secular Arab governments and throw open the door for a return to religious rule.

Iran under the ayatollahs and Afghanistan under the Taliban give us a pretty clear idea of what such religious rule entails: the repression of women, the obliteration of freedom of conscience, and the triumph of a narrow interpretation of Islam. Its implementation also empowers a band of retrograde clerics whose views and whose interests prevail in the face of the modernist enemy.

The enemies of these extremists are clear enough: first there are the many Islamic modernists and reformers who would put religion in a different space and place; who are open to new technologies, ideas and cultures; who allow, even promote, the equality of women and men; and who accept the existence and rights of non-Muslims. So the first line of engagement is within the Mulim world itself. The rest of the world cannot be indifferent to the outcome. The second line of attack is the West and Israel. On February 14, 2003, Osama bin Laden delivered a statement entitled "Among a Band of Knights." It was framed as a sermon:

> As I speak, the blood of Muslims continues to be shed in vain in Palestine, Chechnya, Philippines, Kashmir and Sudan . . . As I speak, our wounds have yet to heal from the Crusader wars of the last century against the Islamic world . . . The Crusaders' agents are still in power to this day, in light of a new Sykes-Picot Agreement, the Bush-Blair axis,

which has the same banner and objective, namely the banner of the Cross and the objective of destroying and looting of our beloved Prophet's *umma*. . . .

The Crusaders are the enemy. So are the Jews: The creation of Greater Israel will entail Jewish domination over the countries of the region. What will explain to you who the Jews are? The Jews are those who slandered the Creator . . . They killed the Prophets and broke their promises . . . These Jews are masters of usury and leaders in treachery. They will leave you nothing, either in this world or the next . . . These are some of the characteristics of the Jews, so beware of them. These, too are some of the features of the Crusader plan, so resist it . . . Our *umma* [the "nation" of Islam] has also been promised victory over the Jews, as our Prophet told us: "The Day of Judgment will not come until the Muslims fight and kill the Jews." . . . This hadith of the Prophet also contains a warning that the struggle against the enemy will be decided by fighting and killing, not by paralysis of the powers of our *umma* for decades through other means, like the deceptive idea of democracy. (Lawrence, 187)

Hitler could hardly have said it better. But the means of battle will not simply be military. It is a long war of ideas and values. It requires strengthening institutions and building the capacity of states. It means improving public education, exposing lies and hatred, and working to improve prospects for training and jobs.

———

Canada's support for the United Nations has been a pillar of our foreign policy since 1945. This internationalism is not based on a fad. It stems from our experience of two world wars, our dependence on the rest of the world for our security and prosperity, the international origins of our population, and the simple fact that the great challenges of our time cannot be solved by us alone. We are in the world and the world is in us.

The founders of the United Nations were not afraid to dream of a world that would marshal the strength to prevent conflict from starting again. But the conflict the UN was set up to tackle was conflict between and among nations, not within them. Sixty-five years later, powerful forces and conflicting ambitions continue to destroy life and limb, homes and hopes. Billions live in poverty, emotions are driven by ancient beliefs and prejudices, and growing scarcity creates the spark and kindling that fuels extremism and still drives the world to war and conflict. The United Nations has not been able to stop these forces, and so it is often pilloried as just as great a failure as the League of Nations before it by those who do not understand the limits of the UN's role.

The UN is two things. The first is the institution itself: the dozens of agencies and hundreds of thousands of people who work around the world on a myriad of issues, from climate change to peacekeeping to improving labour standards and preventing disease. Like all large bureaucracies, the UN has its flaws and imperfections. The body that is supposed to be the world's parliament, the General Assembly, has little power and a capacity for endless rhetoric. The Security Council, with its five permanent members representing the most powerful victors of the Second World War, no longer represents the power structure of the world. But changing the formal structures and constitution of the UN is almost impossible. The UN's agencies, such as the World Health Organization and the International Labour Organization, do vital work, and it is hard not to be impressed with the dedication and expertise of UN workers who are trying to improve the human condition around the world. Others, such as the UN Human Rights Council, are immersed in the politics of the moment, and are notoriously ineffective at dealing with underlying issues.

The second meaning of the UN is as shorthand for the countries of the world attempting to work collectively. It has proven impossible to sustain or recreate the idealism and determination the world showed in forming the UN in the first place, but it has been tried. The passage of the Convention on Genocide in 1948, the Universal Declaration of Human Rights, the creation of the International Criminal Court in 1998, all speak to the emergence of a world order that stems not from the force of a superpower but from the collective will of all nations.

More than 150 heads of state have committed themselves under the auspices of the United Nations to protect those who are unable to protect themselves. The difficulty is, to echo Churchill, that good laws require a good constabulary. A victim-centred approach to conflict prevention is a fine objective, but the commitment each nation has made rings hollow in the wake of Cambodia, Rwanda, Congo, and the other bloodbaths that have been such a feature of the world in the last six decades. The protection of vulnerable nations is a vital principle, but it must be admitted that enforcement and the necessary will to intervene are in their infancy.

The Responsibility to Protect, or "R2P," is the product of a long evolution and the extension of international law. It expresses the notion that the rule of law sits above all national state structures and contributes to a broader understanding of what international law is and can be. Yet the fact that these institutions are so frail is a huge problem. Too many countries – even the United States – do not accept the jurisdiction of the International Criminal Court.

But despair and cynicism are luxuries we cannot afford if we are to strengthen international co-operation. Nor can we retreat to a world of pure power politics, where military might is seen as the test of right. Superior firepower is not sufficient to defeat armed extremists or guerrillas who have a strong level of support from local populations, even when that support is the result of intimidation. Very recently my colleague and friend David Cameron had these very wise words to say based on his experiences in advancing better governance:

> Societies and human beings live in and through time. Often too little heed is paid to this simple and obvious reality. International experts will frequently approach a country in need of help with a brisk sense that the problem can be readily identified, rather in the way that one approaches the formation of public policy within a familiar national context, and, with the help of an all-purpose tool box of institutional and policy instruments, one gets on with solving the problem and fixing the matter. But it is difficult to believe that beneficial measures can rest on a platform of ignorance. . . .
>
> Whatever the political and social achievements of Western societies may be, they are the product of generations of experience, trial and error, wrong turns corrected, and social and political struggle. An awareness of that fosters modesty in counsel, and openness to different ways of achieving desired outcomes. It points to the virtue of humility, and to the need to recognize that it will not be the expert from abroad who will bear the costs of failure, or indeed the costs associated with whatever turmoil is associated with success. It is not our society; it is theirs. . . .
>
> A more acute awareness of one's own imperfections, a stronger sense that in some important ways we are all in the same boat, a deeper and more genuine interest in the logic and character of the societies we are seeking to assist – these sentiments might help to set the stage for a more productive dialogue and exchange, rather than leading us down a hortatory one-way street.

This book begins with an argument between Thomas Paine, democracy's icon, and Edmund Burke, conservative statesman. We need the passion and wisdom of each, as well as an appreciation of the millions of women and men who aspire to a better life. When women are being stoned to death and real equality remains a taboo in too many places, it is impossible to sit on the sidelines. But it is equally impossible to expect immediate results or immediate justice. As Nelson Mandela has said, it is a long walk to freedom. To which we must add, it is an arduous journey that takes us through difficult terrain. We shall need much courage and wisdom along the way.

Brute force is not enough to sustain governments over time. Legitimacy and authority are the real coin of politics, and that is what the democratic conversation is about. The struggle for democracy goes on all about us, in advanced industrial societies as well as in the poorest and most divided of countries. We shall face setbacks, just as our ancestors did over the centuries since the democratic idea was born. But none of us can remain aloof from the struggle, nor can we be indifferent to the result.

The thinking behind this book has been a long time coming, and yet it is very much a work in progress. I have described in a previous book, *From Protest to Power*, the world in which I was raised and how my father Saul, a diplomat for forty years, wrote a book with pollster George Gallup called *The Pulse of Democracy*, before he began his foreign service career. I once asked him why he switched jobs. His answer was, as usual, direct: "It was the war. And turning heads mattered more than counting heads."

A continuing theme in my own life has been the public values I care about – democracy, diversity, human rights, the rule of law – and the challenge of sharing them in a world that is divided and where people forcefully disagree.

Looking back I realize how much I learned from great teachers. Bob Smith, my history teacher at Gordon Junior High School in Washington D.C. at the time of the Kennedy inauguration, was the first to really bring history and politics alive. He was followed by wonderful mentors at the International School in Geneva, the most important among them Michael Knight. John Beattie, Carl Berger, Jacques Kornberg, and Gad Horowitz enlivened my undergraduate days at the University of Toronto, and I was lucky enough at Oxford with John Plamenatz, Philip Williams, Bill Weinstein, and Steven Lukes. Sir Isaiah Berlin was a magisterial presence in my life, and I shall always remember our tutorials on Hegel and Marx. Allan Mewett was an unforgettable inspiration at the University of Toronto law school. I am increasingly aware of what I owe to others.

As always, I am especially grateful to my wife, Arlene, whose love and support have been wonderfully present in a public life that has had its share of downs as well as ups. Her advice has helped me to write a better book as well as live a better life. My daughters Judith, Lisa, and Eleanor have helped me go from ideas to words on paper, and my mother, Lois, and sister, Jennifer, continue to give me love and encouragement. My late brother David's life has been a source of warm memory and continuing inspiration, which I can see in the eyes of his two wonderful sons, Christopher and Jonathan. I have been discussing politics and life with my brother, John, our whole lives. Long may we continue.

My assistants Cynthia Diamond, Kate Purchase, Jen Ehrlich, Denise Lam, and Phil Ozga have organized my political life in such a way that I have been able to find time to finish this project, even though there were many times when this seemed most unlikely. I am grateful to them all for their help and insight. Others who have volunteered their time include Adam Lambert, Philippe Legault, Louis-Philippe Champagne, Fraser Egerton, and Michelle Sample. Gerald Schmitz of the Parliamentary Library prepared a report on corruption in Afghanistan that was comprehensive and thoughtful.

I have discussed these ideas over the years extensively with my friend and now leader Michael Ignatieff. Irwin Cotler, Glen Pearson, and many other members of Parliament and political colleagues have shared their views and ideas with me, and I am deeply appreciative of their friendship.

Fifteen years ago, I resigned as both the leader of the Ontario New Democratic Party and a member of the Ontario Legislature. I was invited by then University of Toronto President Rob Prichard and Massey College Master John Fraser to teach at the university, an offer I quickly accepted. With the help of many able teaching assistants, I taught a course called "Thinking about Politics" in the faculty of arts and sciences, together with some special seminars in the faculties of business and law on globalization, social change, and public policy.

At the same time Prime Minister Chrétien discussed with me the need to broaden the debate about federalism. His new Minister of Interprovincial Affairs Stéphane Dion also called to invite me to a dinner, where the idea Mr. Chrétien and I had discussed – the creation of a Canadian-based international organization that would focus on federal governance – was born. I worked at the Forum for nearly ten years as its first chairman and president. I have spent time then and since in Sri Lanka, Iraq, Pakistan, Afghanistan, Sudan, Nigeria, Kenya, Nepal, and many other countries learning and advising on conflict resolution, governance, and constitutional change.

Ron Watts, known worldwide as the dean of federalist studies, has been a source of much guidance. Ralph Lysyshyn, now Canada's ambassador to Russia, organized the first international conference on the federal idea and ran the Forum from its infancy to a full-fledged international NGO. My successors at the Forum, Arnold Koller as chair and George Anderson as president, have inspired and educated me, as have many wonderful Forum staffers.

David Cameron, now chair of the political science department at the University of Toronto, has worked closely with me in Sri Lanka and Iraq. We had the chance to work together on Canadian constitutional issues in an earlier life, and I am grateful for his patience, wisdom, and courage. I hope there is something in these pages that captures our shared experience and that this draft is an improvement on an earlier one about which he said, "There's a book in there somewhere, but it's not there yet."

I am grateful to my friends at Hebrew University in Jerusalem and the American University in Beirut, especially my dear friend of nearly fifty years, Rami Khouri, for giving me the opportunity to try out some of these ideas. The discussions will continue.

My editor at McClelland and Stewart, Dinah Forbes has helped me get to a finish line that at many points seemed very far off. Her prodding, questions, and advice have forced me to go back to the drawing board many times.

I have dedicated this book to the memory of my father, Saul Forbes Rae, who was a scholar, diplomat, musician, entertainer, humourist, and wonderful dad. His life was dedicated to diplomacy and public service, and like many others of his generation he was present at the creation of the political world which we are now navigating. I have deep and warm memories of time well spent and lessons learned. He shared his own memories, took me to the East Block, Canada House, the UN, everywhere in Washington (including the Kennedy inauguration) and, without being didactic, was an early example of what happens when you take your kid to work. He was my tennis and music teacher and taught me how to fish. He also reminded me that "fishing's not fair," which I now realize is a larger metaphor for life itself. He would be pleasantly surprised at many of my conclusions in this book, although the adage "too soon old, too late smart" might occur to him, and would certainly not have gone unexpressed.

The pulse of democracy needs to beat stronger in the world. The point is not just to measure it, but to figure out how to keep it going.

Toronto, Ottawa, Portland, July 2010

REFERENCES

CHAPTER 1

Dunn, John. *Democracy: A History*. London: Penguin, 2005.

Judicial Committee of the Privy Council. *Edwards v. AG of
Canada*. [1930], AC 124. Judgment of Lord Sankey LC.
Available at: *www.chrc-ccdp.ca/en/browseSubjects/edwardspc.asp*.

Supreme Court of Canada. *Edwards v. Canada (Attorney General)*.
[1928], SCR 276. Anglin CJC Decision. Available at: *www.
chrc-ccdp.ca/en/browseSubjects/edwardscc.asp*.

Supreme Court of the United States. *Dred Scott, Plaintiff in Error v.
John F. A. Sandford*. 60 U.S. 393; 15 L. Ed. 691. December,
1856.

CHAPTER 2

Burke, Edmund. *Selected Writings and Speeches by Edmund Burke*.
Edited by Peter J. Stanlis. Garden City, NY: Anchor Books,
1963.

Lindsay, Alexander Dunlop. *Essentials of Democracy*. London:
Clarendon Press, 1971.

Paine, Thomas. *The Thomas Paine Reader*. Edited by Michael
Foot and Isaac Kramnick. London: Penguin Books, 1987.

Tawney, R.H. *Religion and the Rise of Capitalism*. London:
Penguin Books, 1965.

CHAPTER 3

Hochschild, Adam. *King Leopold's Ghost: A Story of Greed, Terror
and Heroism in Colonial Africa*. New York: Houghton
Mifflin, 1998.

Keynes, John Maynard. *The Economic Consequences of the Peace*.
New York: Harcourt, Brace and Howe, 1920.

MacMillan, Margaret. *Paris 1919*. Toronto: Random House, 2003.

Marx, Karl. *Political Writings*, Volume 1. Edited by David Fernbach. London: Penguin, 1973.

Nicolson, Harold. *Peacemaking 1919*. New York: Grosset and Dunlap, 1965.

Orwell, George. *Homage to Catalonia*, Volume 6 of *The Complete Works of George Orwell*. Edited by Peter Davison. London: Secker and Warburg, 1998.

——— . *Facing Unpleasant Facts*, Volume 11 of *The Complete Works of George Orwell*. Edited by Peter Davison. London: Secker and Warburg, 1998.

CHAPTER 4

Cooke, Alistair. *A Generation on Trial: USA v. Alger Hiss*. New York: Penguin Books, 1968.

CHAPTER 5

Brandon, Piers. *The Decline and Fall of the British Empire*. London: Knopf Doubleday Publishing, 2010.

Fanon, Frantz. *Les Damnés de la Terre*. Edited by François Maspéro. Paris: Présence Africaine Editions, 1961.

Prunier, Gérard. *Africa's World War: Congo, the Rwandan Genocide, and the Making of a Continental Catastrophe*. New York: Oxford University Press. 2009.

Zhao Ziyang. *Prisoner of the State: The Secret Journal of Premier Zhao Ziyang*. Translated and edited by Bao Pu, Renee Chiang, and Adi Ignatius. New York: Simon and Schuster, 2009.

CHAPTER 6

Building on Success: The London Conference on Afghanistan. "Afghanistan Compact." Available at: *www.nato.int/isaf/docu/epub/pdf/afghanistan_compact.pdf* .

"Hizbullah: Views and Concepts." Contributed by Hizbullah through Manar TV, Beirut, June 20, 1997. Available at: *almashriq.hiof.no/lebanon/300/320/324/324.2/hizballah/hizballah-background.html*.

Karzai, Hamid. Quoted in "Afghanistan: Karzai's Corruption

Comments Could Lead to Cabinet Shakeup," by Ron Synovitz , Radio Free Europe/Radio Liberty, November 16, 2007. Available at: *www.rferl.org/content/article/1079143.html*.

Sultanzoy, Daoud. Comments, July 2008. Available at: *www. argoriente.it/arc/paesi/afghanistan/AFGHANISTAN-Interview-Sultanzoy-EN.pdf*.

Fulbright, William J. *The Arrogance of Power*. New York: Random House, 1966.

Luttwak, Edward N. "Dead End: Counterinsurgency Warfare as Military Malpractice." *Harper's*, January 2007. Available at: *harpers.org/archive/2007/02/0081384*.

Stein, Janice Gross, and Eugene Lang. *The Unexpected War: Canada in Kandahar*. Toronto: Viking, 2007.

Stewart, Rory. *The Places In Between*. New York: Harcourt, 2006.

CHAPTER 7

Burns, E.L.M. *Between Arab and Israeli*. New York: Ivan Obolensky, 1962.

Morris, Benny. "Obama's Impossible Ambition." *Guardian*, September 11, 2009. Available at: *www.guardian.co.uk/commentisfree/2009/sep/11/middle-east-obama-peace*.

CHAPTER 8

Brahimi, Lakhdar, and Edward Mortimer. "Let's Help Sri Lanka Win the Peace." *Globe and Mail*, September 16, 2009. Available at: *www.theglobeandmail.com/news/opinions/lets-help-sri-lanka-win-the-peace/article1290021/*.

Comments by UN Secretary General Ban Ki-moon can be found at: *www.cnn.com/2009/WORLD/asiapcf/05/23/sri.lanka.united.nations/index.html* and *www.nytimes.com/2009/08/16/world/asia/161anka.html*.

De Votta, Neil. *Blowback: Linguistic Nationalism, Institutional Decay and Ethnic Conflict in Sri Lanka*. Palo Alto, CA: Stanford University Press, 2003.

McGee, Thomas D'Arcy. *Confederation Debates*. Ottawa: Queen's Printer, 1865.

Polgreen, Lydia. "Downpours Flood the Camps of Sri Lankan Refugees." *New York Times*, August 15, 2009. Available at: *www.nytimes.com/2009/08/16/world/asia/161anka.html*.

"UN Secretary General: Sri Lanka Sites for the Displaced 'Appalling.'" CNN, Sunday May 24, 2009. Available at: *www.cnn.com/2009/WORLD/asiapcf/05/23/sri.lanka.united. nations/index.html*.

Wilson, A.J. *Sri Lankan Tamil Nationalism: Its Origins and Development in the Nineteenth and Twentieth Centuries.* Vancouver: UBC Press, 2000.

Worldwide Press Freedom Index 2009. Available at: *www. freedomhouse.org/uploads/fop/2009/FreedomofthePress2009_ tables.pdf* .

CHAPTER 9

Supreme Court of Canada. *Canada (Justice) v. Khadr* (2008) 2 SCR 125. 2008 SCC 28 (paragraph 24). Available at: *csc. lexum.umontreal.ca/en/2008/2008scc28/2008scc28.html*.

Welsh, Jennifer. *At Home in the World: Canada's Global Vision for the 21st Century.* Toronto: HarperCollins Canada, 2004.

CHAPTER 10

Ignatieff, Michael. *Blood and Belonging: Journeys into the New Nationalism.* London: Penguin, 1993.

———. *Isaiah Berlin.* London: Penguin, 1999.

Lawrence, Bruce (Editor). *Messages to the World: The Statements of Osama bin Laden.* "Bin Laden – Among a Band of Knights," February 14, 2003. London: Verso, 2005.

There are countless books, articles, and websites on the themes touched on in this book. Wikipedia is at once invaluable and not entirely reliable.

The following organizations have great websites: IDEA, The Democracy Digest, International Crisis Group, Amnesty International, Human Rights Watch, Democratic Index, Forum of Federations, Transparency International, Carnegie Endowment for Peace, to mention just a few. The foreign affairs departments of most governments and development agencies around the world are making an effort to be more transparent. Their websites are worth visiting, as are those of the United Nations and its many agencies.

John Keane's *Life and Death of Democracy* (W.W. Norton, 2009) is the most provocative survey of the state of democracy. He has also written an excellent biography of Thomas Paine, *Tom Paine: A Political Life* (Little, Brown, 1996), one of several that has appeared in the last few years, as well as a biography of another great democrat, Vaclav Havel: *Vaclav Havel: A Political Tragedy in Six Acts* (Basic Books, 2000).

Patrick Watson and Benjamin Barber collaborated on a book and a television series some years ago on the rise of democracy, *The Struggle for Democracy* (Little, Brown, 1990). Larry Diamond's *The Spirit of Democracy* (Times Books, 2008) is worth a look, and so is James Traub's *The Freedom Agenda: Why America Must Spread Democracy (Just Not the Way George Bush Did)* (Picador, 2009). Benjamin Barber's *"Jihad vs McWorld"* (Ballantine Books, 1995) is also a helpful read.

In addition to C.B. Macpherson's *The Real World of Democracy* (House of Anansi, 1992), see his *Possessive Individualism* (Oxford University Press, 1964) and *Democratic Theory* (Oxford University Press, 1973).

Conor Cruise O'Brien's *The Great Melody* (Sinclair Stevenson, 1992) is a good read and the best modern introduction to Edmund

Burke. The great English Liberal John Morley wrote a good little book on Burke, and his article in the *Encyclopaedia Britannica* (12th ed.) is an excellent summary, albeit from a nineteenth-century Liberal perspective.

Hilary Mantel's novel *Wolf Hall* (HarperCollins, 2009) and Peter Ackroyd's *The Life of Sir Thomas More* (Sinclair Stevenson, 1998) give fascinating accounts of life in Henry VIII's England, as one world was falling apart and another was slowly being built. Christopher Hill's accounts of the civil war in England grew more textured and nuanced as he got older: *The World Turned Upside Down* (Penguin 1975), *Cromwell* (Penguin, 1970), and *Milton and the English Revolution* (Faber and Faber, 1977) are my personal favourites. A new good survey is Michael Braddick's *God's Fury, England's Fire* (Penguin Books, 2009). Simon Schama's book on the French Revolution, *Citizens* (Vintage 1990), is a great read. His three-volume *History of Britain* based on his TV series for the BBC puts things in a broad and very readable perspective. E.P. Thompson's *Making of the English Working Class* (Penguin, 1991) is a classic, and explains where Paine fit into the pantheon of English radicals and democrats.

The Congress of Vienna (Grove Press, 2001) by Harold Nicolson is a slim, gossipy volume but has some good insights into the world of diplomacy at the time. Adam Zamboyski's *Rites of Peace* (HarperCollins, 2007) is the modern, bigger book, which has the benefit of being far more comprehensive. It is also readable. Jacob Talmon's *The Origins of Totalitarian Democracy* (Secker and Warburg 1952) is not widely read these days. It should be. So should Hannah Arendt's *Origins of Totalitarianism* (Houghton Mifflin Harcourt, 2001), as well as her *Eichmann in Jerusalem* (Penguin, 2006). Richard Evans has written a very readable and comprehensive account of the rise and fall of Hitler and Nazism in his three-volume account, all published in paperback by Penguin: *The Coming of the Third Reich* (2004), *The Third Reich in Power* (2005), and *The Third Reich at War* (2009). It is an excellent survey. Piers Brendon's *The Dark Valley* (Knopf, 2000) describes the slide of the 1930s.

I benefited many years ago from a simple put-down by Leszek Kolakowski, the Polish political philosopher, who interrupted a point I was trying to make at a seminar to say, "There is a difference between saying something and proving something." His three-volume series on Marxism, *Main Currents of Marxism* (Oxford, 1978), is a tour de force, and clears the head of much clouded thinking. So does François Furet's *The Passing of an Illusion* (University of Chicago, 1999). Donald Sassoon's *One Hundred Years of Socialism* (HarperCollins, 1997) looks at social democracy in Europe over the last century. Francis Fukuyama's books, *The End of History* (Free Press, 2006), *Trust* (Free Press, 1995) and *State Building* (Cornell University Press, 2004), are a useful Burkean perspective.

Alexis de Tocqueville's *Democracy in America* (Knopf Everyman, 1994) is a classic. It has an often overlooked chapter on the treatment of aboriginal and black people in early America. Richard Hofstadter's *Social Darwinism in America* (Beacon Press, 1992) shows how hospitable the U.S. was to Herbert Spencer and his ilk. John Burrows's *Evolution and Society* (Cambridge University Press, 1970) is a less pungent account of the same debate in Britain. The best account of the modern civil rights movement in the United States is Taylor Branch's two volumes, *Parting the Waters* and *Pillar of Fire* (Simon & Schuster, 1988 and 1998).

Piers Brandon's *The Decline and Fall of the British Empire* (Vintage, 2008) is a great read and a brilliant overview of the conflicting ambitions behind British expansion. Thomas Pakenham's *The Scramble for Africa* (Weidenfeld and Nicolson, 1991) is also a good account. Martin Meredith's *Diamonds, Gold, and War* (Simon & Schuster, 2007) and *The State of Africa* (Free Press, 2005) are insightful on both historical and contemporary issues. On the endgame of empire see Peter Clarke's *The Last Thousand Days of the British Empire* (Penguin, 2007).

Arthur Herman's *Gandhi and Churchill* (Bantam Dell, 2008) looks at the conflict between competing ideas and personalities in an entertaining way, as does his *How the Scots Invented the Modern World* (Crown, 2001), which is not simply an exercise in ethnic triumphalism, but a good insight into the role of Protestantism and literacy in the rise of democratic thinking.

John Reader's *Africa: A Biography of the Continent* (Vintage, 1997) is indispensable. A compelling account of corruption in

Kenya is Michela Wrong's *It's Our Turn to Eat* (HarperCollins, 2009). Stephen Lewis's *Race Against Time* (House of Anansi, Massey Lectures, 2007) is an eloquent cri de coeur.

Henry Kissinger's *Diplomacy* (Simon & Schuster, 1995) is important both for its range and the insight it gives into the man writing it.

The best biography of Orwell (there are several) is D.J. Taylor's *Orwell: The Life* (Henry Holt, 2003). There is a handy four-volume survey of his letters and journalism published by Penguin (*The Penguin Essays of George Orwell*) that is more accessible than the massive twenty-volume *Complete Works* edited by Peter Davison and published in full in 1998 by Secker and Warburg.

There is a good account of a young Bill Clinton's relationship with Senator Fulbright in the former president's autobiography, *My Life* (Knopf, 2004). The best single volume on Kennedy's foreign policy is Lawrence Freedman's *Kennedy's Wars* (Oxford, 2000).

The literature on Iraq and Afghanistan is massive, and is being added to on a daily basis. Steve Coll's two books, *Ghost Wars* (Penguin, 2004) and *The Bin Ladens* (Penguin, 2008), are indispensable background. Seth Jones's *In the Graveyard of Empires* (Norton, 2009), and Ahmed Rashid's *Descent into Chaos* (Viking, 2008) both provide strong insight into the challenges of Afghanistan. Barnett Rubin's *The Fragmentation of Afghanistan* (Yale, 2002) is scholarly. George Crile's *Charlie Wilson's War* (Grove Press, 2003) is thoroughly entertaining. For a more personal perspective see Rory Stewart's *The Places In Between* (Paw Print, 2008) and Greg Mortensen's *Three Cups of Tea* (Penguin, 2006). On Canada in Afghanistan, read Janice Gross Stein and Eugene Lang's *The Unexpected War: Canada in Kandahar* (Viking, 2007).

Peter Galbraith looks at Iraq from a critical perspective, drawing on his role as an advisor to the Kurds in *The End of Iraq* (Simon and Schuster 2006). A more positive perspective can be found in Bouillon, Malone and Roswell's (eds.) *Iraq: Preventing a New Generation of Conflict* (Rienner, 2007). Thomas E. Ricks's *Fiasco: The American Military Adventure in Iraq* (Penguin, 2006), and Dexter Filkins's *The Forever War* (Knopf, 2008), which covers both Iraq and Afghanistan, is a moving and graphic account by a war correspondent. Richard Clarke's *Against All Enemies* (Free

Press, 2004) is the strongest argument on the costs of taking the eye off Afghanistan and invading Iraq.

On modern-day India, a good comprehensive account is Ramachandra Guha's *India After Gandhi* (Picador, 2007). A good way to assess the changing views of Mao Tse-tung is to read Edgar Snow's famous account of his interview with Mao in *Red Star over China* and Jung Chang and Jon Halliday's study, *Mao: The Unknown Story* (Jonathan Cape, 2002).

On Sri Lanka, there is a recently published, definitive account of efforts at reconciliation over the past century, *Power Sharing in Sri Lanka: Constitutional and Political Documents 1926-2008* (Centre for Policy Alternatives, 2008). K.M. de Silva's *History of Sri Lanka* (Penguin, 2005) is good for background. Michael Ondaatje's memoir *Running in the Family* (Vintage, 1993) describes a world now lost, and his novel *Anil's Ghost* (Vintage, 2001) evokes the violence and emotion of the conflict. Adele Balasingham's *The Will to Freedom* (Fairmax, 2003) is an insider's account and plea for the Tamil Tigers. The Indian journalist Cho Ramaswamy has two good books, *The Tigers of Sri Lanka* and a biography of Velupillai Prabhakaran. A.N. Wilson's book *Sri Lankan Tamil Nationalism: Its Origins and Development in the Nineteenth and Twentieth Centuries* (UBC Press, 2000) helps explain the origins of Tamil nationalism.

On the Middle East, Tom Segev's *One Palestine Complete* (Picador, 2001) is a good account of the origins of the conflict. Thomas L Friedman's *From Beirut to Jerusalem* (Anchor, 1990) is also excellent. Avi Shlaim's *The Iron Wall* (Norton, 2000) and *Lion of Jordan* (Penguin, 2007) are strong accounts. For the evolution of the thinking of Israeli historian Benny Morris, see his *Righteous Victims* (Vintage, 1999) and *1948: A History of the First Arab-Israeli War* (Yale University Press, 2008), and a recent account of the futility of the current situation, *One State, Two States* (Yale University Press, 2009). Paul Berman's *Terror and Liberalism* (W.W. Norton, 2003) should be read side by side with *Messages to the World: The Statements of Osama bin Laden*, edited by Bruce Lawrence (Verso, 2005).

Fareed Zakaria's two recent books, *The Future of Freedom* (W.W. Norton, 2003) and *The Post-American World* (W.W. Norton, 2009) have affected my thinking, as has Parag Khanna's *The Second World*

(Random House, 2006). On the utility of aid and foreign assistance, the best introduction to the debate is Paul Collier's *The Bottom Billion* (Oxford, 2007) and Dambisa Moyo's *Dead Aid* (Farrar, Strauss and Giroux, 2009).

Samantha Power's *The Problem from Hell* (Harper Perennial, 2003) describes the history of the law on genocide. Brian Urquhart's memoir, *A Life in Peace and War* (HarperCollins, 1987), gives a strong sense of the history of the UN, usefully supplemented by Dag Hammarskjöld's *Markings* (Ballantine 1985). Romeo Dallaire's more recent *Shake Hands with the Devil* (Random House, 2003) is a moving personal account of the war in Rwanda. *Mobilizing the Will to Intervene: Leadership to Prevent Mass Atrocities* by Frank Chalk, Kyle Matthews, Carla Barqueiro and Simon Doyle (McGill-Queen's University Press, 2010) and *Eliminating Nuclear Threats: A Practical Agenda for Global Policymakers* by Gareth Evans and Yoriko Kawaguchi (International Commission on Nuclear Non-Proliferation and Disarmament, 2009) are both useful reads. On Canadian foreign policy, see the following: *Intent for a Nation: What is Canada for?* by Michael Byers (Douglas and McIntyre, 2007), *While Canada Slept: How We Lost Our Place in the World* by Andrew Cohen (McClelland & Stewart, 2005), *At Home in the World, Canada's Global Vision for the 21st Century* by Jennifer Welsh (HarperCollins, 2005), *The World in Canada: Diaspora, Demography and Domestic Politics* edited by David Carment and David Bercuson (McGill-Queen's University Press, 2008) and *Environment, Scarcity and Violence* by Thomas F. Homer-Dixon (Princeton University Press, 1999) are recommended.

On federalism, start with *The Federalist Papers*, available in innumerable paperback versions. Ron Watts has written a good update for McGill-Queens University Press, and George Anderson's little book, *Federalism* (Oxford University Press, 2008) is excellent. The Forum of Federations, in addition to its website, www.forumfed.org, has produced several monographs published by McGill-Queen's University Press.

Lastly, Nelson Mandela's memoir *The Long Walk to Freedom* (Abacus, 1994) should be read by everyone. For anyone wanting to know the meaning of dignity, persistence, and the triumph of the human spirit, this is a good place to start.